Body Language

FOR

DUMMIES®

2ND EDITION

by Elizabeth Kuhnke

 **WILEY**

A John Wiley and Sons, Ltd, Publication

Body Language For Dummies,® 2nd Edition

Published by
John Wiley & Sons, Ltd
The Atrium
Southern Gate
Chichester
West Sussex
PO19 8SQ
England
www.wiley.com

WILEY

About the Author

Elizabeth Kuhnke holds a Bachelor's degree in Speech and Communications from Northwestern University, and a Masters degree in Theatre Arts. For over 20 years, Elizabeth has worked with individuals and groups to bolster their personal impact and communication skills.

Before moving to Britain, Elizabeth acted throughout the United States on the stage, radio, and television. In addition to designing and delivering university programmes in voice and movement, she also taught acting skills to students and professionals.

In the United Kingdom, Elizabeth applies her theatrical expertise and psychological insight with a rock-solid business approach. She works at top level with FTSE 100 companies and leading professional firms to provide both one-to-one and group coaching in key areas relating to interpersonal communication and image projection. Coming from diverse backgrounds including accountancy, law, construction, and telecommunications, Elizabeth's clients consistently achieve their goals and have fun getting there. Her keys to communication are based on the simple principle of demonstrating respect, establishing rapport, and achieving results.

A highly entertaining speaker, Elizabeth is a popular choice on the conference circuit, and is often quoted in the media addressing issues concerning confidence, voice, body language, and communication skills – all the ingredients that create a positive impact.

For further information about Elizabeth, visit her website at www.kuhnke communication.com.

Author's Acknowledgements

They say you should be careful what you dream for, as it may come true. When I wrote the first edition of *Body Language For Dummies,* I harboured an unspoken dream that the book would be a runaway bestseller with translations across the globe. My dream came true – and then some! Apps, DVDs, enhanced e-books, and international speaking engagements all followed.

Thank you, Kate, for introducing me to the wonderful world of Wiley, and for helping me to surpass my goals. My thanks also go to Kaiser Karl, whom I love with all my heart, for supporting me in weird and wonderful ways; to my precious angels, Max and Kristina, who bring me peaceful love and nurturing challenges; to Katie and Charlotte, who keep me on track and bring joy to my days; to Tom, who keeps his eye on the pounds and pennies; and to Kerry, Steve, Jo, and the whole *For Dummies* crew. You're stars.

Most of what you read in these chapters I have learned from valued colleagues, clients, friends, and family members. To name them all would take more pages than I am allowed, so those of you who know me, know you're in my heart as I write these words. Finally, to you, my readers. My wish for you is that you enjoy the read, gain some knowledge, and free your expressive bodies in the name of clear, congruent communication.

Publisher's Acknowledgements

We're proud of this book; please send us your comments at `http://dummies.custhelp.com`. For other comments, please contact our Customer Care Department within the U.S. at 877-762-2974, outside the U.S. at 317-572-3993, or fax 317-572-4002.

Some of the people who helped bring this book to market include the following:

Acquisitions, Editorial, and Vertical Websites

Project Editor: Steve Edwards
(Previous Edition: Rachael Chilvers)

Commissioning Editor: Kerry Laundon

Assistant Editor: Ben Kemble

Development Editor: Andy Finch

Proofreader: Kim Vernon

Production Manager: Daniel Mersey

Publisher: David Palmer

Cover Photo: © iStock/hammondovi

Photography: Stephen Walby
(`www.stephenwalby.com`)

Cartoons: Rich Tennant
(`www.the5thwave.com`)

Composition Services

Project Coordinator: Kristie Rees

Layout and Graphics: Carrie A. Cesavice

Proofreader: Jessica Kramer

Indexer: Christine Karpeles

Publishing and Editorial for Consumer Dummies

  Kathleen Nebenhaus, Vice President and Executive Publisher

  Kristin Ferguson-Wagstaffe, Product Development Director

  Ensley Eikenburg, Associate Publisher, Travel

  Kelly Regan, Editorial Director, Travel

Publishing for Technology Dummies

  Andy Cummings, Vice President and Publisher

Composition Services

  Debbie Stailey, Director of Composition Services

Contents at a Glance

Introduction 1

Part I: In the Beginning Was the Gesture 7
Chapter 1: Defining Body Language...9
Chapter 2: Looking Closer at Non-verbal Gestures 37

Part II: Starting at the Top... 47
Chapter 3: Heading to the Heart of the Matter 49
Chapter 4: Watching Facial Expressions..67
Chapter 5: The Eyes Have It 83
Chapter 6: Mastering Lip Reading 103

Part III: The Trunk: Limbs and Roots........................... 119
Chapter 7: Taking It From the Torso 121
Chapter 8: Arming Yourself 139
Chapter 9: It's in the Palm of Your Hand 157
Chapter 10: Standing Your Ground 185
Chapter 11: Playing with Props 201

Part IV: Putting the Body into Social and Business Context 217
Chapter 12: Being Aware of Territorial Rights and Regulations 219
Chapter 13: Rating, Dating, and Mating: Using the Body in Courting Behaviour....241
Chapter 14: Interviewing, Influencing, and Playing Politics 263
Chapter 15: Crossing the Cultural Divide 289
Chapter 16: Reading the Signs..307

Part V: The Part of Tens 315
Chapter 17: Ten Ways to Spot Deception 317
Chapter 18: Ten Ways to Reveal Your Attractiveness 325
Chapter 19: Ten Ways to Find Out About Someone Without Asking 331
Chapter 20: Ten Ways to Improve Your Silent Communication 339

Index 345

Table of Contents

Introduction *1*

About This Book..2
Conventions Used in This Book.....................................2
Foolish Assumptions..3
How This Book is Organised 3
    Part I: In the Beginning was the Gesture....................3
    Part II: Starting at the Top 3
    Part III: The Trunk: Limbs and Roots 3
    Part IV: Putting the Body into Social and Business Context 4
    Part V: The Part of Tens...............................4
Icons Used in This Book 4
Where to Go from Here.....................................5

Part 1: In the Beginning Was the Gesture *7*

Chapter 1: Defining Body Language **9**

Discovering How Body Language Conveys Messages 10
    Projecting an image in the first 30 seconds........................11
    Transmitting messages unconsciously.....................12
    Substituting behaviour for the spoken word 13
    Gesturing to illustrate what you're saying 15
    Physically supporting the spoken word 16
    Revealing thoughts, attitudes and beliefs 18
Examining Key Types of Gestures 21
    Unintentional gestures.....................................21
    Signature gestures: Gestures that define who you are 23
    Spotting fake gestures: Pulling the wool........................25
    Micro gestures: A little gesture means a lot.....................26
    Displacement gestures 27
    Universal gestures 28
Getting the Most Out of Body Language.....................................31
    Becoming spatially aware.....................................32
    Anticipating movements 32
    Creating rapport through reflecting gestures 33
    Becoming who you want to be.....................................33
    Reading the signs and responding appropriately.....................35
Appreciating Cultural Differences 36

Chapter 2: Looking Closer at Non-verbal Gestures 37

Observing the History of Body Language...37
Aping our ancestors 38
Gestures first, language second 38
Understanding the Nuts and Bolts of Body Language 39
Kinesics: The categories of gesture...........................40
Inborn responses 43
Learned gestures 44
Hearing a Final Word on Non-Verbal Gestures 46

Part II: Starting at the Top 47

Chapter 3: Heading to the Heart of the Matter 49

Demonstrating Power and Authority 49
Signalling superiority 50
Demonstrating arrogance 50
Displaying aggression..51
Showing disapproval..52
Conveying rejection..53
Catapulting for intimidation 54
Tossing your head in defiance 55
Beckoning with your head 55
Touching someone on the head...................................55
Showing Agreement and Encouragement: The Nod..................56
Encouraging the speaker to continue 56
Showing understanding..57
Micro nodding...57
Displaying Attention and Interest...58
Tilting and canting 58
The head cock 60
Sitting tête à tête 60
Indicating Submissiveness or Worry 61
Dipping and ducking..61
Cradling for comfort 62
The head clasp 63
Showing Boredom 63
Showing You're Deep in Thought..64
Head resting on hand 65
Chin stroking 65

Chapter 4: Watching Facial Expressions 67

Communicating Feelings When Words Are Inappropriate..................67
Recognising Facial Expressions that Reinforce the Spoken Message.....69

Masking Emotions 73
Expressing a Range of Emotions................................ 75
    Showing happiness 75
    Revealing sadness.. 77
    Demonstrating disgust and contempt.................... 78
    Showing anger 79
    Recognising surprise and revealing fear................ 80
    Demonstrating interest 82

Chapter 5: The Eyes Have It **83**

The Power of the Held Gaze................................... 83
    To show interest 85
    To show disapproval, disagreement,
        and other not-so-pleasant feelings................... 88
    Showing dominance... 89
    Effective gazes in business situations 92
The Wandering Eye: Breaking Eye Contact................. 93
    The eye shuttle... 94
    The sideways glance.. 95
    The eye dip 97
Other Ways Your Eyes Tell a Tale............................ 97
    Winkin' and blinkin'.. 97
    Active eyebrows: The Eyebrow Flash 99
    Widening your eyes 100
    Flicking, flashing, and fluttering........................ 101

Chapter 6: Mastering Lip Reading. **103**

Revealing Thoughts, Feelings, and Emotions 103
    Tight lips 104
    Loose lips 105
    Chewing on lips 105
    Maintaining a stiff upper lip.............................. 106
    Pouting for effect.. 107
    Pursing as a sign of disagreement 109
    Tensing your lips and biting back your words 110
    Changing thoughts and behaviours 111
Differentiating Smiles 112
    The tight-lipped smile 112
    The lop-sided smile 113
    The drop-jaw smile 113
    The turn-away smile 115
    The closed-lip grin 115
    The full-blown grin.. 116
Remembering that Laughter's the Best Medicine 117

Part III: The Trunk: Limbs and Roots 119

Chapter 7: Taking It From the Torso 121
Gaining Insights into the Impact of Posture 121
    Evaluating what your own posture says about you 122
    Showing intensity of feelings 124
    Revealing personality and character 126
Knowing the Three Main Types of Posture 127
    Standing 128
    Sitting 129
    Lying down 130
Changing Attitudes by Changing Posture 130
Using Posture to Aid Communication 131
    Showing high and low status through postural positions 132
    Leaning forward to show interest and liking 134
Shrugging Signals 136
    Signalling lack of knowledge 137
    Showing unwillingness to get involved 137
    Implying a submissive apology 138

Chapter 8: Arming Yourself 139
Building Defensive Barriers 139
    Arms crossed on your chest 140
    Touching yourself: Hugs, strokes, and more 144
    Placing objects in front of yourself 144
    Giving the cold shoulder 146
Conveying Friendliness and Honesty 146
Touching to Convey Messages 148
    Creating a bond 149
    Demonstrating dominance 151
    Reinforcing the message 152
    Increasing your influence 153
    Embracing during greetings and departures 155

Chapter 9: It's in the Palm of Your Hand 157
Up or Down: Reading Palms 157
    The open palm 158
    The downward facing palm 161
    Closed-palm, finger-pointed 162
Hands Up! 163
    Hiding your hands 164
    The hand rub: Good for you or good for me? 164
    The folded hand 165
    Hands clenched 166

Letting the Fingers Do the Talking 167
The precision grip.. 168
The power grip... 170
The power chop.. 171
The steeple 172
Gripping hands, wrists, and arms.. 173
Gesturing with your thumbs 173
Analysing Handshakes 174
Deciding who reaches out first 175
Conveying attitude... 176
Displacing Your Energy 181
Drumming for relief 182
Fiddling for comfort 182
Hand to nose... 182
Hand to cheek... 183
Hand to chin 184

Chapter 10: Standing Your Ground **185**
Showing Commitment and Attitude through Your Stance.................... 185
Straddle stance... 187
Parallel stance.. 189
Buttress stance 190
Scissor stance... 192
Entwining your legs 194
Reflecting Your Feelings by the Way You Position Your Feet 195
Pointing towards the desired place... 195
Fidgeting feet 196
Knotted ankles 197
Twitching, flicking, or going in circles 198
Walking Styles 199

Chapter 11: Playing with Props **201**
Using Accessories to Reflect Mental States 201
Showing inner turmoil.. 202
Pausing for thought 203
Through the Looking Glasses 204
Stalling for time 204
Scrutinising the situation.. 205
Controlling the conversation 206
Showing resistance 206
Appearing cool 206
Spectacles at the office 207
Holy Smokes... 208
Smoking and sexual displays... 208
Ways of smoking 209

Making It Up as You Go Along..211
    Make-up at the office...212
    Making up for play..212
Clothing: Dressing the Part..213
    Women's accessories..213
    Men's accessories...214

Part IV: Putting the Body into Social and Business Context.................................. 217

Chapter 12: Being Aware of Territorial Rights and Regulations....219

Understanding the Effect of Space...219
Knowing Your Space..221
    The five zones..221
    Other territorial positions...222
Using Space...225
    Demonstrating ownership..225
    Showing submission..226
    Guarding your space..226
    Revealing comfort or discomfort..227
    Maintaining your personal space..228
Seating Arrangements...229
    Speaking in a relaxed setting...230
    Cooperating..230
    Combating and defending...231
    Keeping to yourself...232
    Creating equality..232
Orientating Yourself...234
    Horizontally...234
    Vertically...235
    Asymmetrically..238

Chapter 13: Rating, Dating, and Mating: Using the Body in Courting Behaviour.........................241

Attracting Someone's Attention..242
    Going courting: The five stages..245
    Highlighting gender differences...246
Showing That You're Available..250
    Looking at the many courting gestures of women...................250
    Examining the few courting gestures of men..........................256
    Recognising dilated pupils: A universal sign of attraction..........258
Progressing Through the Romance...259
    Matching each other's behaviours..259
    Displaying that you belong together......................................259

Chapter 14: Interviewing, Influencing, and Playing Politics **263**

Making a Great First Impression: The Interview.......................................264
   Perfecting your interview behaviour...264
   Using minimal gestures for maximum effect...............................268
Creating a Positive Environment 269
   Demonstrating respect...269
   Establishing rapport...270
   Standing tall and holding your ground 273
   Moving with purpose..275
Pointing Your Body in the Right Direction..276
   Creating a relaxed attitude with the 45-degree angle................277
   Facing directly for serious answers...278
   Picking the power seats 279
Negotiating Styles 281
   Claiming your space 282
   Displaying confidence 284
   Avoiding nervous gestures 285

Chapter 15: Crossing the Cultural Divide **289**

Recognising the Different Strokes for Different Folks.............................290
   Positioning yourself and setting boundaries 290
   Getting up close and personal 291
   Gearing up your greetings 293
   Acknowledging the no-touching rule..294
   Waving farewell...295
Observing the Conventions of Higher- and Lower-Status Behaviour.....295
   Bowing, kneeling, and curtseying 297
   Standing to attention..298
Getting Specific: Common Gestures, Multiple Interpretations 299
   Giving the thumbs up . . . cautiously..299
   Ensuring that the okay sign really is okay...................................300
   Laughing your way into (and out of) trouble................................300
Avoiding Problems and not Causing Offence..301
   Smoothing over difficult situations 302
   Playing by the local rules: Eye contact 302
   Adapting your style for clear communication 304

Chapter 16: Reading the Signs **307**

Taking an Interest in Other People 307
Drawing Conclusions from What You Observe 309
   Looking at the sum total of the gestures 309
   Dealing with a mismatch between spoken
     and non-verbal messages...311
   Considering the context..313
Practice Makes Perfect: Improving Your Reading....................................313

Part V: The Part of Tens *315*

Chapter 17: Ten Ways to Spot Deception. .317
Catching Fleeting Expressions Crossing the Face 317
Suppressing Facial Expressions...318
Eyeing Someone Up...319
Covering the Source of Deception...319
Touching the Nose 320
Faking a Smile...321
Minimising Hand Gestures 321
Maximising Body Touches..322
Shifting Positions and Fidgeting Feet...323
Changing Speech Patterns...323

Chapter 18: Ten Ways to Reveal Your Attractiveness. 325
Using Eye Contact...325
Showing Liveliness in Your Face 326
Offering Encouragement..326
Using Open Gestures..327
Showing Interest Through Your Posture...327
Positioning Yourself...328
Touching to Connect...328
Being on Time 329
Synchronising Your Gestures 330
Balancing Your Non-Verbal Aspects of Speech 330

Chapter 19: Ten Ways to Find Out About Someone
Without Asking. 331
Observing Eye Movements...331
Looking at Facial Expressions...332
Watching for Head Movements 333
Noticing Hand and Arm Gestures 333
Observing Posture..334
Considering Proximity and Orientation...334
Paying Attention to Touching 335
Responding to Appearance 335
Checking Timing and Synchronisation...336
Scrutinising Non-verbal Aspects of Speech 337

Chapter 20: Ten Ways to Improve Your Silent Communication. . . .339
Taking an Interest...339
Knowing What You Want to Express 340
Modelling Excellence 340
Mirroring Others..341

Practising Gestures 341
Developing Timing and Synchronisation...341
Dressing the Part 342
Acting the Way You Want to Be Perceived 343
Demonstrating Awareness 343
Asking for Feedback...344

Index.. 345

Introduction

Body language speaks more loudly than any words you can ever utter. Whether you're telling people that you love them, you're angry with them, or don't care about them, your body movements reveal your thoughts, moods and attitudes. Both consciously and sub-consciously, your body tells observers what's really going on with you.

All day, every day, your body is relaying messages about your attitude, your mood and your general state of being. You can determine what messages you relay by the way you use your body.

Although body language began with our ancient ancestors and long before vocal sounds turned into sophisticated words, phrases and paragraphs, only in the last 60 years or so has body language been seriously studied. During that time, people have come to appreciate the value of body language as a tool for enhancing interpersonal communication. Politicians, actors and high-profile individuals recognise the part that their bodies play in conveying their messages.

Each chapter of this book addresses a specific aspect of body language. In addition to focusing on individual body parts and the role they play in communicating your thoughts, feelings and attitude, you discover how to interpret other people's body language, giving you an insight into their mental state before they may be aware of it themselves. Remember that you need to read body language in clusters and context. One gesture doesn't a story tell any more than does one word.

By performing specific actions and gestures, you can create corresponding mental states. By practising the gestures, you experience the positive impact of body language and discover how to create the image you want. You may actually become the person you want to be.

Are you ready? Read on.

About This Book

For a subject that's relatively new to the study of evolution and social behaviour, you can find a sizeable amount of research on body language. As businesses expand across the globe and international travel is more accessible than ever before, people are recognising the impact of culture, gender and religious customs on body language and communication. While I've written the second edition of *Body Language For Dummies* from a mostly English-speaking western perspective, Chapter 15 has been expanded to include body language in different cultures – what's acceptable and what could cause offence. Because of the vastness of the subject, I've been selective in what I've chosen to include and focused on using body language to enhance your non-verbal communication for your personal and business relationships.

In this book I explain ways of recognising and identifying specific gestures, actions and expressions that convey and support both the spoken and non-spoken message. By improving your reading of body language, understanding how your body conveys messages and recognising how mood and attitude are reflected in your gestures and expressions, you have the upper hand in your interpersonal communications. By recognising and responding to body signals, you can direct the flow of the conversation and facilitate meetings easily and effectively. I show you the impact of thoughts and feelings on gestures and expressions – both yours as well as others.

The point of the book is for you to become conscious of body language, whether it's your own or that of other people. The book is also intended to help you interpret gestures, movements and expressions. Finally, this book identifies the signs and signals you can send out to enhance your communication.

Conventions Used in This Book

This book is a jargon-free zone. When I introduce a new term, I *italicise* it and then define it. The only other conventions in this book are that Web and email addresses are in `monofont` and the action part of numbered steps and the key concepts in a list are in **bold**. I alternate between using female and male pronouns in odd- and even-numbered chapters to be fair to both the men and women who read through these pages.

Foolish Assumptions

I assume, perhaps wrongly, that you:

✔ Are interested in body language and know a little bit about it

✔ Want to improve your interpersonal communications

✔ Are willing to reflect and respond

✔ Expect the best

How This Book is Organised

The cool thing about the *For Dummies* books is that you can dip in and out as you please. You don't need to read the first chapter to understand the last and if you read the last chapter first you won't ruin the story. The table of contents and index can help you find what you need. If you prefer to just dive in, please do – there's water in the pool. Read on for what lies ahead.

Part 1: In the Beginning Was the Gesture

In this part I explore the foundations of body language, the silent communicator. You discover the origins of body language, how it evolved and the impact it has on all your communications and relationships.

Part 11: Starting at the Top

Focusing on the head and its parts and positions, I continue exploring body language and the messages it conveys. You discover how the tilt of your head, the lift of your brow and the tremble of your lip reveal more than the words that tumble from your mouth.

Part 111: The Trunk: Limbs and Roots

In this part I explore the impact of your posture on your thinking, attitudes and perceptions. You see how feelings, behaviour and perceptions are intertwined. I look at the body's limbs, its arms, legs, feet, hands and fingers and how their movements reflect inner states and create impressions. Finally, you see how your accessories add to the picture of who you are.

Part IV: Putting the Body into Social and Business Context

In this part you discover how to gesture effectively and appropriately according to the situation you're in. You find out where to place and position yourself for greatest effect. You discover how to read and reveal signs of interest and dismissal and how to engage with a possible romantic partner. Back at the office, you discover the power positions and how to demonstrate confidence and positive impact.

Addressing cultural diversity, you get a glimpse into behaviours different from your own and pick up adaptive strategies for avoiding potential pitfalls.

Part V: The Part of Tens

If you're keen to get a handle on body language quickly and concisely, start with Part V. Stop here if you want top ten tips for spotting when someone's being economical with the truth. I also show you how to enlarge your fan base and engage with your admirers. For developing your skills as a silent communicator, gaining self-awareness and honing your observation skills, this is the place to be.

Icons Used in This Book

For sharpening your thinking and focusing your attention, let these icons be your guide.

This icon highlights stories to entertain and inform you about people I know, or people I've observed and the clues they've revealed through body language.

Here's a chance for you to stand back and observe without being seen. By distancing yourself and taking a bird's eye view, you can watch how others behave and reflect on the outcome.

This icon underscores a valuable point to keep in mind.

These are practical and immediate remedies for honing your body language skills.

Here, you can have a go at putting theory into practice. Some of the practical exercises are designed to enhance your image and create an impact.

Where to Go from Here

Although all the material in this book is designed to support you in being yourself at your best, not all the information may be pertinent to your specific needs or interests. Read what you want, when you want. You don't have to read the book in order, nor is there a sell by date for covering the material.

If you're interested in how body language conveys messages, begin with Part I. If you're seeking to improve your body language for a job interview or for playing the political and corporate game at work, have a look at Chapter 14. If you're curious about facial expressions have a look at Chapter 4. And if you want to know how to behave appropriately in cultures different from yours, turn to Chapter 15.

Now, flip to a page, chapter, or section that interests you and read away. Feel free to dip and dive from section to section and page to page. Most importantly, enjoy the read.

Part I
In the Beginning Was the Gesture

The 5th Wave   By Rich Tennant

"I assume that means either 'rub my feet,' or 'find my socks.' Any other meaning will require a spoken word or another body part."

In this part . . .

Here's where we explore the foundations of body language, the way of silently communicating that can improve your impact factor and relationships once you grasp the basics. In this part, we go back in time to the origins of body language, how it's evolved, and its ability to reveal thoughts, feelings, and attitudes.

Chapter 1

Defining Body Language

- -

In This Chapter

▶ Finding out how body language speaks for you

▶ Gesturing for a purpose

▶ Understanding what you're communicating

- -

The science of body language is a fairly recent study, dating primarily from around 60 years ago, although body language itself is, of course, as old as humans. Psychologists, zoologists and social anthropologists have conducted detailed research into the components of body language – part of the larger family known as non-verbal behaviour.

If you're quiet for a moment and take the time to pay attention to body language movements and expressions that silently communicate messages of their own, you can cue in on gestures that convey a feeling and transmit a thought. If you pay close attention, you can identify gestures that you automatically associate with another person, which tell you who she is. In addition, you may notice other types of gestures that reveal a person's inner state at that moment.

In this chapter, you discover how to interpret non-verbal language, exploring the gestures and actions that reveal thoughts, attitudes and emotions. Also, you have a quick glance at some of the research into this unspoken language and recognise similarities and differences throughout the world. In addition, you find out how you can use gestures to enhance your relationships and improve your communication.

Discovering How Body Language Conveys Messages

When cave-dwellers discovered how to decipher grunts and to create words to convey their message, their lives became a lot more complex. Before verbal communication, they relied on their bodies to communicate. Their simple brains informed their faces, torsos and limbs. They instinctively knew that fear, surprise, love, hunger and annoyance were different attitudes requiring different gestures. Emotions were less complex then, and so were the gestures.

Speech is a relatively new introduction to the communication process and is mainly used to convey information, including facts and data. Body language, on the other hand, has been around forever. Without relying on the spoken word for confirmation, the body's movements convey feelings, attitudes and emotions. Like it or not, your body language, or non-verbal behaviour, says more about you, your attitudes, moods and emotions, than you may want to reveal.

According to research conducted by Professor Albert Mehrabian of the University of California, Los Angeles, 55 per cent of the emotional message in face-to-face communication results from body language. You only have to experience any of the following gestures or expressions to know how true the expression is, 'Actions speak louder than words':

- Someone pointing her finger at you
- A warm embrace
- A finger wagging in your face
- A child's pout
- A lover's frown
- A parent's look of worry
- An exuberant smile
- Your hand placed over your heart

Figure 1-1 shows two different gestures conveying two very different messages.

Figure 1-1:
A pointing
finger and
hand over
the heart
convey
different
messages.

Projecting an image in the first 30 seconds

You can tell within the first seven seconds of meeting someone how she feels about herself by the expression on her face and the way she moves her body. Whether she knows it or not, she's transmitting messages through her gestures and actions (check out the *Body Language For Dummies* app for an example).

You walk into a room of strangers and from their stance, movements and expressions, you receive messages about their feelings, moods, attitudes and emotions. Look at the teenage girl standing in the corner. From her slouching shoulders, her lowered head and the way her hands fidget over her stomach, you can tell that this little wallflower is lacking in self-confidence.

Another young woman in this room of strangers is standing in a group of contemporaries. Her eyes twinkle, she throws her head back as she laughs, her hands and arms move freely and openly and her feet are planted firmly beneath her, hip width apart. This woman is projecting an image of self-confidence and joie de vivre that draws people to her.

Early observations about body language

Before the 20th century, a few forays were made into identifying and analysing movement and gesture. The first known written work exclusively addressing body language is John Bulwer's *Chirologia: or the Natural Language of the Hand,* published in 1644. By the 19th century, directors and teachers of drama and pantomime were instructing their actors and students how to convey emotion and attitude through movement and gesture.

In *The Expression of the Emotions in Man and Animals* (1872), Charles Darwin discusses the connection between humans, apes and monkeys. These species use similar facial expressions, inherited by a common ancestor, to express certain emotions. Out of Darwin's work grew an interest in *ethology*, the study of animal behaviour.

In the late 1960s, Desmond Morris created a sensation when his interpretations of human behaviour, based on ethological research, were published in *The Naked Ape* and *Manwatching*. Further publications and media presentations continue to reveal how much our non-verbal behaviour is based on our animal nature.

How you position your head, shoulders, torso, arms, hands, legs and feet, and how your eyes, mouth, fingers and toes move, tell an observer more about your state of being, including your attitude, emotions, thoughts and feelings, than any words you can say.

Transmitting messages unconsciously

Although you're capable of choosing gestures and actions to convey a particular message, your body also sends out signals without your conscious awareness. Dilated or contracted eye pupils and the unconscious movements of your hands and feet are examples of signals that reveal an inner emotion that the person signalling may prefer to conceal. For example, if you notice that the pupils of someone's eyes are dilated, and you know that she's not under the influence of drugs, you'd be correct in assuming that whatever she's looking at is giving her pleasure. If the pupils are contracted, the opposite is true.

Be careful when ascribing feelings and attitudes based on body language as individual signals can be easily overlooked or misidentified if they're taken out of their social context, or if they're not identified as part of a cluster of gestures involving other parts of the body.

At times in life, you may want to conceal your thoughts and feelings, so you behave in a way that you believe hides what's going on inside. And yet, wouldn't you know it, out pops a slight giveaway gesture, often invisible to the untrained eye, sending a signal that all's not what it appears. Just because these micro gestures and expressions are fleeting doesn't mean that they're not powerful.

In the 1970s, Paul Ekman and W V Friesen developed the Facial Action Coding System (FACS) to measure, describe and interpret facial behaviours. This instrument is designed to measure even the slightest facial muscle contractions and determine what category or categories each facial action fits into. It can detect what the naked eye can't and is used by law enforcement agencies, film animators and researches of human behaviour.

University of California, Los Angeles (UCLA) Professor Albert Mehrabian's classic study of how messages are received and responded to during face-to-face communication, when discussing feelings and emotions, shows that when an incongruity exists between the spoken word and how you deliver it, 7 per cent of the message is conveyed through your words, 38 per cent is revealed through your vocal quality and a whopping 55 per cent of your message comes through your gestures, expression and posture. Mehrabian's premise is that the way people communicate is inseparable from the feelings that they project, consciously or not, in daily social interactions. Although some people contest Mehrabian's figures, the point remains that body language and vocal quality significantly contribute to the meaning of the message and determine the effectiveness of our relationships.

Arthur is the chief executive of a global telecoms company. Highly accomplished and rewarded for his successes, he still harbours some self-doubt and insecurity. This uncertainty is particularly evident when he's making formal presentations. He holds a pad of paper in front of himself as if it were a protective shield. When he's unsure of the word he wants to use, he quickly and briefly rubs the skin under his nose with his index finger. When he moves from one point to the next in his presentation, he quickly taps his forehead with his left index finger as if to remind himself that he's about to move to the next point. Seeing himself on DVD, he recognised how these meaningless gestures were revealing his lack of security and how uncomfortable he feels in front of a large audience. By visualising himself presenting at his best and modelling specific behaviours of presenters who Arthur thinks are excellent, he developed ways of eliminating his unconscious negative gestures.

Substituting behaviour for the spoken word

Sometimes a gesture is more effective in conveying a message than any words you can use. Signals expressing love and support, pleasure and pain, fear, loathing and disappointment are clear to decipher and require few, if any, words for clarification. Approval, complicity or insults are commonly communicated without a sound passing between lips. By frowning, smiling, or turning your back on another person, your gestures need no words to clarify their meaning.

When words aren't enough or the word mustn't be spoken out loud, you gesture to convey your meaning. Some examples are:

- ✔ Putting your index finger in front of your mouth while at the same time pursing your lips is a common signal for silence.
- ✔ Putting your hand up sharply with your fingers held tightly together and your palm facing forward means 'Stop!'.
- ✔ Winking at another person hints at a little secret between the two of you.

Figure 1-2 illustrates these behaviours, and Figure 1-3 shows another example of a situation in which words just aren't enough.

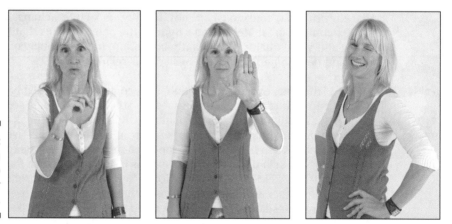

Figure 1-2:
Using
gesture to
convey your
meaning.

When Libby, the well loved and highly successful Artistic Director of the Oregon Shakespeare Festival was honoured for her years of service, she felt proud and humbled. Looking around the room filled with colleagues, friends and major financial contributors, Libby placed her right hand over her heart as she thanked them all for their years of support, belief and dedication. Around the room, many people's eyes were moist and they held their fingers to their lips to prevent themselves from crying out loud. Libby's hand to her heart reflected her deeply felt appreciation.

Figure 1-3:
These people are witnessing something that has shocked them. Open mouths and hand positions show how people attempt to keep emotions in check.

Gesturing to illustrate what you're saying

When you describe an object, you frequently use gestures to illustrate what the object is like. Your listener finds it easier to understand what you're saying when you let your body create a picture of the object rather than relying on words alone. If you're describing a round object, like a ball, for example, you may hold your hands in front of yourself with your fingers arched upward and your thumbs pointing down. Describing a square building, you may draw vertical and horizontal lines with a flat hand, cutting through the space like a knife. If you're telling someone about a turbulent ride on a boat or plane, your arms and hands may beat up and down in rhythmic fashion. Describing a large object may entail holding your arms out wide. If you're illustrating a small point, you may hold your fingers close together (see Figure 1-4). The point is that gesturing is a useful means of conveying visual information.

Figure 1-4:
Gestures
help clarify
your
message.

Because some people take in information more effectively by seeing what's being described, illustrating your message through gestures helps create a clear picture for them. To help a blind person experience what you're describing, hold her hands in the appropriate position.

Lotsie, my daughter's godmother, is a world explorer and frequently speaks to students about her adventures. As Lotsie was describing her climb up Mount Kilimanjaro, she acted out those moments when the air felt so thin that she was hardly able to breathe and when she struggled to put one foot in front of the other. She mimed leaning on her walking stick, bending over with the weight of her equipment, gasping for air and pausing between shuffled steps as she put one foot in front of the other. Her gestures painted the combined picture of a woman who was both fit and exhausted.

Physically supporting the spoken word

Gesturing can add emphasis to your voice, clarify your meaning and give impact to your message. Whether your point requires a gentle approach, or a firm telling off, your body's instinct is to reflect and move in harmony with the emotion.

In addition to reinforcing your message, hand signals especially reflect your desire for your message to be taken seriously. Watch a well-schooled politician standing at the podium. See how their hands move in a precise, controlled manner (see Figure 1-5). No wasted gestures, just those specific ones that paint a clear picture and accurately convey the message.

Figure 1-5:
Clear, sharp
gestures
let the
audience
know that
you mean
business.

When you're making a formal presentation, use illustrative gestures to help your audience remember the points you're making.

During the introduction to your presentation, as you establish the points to be covered, list them separately on your fingers. You may hold your fingers up in front of you, or touch them individually on one hand with a finger from your other hand as you say the point. (Note: Many British and American people begin counting with their index finger. Many Europeans begin counting with their thumb. See Chapter 15 for more on cultural differences in body language.) When talking about point one in your presentation, point to the first finger, or gesture to it; when you reach point two, point or gesture to your second finger, and so on.

Experienced lawyers, celebrities and anyone in the public arena are also adept at emphasising their messages through considered movements and gestures. By carefully timing, focusing and controlling their actions, moving in synchronicity with their spoken words and responding appropriately to the atmosphere in their environment, they court and woo the people they want and dismiss others with aplomb.

Observe movie stars and celebrities at red carpet events as well as politicians at global conferences and notice what messages they're conveying through their body language.

When you're giving bad news and want to soften the blow, adapt your body language to reflect empathy. Move close to the person you're comforting and tilt your body towards hers (see Figure 1-6). You may even touch her on the hand or arm or place your arm around her shoulder.

Figure 1-6: Empathic gestures create a feeling of care and concern.

Revealing thoughts, attitudes and beliefs

You don't have to tell people how you're feeling for them to know. Look at Rodin's sculpture of *The Thinker.* There can be no doubt about that person's state of mind: thoughtful, serious and contemplative. Equally so is a child throwing a tantrum with stomping feet, clenched fists and a screwed up face is letting you know that she's not happy.

Think of your body as if it were a movie screen. The information to be projected is inside you and your body is the vehicle onto which the information is displayed. Whether you're anxious, excited, happy or sad, your body shows the world what's going on inside. Here are some examples:

- ✔ People who feel threatened or unsure of themselves touch themselves as a means of self-comfort or self-restraint. Gestures, such as rubbing their foreheads, crossing their arms and holding or rubbing their fingers in front of their mouths, provide comfort and protection (see Figure 1-7).

- ✔ People who perform specific gestures reserved for religious rituals reveal their beliefs and values. Upon entering a Catholic church, the congregation dip their fingers into holy water and cross themselves. Before entering the home of many Jewish people, you may touch the mezuzah by the front door. Muslims bow in prayer facing east. By performing these gestures, people are demonstrating their respect for the culture, its traditions and values. See Chapter 15 for more about cultural differences and body language.

- ✔ People in a state of elation often breathe in deeply and gesture outwards with expanded arms. Pictures of winning sportspeople frequently show them in the open position with their arms extended, their heads thrown back and their mouths and eyes opened in ecstasy.

- ✔ Footballers who miss the penalty kick and city traders who get their numbers wrong often walk dejectedly with their heads down and their hands clasped behind their necks. The hand position is a comforting gesture and the head facing downwards shows that the individual's upset.

- ✔ People in despair, or feeling down and depressed, reveal their thoughts and attitudes by the slouch in their step, their drooping heads and their downward cast eyes. Positive people, on the other hand, reveal their thoughts and attitudes with an upright stance, a bounce in their step and eyes that appear lively and engaged.

- ✔ Not every bent head signals depression. Sometimes it just means that you're reflecting, thinking or absorbing information. If you're demonstrating the behaviour of someone who's thinking hard, your head most likely rests in your hand or on your fingertips, like Rodin's *The Thinker*. You can find out more about body language and mental states in *Persuasion & Influence For Dummies* by Elizabeth Kuhnke (Wiley).

Figure 1-7: These two men are telling us they're holding back and seeking comfort.

At Peter and Louise's wedding anniversary celebrations, Peter stood up to toast his wife and children. As he raised his glass to the family members, his feelings for them were clear. By the way he slightly leaned forward toward his son, Sebastian, you were able to sense the great warmth and tenderness he held for him. As he turned to his daughter Olivia, to express his amazement at her joyous spirit, he slightly lifted his head and tossed it back. When he turned to gaze at his wife, Louise, his eyes softened and a gentle smile played at the sides of his mouth. He stood upright, held his arm forward and raised his glass high in a display of love and appreciation for his family.

Noticing your own body language

My husband suggested that people may only demonstrate body language when someone else is around to see and respond to it. I found that an interesting thought and retired to my office to consider the implications on my own. As I sat at my desk reflecting on what he said, I noticed I was leaning back in my chair with my head tilted upwards, one arm folded over my body supporting the elbow of my other arm. My chin was resting lightly on my thumb as my index finger gently stroked my cheek. I couldn't help but think of the saying about falling trees in the forest making noise if no one's around to hear it.

Holding your hands over or near your heart, as shown in Figure 1-8, is an expression of how much something means to you.

Figure 1-8:
The hands
over the
heart, the
tilted head
and the
open smile
indicate
apprecia-
tion.

Examining Key Types of Gestures

Humans are blessed with the ability to create a wide variety of gestures and expressions from the top of the head to the tips of the toes. Gestures can show intention, such as leaning forward just before rising out of a chair; as well as showing no intention, such as crossing arms and legs. Some gestures belong to you, because you've become identifiable by them. Some gestures are displacement gestures: you perform them for no reason other than to shift some energy. Some gestures are specific to local customs and some are universal gestures that everyone does.

Unintentional gestures

Unintentional gestures are behaviours that inhibit your ability to act. The unintentional gestures imply that you have no intention of moving from where you are. They hold you back, won't let you go and your body says that you're not budging. And no amount of outside influence to get you to move is going to succeed.

Examples of unintentional gestures are:

- Folded arms
- Lips pressed together
- A hand or finger in front of the mouth
- Crossed legs

These actions all keep you in place. You can't walk when your legs are crossed. You can't speak with your hand in front of your mouth. You can't reach out when your arms are crossed in front of you.

Standing or sitting with your legs crossed is no position to take if you want to get somewhere quickly. The scissor stance is a prime example of a gesture that keeps you in your place. One leg is crossed over the other, rendering you immobile (see Figure 1-9). When someone adopts this position you know she's staying put.

Figure 1-9: The finger over the mouth, the arm across the body and the scissored legs indicate that she's holding back.

Because the scissor stance contains no sign of impatience, the gesture can come across as submissive. The person has no forward movement in her body as does the body of a person about to take action. The person who acts is usually considered to be dominant. Therefore, the person who stays put is usually considered to be submissive.

Signature gestures: Gestures that define who you are

A signature gesture is one that you become known by, a common gesture that you perform in a particular way. Some examples are:

- Twirling your hair around your finger
- Thumb sucking
- Eyebrow patting
- Throat stroking

These gestures give us clues into the person's personality.

Signature gestures set you apart from all others. Think Napoleon Bonaparte and his mighty stance (see Figure 1-10) – on the canvas, not the battlefield. Standing with his hand tucked into his waistcoat, he looks the picture of pride and authority. Who knows if he ever really stood in that position. The artist created the image and we believe the artist.

One of Diana, Princess of Wales's most vividly remembered signature gesture's was the lowered head with her eyes looking upward from underneath her eyebrows. This look is commonly referred to as the Shy Di look (see Figure 1-11).

Sophie is a delightful woman in her early twenties. Pretty, vivacious and polite, Sophie's signature gesture is thumb-sucking. I first noticed this gesture when she spent several days at our home. Curled up on the couch, Sophie slipped her right thumb into her mouth, lightly rubbing her nose with her index finger. Claire, a woman in her forties, also sucks her thumb. Her variation on this gesture is a small piece of soft fabric that she rubs in the palm of her cupped hand. Both women are indicating a need for nurturing and succour by this gesture.

Figure 1-10:
The Bonaparte pose conveys stature and authority.

Figure 1-11:
A downward tilted head and upcast eyes looks vulnerable and pleading.

Martyn is a quiet, thoughtful, focused man. His boss, Annie, is highly energetic with a mind that skips and leaps from one project to the next. Frequently, Annie asks Martyn to do one task, only to interrupt his concentration by asking him to do something else, often unrelated. When Martyn pats his eyebrows with the tips of his fingers, Annie knows that the time's come for her to back off and let him get on with what he has to do.

Some examples of signature gestures can be seen in a person's:

- ✔ Posture
- ✔ Smile
- ✔ Hand clap
- ✔ Pointing finger
- ✔ Clothes tugging

Some sportspeople perform specific actions as an anchor to get them grounded and focus their energy. Before serving, the tennis player Rafael Nadal tugs at the back of his shorts. This gesture is so closely associated with this gifted sportsman that other players have been known to mock him on the courts and in the dressing rooms by performing it in front of him.

By recognising signature gestures, you can tell what kind of person you're dealing with. Certain gestures, like clapping the hands together once, show a mind that's organised. The hair twirling gesture indicates that the person may be a day dreamer. When you successfully read the signs, you can figure out how best to interact with the person.

If you want to be easily identified and remembered, you can create your own signature gesture. Victoria Beckham's sexily defiant pout has become her signature gesture, as has Hugh Grant's foppish head toss.

Spotting fake gestures: Pulling the wool

Fake gestures are designed to camouflage conceal and fool. They deliberately point you in one direction to make you believe something that isn't so. Fake gestures pretend to be something when they're actually something else.

You're able to tell a fake gesture from a real one because some of the real gesture's parts are missing.

Some gestures that are commonly faked are:

- ✔ Smiling
- ✔ Frowning
- ✔ Sighing
- ✔ Crying
- ✔ Holding your body as if in pain

Anna is a highly motivated recently qualified lawyer in a large London firm. She knows that, in part, her success depends on her ability to get on well with clients and colleagues. One day, her supervising partner invited her to attend a client meeting and to put together the remaining briefs that a previous trainee had begun and hadn't had time to finish. Anna, already overloaded with work, stayed at the office until well past midnight. In spite of little sleep and over an hour's commute that morning, she arrived, shortly before the meeting's 8 a.m. start looking smart and ready to go. At one point during the session, the client remarked that some information seemed to be missing. The partner shot Anna a glance of annoyance before covering up his feelings with the hearty remark, 'Well, she's new on the job. We'll let her get away with it just this once.' To cover her fury and shame, Anna put on what she calls her 'smiley face', a big toothy grin and offered to find the missing materials. Anna's teeth were clenched, and her eyes didn't crinkle (a sign of a sincere smile). She was tired, hurt and humiliated and anyone paying attention would have seen she was giving a fake grin.

You can't spot a true emotion by one gesture or expression alone. Look for all the signs. Fake gestures are meant to deceive.

Micro gestures: A little gesture means a lot

Teeny weeny, so small that they sometimes take highly specialised equipment to see them, micro gestures are flashes of emotion that flicker across your face faster than a hummingbird, revealing feelings that you may prefer to keep to yourself. These gestures aren't ones that you purposely choose. Micro gestures give a brief hint of what's going on inside. You choose to smile, wave and rise from a chair. You don't choose to have a micro gesture flicker across your face. No one is immune to them.

A list of the more common micro gestures include:

- ✔ Movement around the mouth
- ✔ Tension at the eyes
- ✔ Flaring of the nose

Mark and Liz met at a party. They were immediately attracted to one another. They stood easily in the other's intimate space. Their facial gestures were controlled, but the occasional flicker around Liz's eyes and hint of a smile around Mark's mouth gave the impression that a frisson existed between the two. Friends and family members recognised the signs and frequently ask about how the relationship between Liz and Mark is progressing.

Displacement gestures

When you're feeling conflicting emotions, you may engage in gestures that have no relation to your immediate goals. These behaviours are mostly self-directed and serve to release excess energy and gain a feeling of comfort, even if only temporary. Drumming fingers, flicking feet, going for a glass of water when you're not even thirsty – these are the behaviours of someone who's looking to burn some pent up energy, or at least, refocus it. Called displacement activities, they're a conduit for excess energy that's looking for a place to go.

Some examples of displacement gestures are:

- ✔ Fiddling with objects
- ✔ Tugging at your earlobe
- ✔ Straightening your clothes
- ✔ Stroking your chin
- ✔ Running your fingers through your hair
- ✔ Eating
- ✔ Smoking

Some smokers light up a cigarette, take a puff or two and then put it out or leave it in the ashtray barely smoked. These people may not actually want the cigarette, but need a gesture to take their mind off something else.

I knew the time had come to stop smoking when I had three cigarettes on the go in a four-room apartment. I was working in New York, living on my own, making barely enough to pay my monthly bills and wondering what I was doing with my life. I was frustrated and feeling anxious. One morning, while I was in the kitchen making coffee, I lit up a cigarette. When the phone rang, I answered it in the living room, leaving the cigarette burning in the kitchen. While speaking on the phone to my soon-to-be ex-husband, I lit another cigarette which, after a drag or two, I stubbed out in the ashtray on my desk. I went to the bathroom to get ready for work. Here, too, I lit a cigarette, which I occasionally puffed on as I applied my make-up. In the course of less than ten minutes I had lit three cigarettes, none of which I was interested in smoking and all of which were props for displacing nervous anxiety.

Rather than stating their feelings verbally, people demonstrating displacement activities are letting their gestures reveal their emotion.

Prince Charles is noted for fiddling with his cufflinks. He crosses his arm over his body and touches his cufflinks in a protective and reassuring gesture. The Prince is displacing his anxiety by making contact with his cufflinks. On honeymoon with Diana, the late Princess of Wales, Charles is purported to have worn cufflinks given to him by his true love and now wife, the Duchess of Cornwall. No wonder that his young bride was upset when she discovered this wedding gift of gold cufflinks with entwined Cs; especially when she saw him fondling them.

Words convey information. Gestures reveal attitude. If someone's feeling anxious, she may fiddle with her keys, twist the ring on her finger or pull at her clothes to compensate for her anxiety.

If you see someone under pressure and being scrutinised, look to see what her hands are doing. If she's gently rubbing her stomach, you may assume that she's feeling the pressure and is calming and comforting himself, the way you comfort a baby or sick child.

Universal gestures

Universal gestures, such as blushing, smiling and the wide-eyed expression of fear, mean the same thing across world cultures. These gestures stem from human biological make-up, which is why you can recognise them spanning the globe. See Chapter 15 for more about gestures across cultures.

Smiling

From the sands of Iraq to the shores of Malibu, humans are born with the ability to smile. From the earliest days in an infant's life, her facial muscles can form the upward turn of the lips and the crinkling around the outer edges of the eyes to create a recognisable smile.

Sure, each person may have her own unique way of smiling. The point remains that anyone with working facial muscles who's conveying a positive message lifts her lips in pleasure (see Figure 1-12).

When you see the sides of the lips turned up and the eyes crinkling at their outer edges, count on that smile being genuine in showing pleasure.

Figure 1-12:
A genuine smile engages the muscles around the mouth and eyes.

The Japanese smile in embarrassment as well as pleasure. Young women giggle behind their hands. Don't expect the Japanese to respond to your humour with a raucous, belly laugh. See Chapter 15 for more on smiling and laughing in different cultures.

Blushing

If you blush, your embarrassment's showing. The blood flows to your chest and cheeks, and you want to drop down and hide. Whether you're in Thailand, Afghanistan, the United Kingdom or another other country across the globe, when you see someone blush you know they're being consumed with embarrassment.

To control the blushing take several slow, deep breaths from your diaphragm to steady your nerves and control the blood flow. For more about how breathing can help control nervous energy, see *Persuasion & Influence For Dummies* by Elizabeth Kuhnke (Wiley).

My Aunt MarNell lives in Dallas, Texas and is the perfect combination of cowgirl and southern belle. When Dad, MarNell's only sibling and adored brother, raised his glass in special toast to her at a recent family reunion, her cheeks flushed like a shy young girl's.

Crying

Crying is a universal sign of sadness. One of a healthy infant's first actions is to let out a walloping great cry when she first enters this world, having been torn from the comfort and safety of her mother's womb. No one had to teach her how to cry, she was born with the innate ability to express her upset. . .

If you feel tears well up in your eyes and you want to stop them from flowing down your face, fix your gaze at that point where the ceiling and wall meet. Performing this action focuses your attention onto a meaningless and unrelated subject and frees your mind of upsetting thoughts. Another way to achieve the same result is to press your tongue firmly against the roof of your mouth as you remind yourself that in a few moments what's troubling you will be over. If, however, you feel the salt of your tears about to splash down your face, you could acknowledge what's happening and move on. Sometimes accepting what's about to occur is enough to make it stop.

Shrugging

Shrugging is a gesture that people use when they need to protect themselves in some way. The full shrug is when your head dips into your rising shoulders, the sides of your mouth turn down, your palms turn upwards and you raise your eyebrows.

The shrug can indicate:

- Indifference
- Disdain
- Lack of knowledge
- Embarrassment

To know which attitude is being expressed, you have to look to see what the other body parts are doing.

Television versus radio

In the early 1960s, there was little knowledge of body language. Yet, John F Kennedy intuitively knew how to use it. Prior to their first televised debate in 1960 JKF and Richard Nixon posed for a media photo call. Kennedy placed himself to the right of Nixon and shook Nixon's hand. The resulting photograph showed Kennedy applying the upper-hand position causing Nixon to appear diminished in stature. This was one of Kennedy's favourite gestures. The Nixon–Kennedy election debate that followed this photo call was a further testimonial to the power of body language. Most of the Americans who only heard the debate on the radio believed that Nixon out-performed Kennedy. However, the majority of those who saw the debate on television believed Kennedy was the victor. Kennedy knew how to use his body to manipulate public perception and did it with grace, charm and unconscious expertise.

Robin was invited to speak at an industry event. She made the mistake of sitting at the panel table before making her presentation, rather than joining the other invited speakers afterwards. When the host introduced Robin, his comments were so glowing that Robin felt embarrassed. She'd set herself up for all to see and, rather than squaring her shoulders and lifting her head with pride, she dropped her head and lifted her shoulders in a humble shrug, as if seeking protection. What saved her from looking like a complete idiot was the sparkle in Robin's eye and the bounce in her step when she took to the stage.

Getting the Most Out of Body Language

Successful people know how to use their bodies for greatest effect. They stand tall, with their chests opened like a well-loved book, smiles on their faces and when they move, they move with purpose. Their moderate and carefully chosen gestures reflect their sense of what they want to project and how they want to be perceived.

Successful people also know where to position themselves in relation to other people. They know that if they stand too close they can be perceived as overwhelming or threatening. They know that if they stand too far away they can be perceived as distant. They know how to anticipate movements – theirs and another's – to avoid (or not) bumping into someone else, depending on their motives and their relationship with the other person. They know that the gestures they use and how they use them have infinitely more of an impact than the words they say.

The people who demonstrate respect for others, who think before acting and who develop the necessary skills to create their desired outcomes, are the ones who feel good about themselves. You can tell by the way they move. Their gestures and actions have purpose and meaning.

If you want to succeed in your career or relationship, using effective body language is part of your foundation. Once you're aware of the impact – of what works and what doesn't – you can move and gesture with confidence, knowing that you and your message are perceived the way you want them to be.

Becoming spatially aware

Understanding how to position yourself in relation to other people is a skill that some people just don't seem to have. Someone is either so up close and personal to you that you can smell their morning coffee breath, or they stand just that bit away that makes them appear uninterested, unengaged or slightly removed. Others, however, know just how to get it right. They understand and respect the different territories and parameters that people have around themselves, and being with them is comfortable.

You have a personal, individual space bubble that you stand, sit and move around in, and it expands and contracts depending on circumstances. Although you may have grown up in the country and have need for a lot of space around you, people who grew up in cities need less.

The study of *proxemics*, how people use and relate to the space around them to communicate, was pioneered by Edward T Hall, an American anthropologist in the 1960s. His findings revealed the different amounts of personal space that people feel they need depending on their social situation. Robert Sommer, an American psychologist, coined the term 'personal space' in 1969. He defined it as the 'comfortable separation zone' people like to have around them.

Chapter 12 takes a look at how circumstances determine at what distance you're most comfortable, and how best to position yourself in relation to another person, whether standing, sitting, or lying down.

Anticipating movements

Movement can be equated to dance. It's more than just the gestures themselves, it's about the timing of them as well. Anticipating an action and registering that an action is about to happen before it does, gives you information that others may not grasp.

The American anthropologist, Ray Birdwhistell, pioneered *kinesics*, the study of body movement and verbal communication. Replaying, in slow motion, films of people in conversation, Birdwhistell was able to analyse people's actions, gestures and behaviours.

Consider these examples:

- ✔ Spotting the subtle gestures a person makes in preparation for rising from a seated position previews what's about to happen.

- ✔ Recognising when a person's about to strike out in anger gives you enough time to protect yourself and others.

- ✔ Feeling your dancing partner shift his weight indicates that a change in movement is about to occur.

Anticipating a movement can save your life. It can keep you from harm. It may also bring you great happiness, like a lover's first kiss which, had you missed the movement, you may have lost. By anticipating gestures, you gain the upper hand in knowing how to respond before the action is completed.

Creating rapport through reflecting gestures

When you talk about establishing rapport, you're talking about accepting and connecting with other people and treating one another with respect. Rapport assures that your communications are effective and lead to results that satisfy both parties' needs.

You have many ways of creating rapport, through touch, word choice and eye contact. Another way is to reflect another person's movements. By mirroring and matching the other person's gestures and behaviours, you're demonstrating that you know what it feels, sounds and looks like to be in her shoes. If connecting with others and behaving respectfully is important to you, mirroring and matching their behaviour helps you achieve that goal.

A fine line exists between reflecting another person's gestures and mimicking her. People who are being mimicked quickly figure out what you're doing and recognise your insincerity.

Becoming who you want to be

How you present yourself, how you move and gesture, how you stand, sit and walk all play their part in creating the image you present and in determining people's perceptions. By adopting a cluster of postures, positions and gestures known for the attitudes they effect, you can create any attitude and make it your own. Positive body language looks and feels strong, engaged and vibrant. Negative body language communicates weaknesses, dullness and a disconnectedness. Sometimes you want to project one image over another. Whatever image you want to project – moving your head, face, torso and limbs with confidence, control and commitment, or creating desired effects with the flick of your wrist or a furrow of your brow – being perceived and responded to in the way you want helps you to achieve your desired results.

Actors know the technique of creating a character from both within and without. Working from the outside in, actors consider how their character sounds, moves and gestures. They ask themselves:

✔ How would the character walk, sit and stand? Would the character move like a gazelle, lumber along like a sleepy bear or stagger in a zigzag pattern like someone who's had one drink too many? Is the posture upright and erect or slouched and limp?

✔ What gestures would be required for conveying a particular mood or emotion? Slow, deliberate and carefully timed gestures create a different impression from those that are quick, spontaneous and unfocused.

By adopting the appropriate behaviours, the actor creates an attitude, emotion or feeling that the audience recognises and understands. The same is true for the lay person. By acting in a particular manner you can create an image and become that character. As Cary Grant said, 'I pretended to be someone I wanted to be until I finally became that person.'

The behaviour you adopt and the gestures that you make leave an impression. How you're perceived – dumb or sultry, champion of the people or chairman of the board – is up to you. The key is to adopt/exhibit/display the right gestures. To do that, keep these points in mind:

✔ **Make sure that your gestures reinforce the impression you want to make:** For example, the higher up the command chain, the more contained the gesture (which is why you never see the chief executive run down the hall).

✔ **You can modify your gestures to suit the situation:** When Charlotte, my PA and I, are working in the office and no one else is around, our body language is loose and relaxed. When a client or another colleague arrives, the body language changes. We both become more formal, the degree of formality depending on how the other person behaves.

Decide what attitude you want to project. If you struggle to project that attitude, model the gestures of a person who you think successfully emulates the image you want to portray.

I recently experienced my first tax audit, which had me in a bit of a state. Tom, my financial director , and my accountant Rashmi, tell me how much and where to sign and I do it. I trust them and Tom's been teaching me about the finances. Tom arrived at the office, wearing a suit and tie, for the meeting with the VAT lady. Our office is normally quite informal and Tom's change of clothes told me that we were to leave out the jokes. Although I was dressed informally, I adjusted my behaviour to mirror Tom's, which was thoughtful, serious and open. We wanted to create the impression that not only does the business have a strong creative base, but also that its financial backbone is firmly in place.

Reading the signs and responding appropriately

Being able to read other's signals is a stepping stone to effective communication. By observing how people move and gesture, you get a glimpse into their emotions. You can tell, for example, the intensity of someone's feelings by the way she stands. You can see what kind of mood a person's in by the speed of her gestures. By having an insight into someone's feelings, you're forewarned and forearmed for whatever may happen next.

Say that you're at a party with a friend. You notice her sitting dejectedly by herself. Seeing her in this position, with her head hanging down and her arms wrapped around her body, you know that she needs a little tender loving care. You gently put your hand on her arm and she begins to feel a bit better.

Later at the party, you observe that some of the younger guests – who have had more than their fair share of drink – are beginning to go from jovial to rowdy. You notice the lads pushing and shoving one another, which is your sign to leave.

By reading body language effectively, you can tell when to stay and when to go.

Edith unexpectedly popped around to have a chat with her neighbours, Tim and Sarah, who were in the middle of a busy morning and had little time to stop for a gossip. Although Tim smiled warmly at Edith, he stood by the entrance without inviting her in. His arms were crossed over his chest, his legs were held closely together and rhythmically he rocked backwards and forwards on his toes. Edith sensed from Tim's closed position that now was not a convenient time for them to speak, and she quickly left.

Appreciating Cultural Differences

How much more exciting, interesting and stimulating it is to live in a world with difference and diversity, rather than one in which everything's the same. Even though you appreciate the differences between cultures and nationalities, you may sometimes find yourself confused, scared or even repelled by displays of body language that are very different from what you're used to.

Because people in one culture act differently than people in another doesn't suggest that one is right and the other is wrong. When it comes to cultural differences, the operative verbs are 'to respect' and 'to value'. Valuing behaviours that vary so much from those that you grew up with, and were taught to believe in, can be hard. To create respectful, positive relationships between different cultures and nationalities, you need to expand the way you think and work, from an attitude of respect. That doesn't mean having to agree with all the behaviours you see in your travels. Instead, accept that differences do exist, and then decide how best to respond.

Chapter 15 looks at different cultures and how behaviour and body language impact upon communication between nations.

Different nationalities and cultures use their bodies differently. An acceptable gesture in one country may land you in jail in another. Before visiting or moving to another country, do your homework and find out what's suitable and what's not. Before making a gesture, think whether this gesture is appropriate and acceptable before doing so.

Chapter 2

Looking Closer at Non-verbal Gestures

In This Chapter

▶ Looking into the origins of body language

▶ Conveying information through body language

▶ Considering gestures – what you can discover from others

*W*hether you like to think of yourself as an animal or not, the truth is, you are. And like all animals, the way you gesture, move, and position your body tells an observer a lot more about you than the words you say.

Throughout the animal kingdom, body language is a constant and reliable form of communication. Whether on two, four, or more legs, homo sapiens and the rest of the animal kingdom are constantly sizing one another up as they prepare for a friendly, or unfriendly, encounter. Because of the structure and programming of the human body, it can send a myriad silent messages, whereas most animals are limited in the number of signals they can convey.

In this chapter, I revisit our ancient ancestors to see where body language began and how it evolved. You discover that the way you use your body conveys how you're feeling, what you're thinking and your general state of being. You find out how body language reveals the feelings and attitudes you may prefer to leave unsaid, as well as how it supports your spoken message.

Observing the History of Body Language

For over 100 years, psychologists, anthropologists, and even zoologists have been studying non-verbal behaviour throughout the animal kingdom to understand its implications and explore its possible applications in the broader field of human communication. These experts recognise that applying that knowledge of non-verbal behaviour in practical settings allows people to communicate more successfully than if they rely purely on the spoken word.

Research into primate behaviour concludes that non-verbal behaviour, including gestures and facial expressions, is a reliable source for conveying messages.

Aping our ancestors

Charles Darwin concluded that humans' ability to express emotions, feelings, and attitudes through posture and gesture, stems from prehistoric apes that most resemble today's chimpanzees. Like humans, chimpanzees are social animals that live in groups. As with humans, chimpanzees' needs are based around successful communication and cooperation in order to survive. As chimpanzees have yet to develop the ability to speak, they primarily rely on non-vocal means such as stance, facial expressions, and touching gestures, to show who's in charge and where there's danger.

Darwin published his findings in *The Expression of the Emotions in Man and Animals* in 1872. Regarded as the most influential pre-20th century work on the subject of body language, this academic study continues to serve as the foundation for modern investigations into facial expressions and non-verbal behaviour. Close to 140 years after its original publication, Darwin's findings about posture, gesture, and expression are consistently validated by experts in the field.

Gestures first, language second

Further research into the foundations of communication suggests that spoken language evolved from gesture. In evolutionary terms, speech is a relatively new means of communication, having only been a part of humans' communication process for somewhere between 500,000 and 2 million years.

According to Frans de Waal of the Yerkes National Primate Research Center in Atlanta, Georgia, gestures appeared first in human development, followed by speech. Babies quickly discover which gestures to use, and how to use them to get what they want.

Studying the behaviour patterns of apes and monkeys, de Waal concludes that gestures used as specific signals are a more recent addition to the communication chain, coming after vocalisations and facial expressions. Apes (which are genetically closer to humans than monkeys are) use specific gestures but monkeys don't.

Although humans' ability to communicate effectively has evolved with the development of speech, body language continues to be the most reliable source for conveying attitude, feelings, and emotions.

Understanding the Nuts and Bolts of Body Language

The primary purpose of the spoken word is to convey information, facts, and data whereas body language is designed to relay attitudes, feelings, thoughts, and emotions. You may argue that words also relay attitudes, feelings, thoughts, and emotions, and you'd be right. Sometimes. Think back to those occasions when you said words like, 'I'm fine; there's no problem; I think you're great; I couldn't be happier' when you really meant, 'I'm annoyed; there's a huge problem; I think you're hideous; I couldn't be more miserable.' If the person you were speaking to was a careful observer, he would have noticed that while your words were giving one message, the way you delivered them signalled a conflicting meaning.

The meaning of a gesture depends on the context in which someone uses it, as well as on what other signals are being sent out at the same time.

Context clues: Studying gestures in chimps and bonobos

Studying humans' closest primate relatives – chimpanzees and the black-faced bonobo chimpanzees – research conducted by Amy Pollick and Frans de Waal concluded that the meaning of a gesture depends on the context in which the gesture's made, as well as other gestures that are occurring at the same time. Observing a captive test group of chimps and bonobos, the researchers identified 31 gestures – defined as any movement of the forearm, hand, wrist, or fingers, used solely for the purpose of communication. In addition, they identified 18 facial or vocal signals and recorded them in the context in which they were made. The facial and vocal signals had practically the same meaning in the two species. The gestures had different meanings.

The common signal for fear in chimps is a 'bared-tooth scream'. The 'up and out' gesture of reaching with the palm facing upward has different meanings. Depending on the context, it can be interpreted as begging for food or money as street beggars do, or begging for a friend's support. The open-handed gesture can frequently be seen after a fight where reconciliation is sought. This versatility demonstrates the necessity for context to be taken into consideration before interpreting the meaning of a gesture.

Kinesics: The categories of gesture

The American anthropologist Ray Birdwhistell was a pioneer in the study of non-verbal behaviour. He labelled this form of communication 'kinesics' as it relates to movement of individual body parts, or the body as a whole. Building on Birdwhistell's work, Professor Paul Ekman and his colleague Wallace V Friesen classified kinesics into five categories: emblems, illustrators, affective displays, regulators, and adapters.

Kinesics convey specific meanings that are open to cultural interpretation. The movements can be misinterpreted when communicating across cultures as most of them are carried out with little if any awareness. In today's global environment, awareness of the meanings of different kinesic movements is important in order to avoid sending the wrong message. (To find out more about kinesics across different cultures, see Chapter 15.)

Emblems

Emblems are non-verbal signals with a verbal equivalent, and are easily identified because they're frequently used in specific contexts. Because emblems are quick to use and unambiguous in their meaning, the person receiving the gesture immediately understands the message – as long as he comes from the same culture as you. Keep in mind that easily understood emblems in one culture may be puzzling in another.

Examples of emblems include:

- **The V-shaped sign.** Winston Churchill made the victory sign popular. The palm of the hand faces forwards with the middle and forefingers held erect.

- **The raised arm and tightly closed fist.** Generally the fist is used as an expression of solidarity or defiance. In 1990, Nelson Mandela walked free of prison holding this position. Among black rights activists in the United States, the raised fist is known as the black power salute.

- **The Finger.** Americans hold the middle finger of the hand in an upright position, with the back of the hand facing out. In Britian, people tend to hold up their index and middle fingers with the back of their hand facing out. Both gestures mean the same thing and the meaning's quite rude.

- **The Sign of the Cuckold.** Your index and little fingers are extended pointing forward with your palm facing down, making 'horns'. Your thumb crosses over your two middle fingers. You're telling an Italian that his partner's been unfaithful. In Texas, this gesture is the sign for fans of the University of Texas Longhorns football team and has nothing to do with infidelity.

✔ **The OK Sign.** A circle made with the thumb and forefinger means 'OK' in many parts of the world, but in other places it can be interpreted as 'zero', 'nothing' or as an obscene gesture representing a body orifice.

Because of different interpretations of the same gesture between cultures, the correct reading is dependent on the context in which the signal occurs.

Illustrators

Illustrators create a visual image that describes, accents or reinforces what the speaker is saying, by pointing to an object or pounding on a table, for example. They indicate interest, help clarify meaning and demonstrate levels of enthusiasm. Illustrators tend to be subconscious movements occurring more regularly than emblematic kinesic movements. People use them widely all around the world, though more or less frequently depending on the culture.

Examples: Holding your hands apart to indicate size; standing tall to demonstrate pride or confidence.

The usage and the amount of illustrators used differ from culture to culture. In general, Latinos use illustrators more than their Anglo-Saxon counterparts, who make more use of illustrators than many Asian cultures. In some Asian cultures, extensive use of illustrators is often interpreted as a lack of intelligence. In Latin cultures, the absence of illustrators indicates a lack of interest.

Affective displays

Affective displays are movements, including your gait and facial expressions, that reveal emotional meaning. For example, bouncing on the balls of your feet indicates excitement, a genuine broad grin signals pleasure and slouching or shuffling along illustrates depression. Because affective displays are spontaneous, they may send out signals you'd rather not have revealed, due to social norms or what you want to achieve in your communication. Less conscious than illustrators and occurring less frequently, affective displays convey universal emotions and can be understood fairly easily, though the degree and frequency with which they occur is determined by cultural mores.

Example: Expressions of love, frustration, or anger.

A lack of affective displays doesn't indicate a lack of emotion. Cultural considerations determine what is considered to be acceptable behaviour. A person from Japan expressing anger shows significantly fewer affective display movements than his Italian counterpart. This doesn't suggest, however, that the Japanese person is feeling any less annoyed. The Japanese are taught to hold in their emotions whereas Italians are encouraged to express them fully.

Regulators

Regulators – body movements that control, adjust and sustain the flow of a conversation – are frequently relied on to feedback how much of the message the listener has understood. Regulators are associated with turn-taking in a conversation and they influence the ebb and flow of the discussion. For example, starting to move away from someone indicates that you want the communication to end; raising a finger or lifting your head indicates that you want to speak, and showing your palm signals that you don't want to speak (see Figure 2-1).

Example: Head nodding and eye movements.

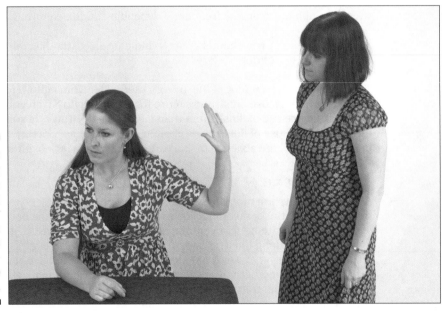

Figure 2-1: Looking away with a palm facing the other person indicates unwillingness to speak.

Because of cultural differences in the use of regulators, the way in which people respond to the flow of information can be confusing. A misinterpreted regulatory signal in international politics and business can lead to serious problems.

Adaptors

Adaptors include changes in posture and other movements, made with little awareness. These body adjustments are to perform a specific function, or to make the person more comfortable. Because they occur with such a low level of awareness, they're considered to be the keys to understanding what someone really thinks. Adaptors principally comprise body-focused movements, such as rubbing, touching, scratching, and so on.

Example: Shifting body and/or feet position when seated. Twisting hair, drumming the fingers, pushing eye glasses up on the nose, swinging a leg, tugging an ear, and scratching and holding oneself are further examples of adaptive behaviours. These adaptors aren't intended to further or support the conversation and are triggered by situational circumstances, increasing as anxiety levels rise.

The significance given to adaptors may be overstated as well as oversimplified. Many adaptor movements, such as shifting position while seated, may be simply a way of resolving a specific physical situation, such as being uncomfortable, rather than revealing emotions and attitudes.

Inborn responses

A newborn baby latches onto its mother's breast and begins to suckle. A child born blind and deaf smiles, frowns, and cries. These reactions aren't taught. Inborn responses to specific stimuli such as these require no practice or knowledge and are performed unconsciously, unprompted, and without self-analysis.

Some movements are so familiar that you take them completely for granted. Asked how to do them and you wouldn't have a clue. Take for example, interlocking fingers. Every person has a dominant thumb, which consistently rests on top of the other when you interlock your fingers. If you were asked which of your thumbs rests on top you probably wouldn't know and would have to have a look to find out. This doesn't mean that you can't reverse the position and put the other thumb on top. Do it and see what happens. Feels strange, awkward, and not quite right, doesn't it?

The study of animal behaviour, especially as it occurs in a natural environment, was pioneered by Irenaus Eibl-Eibesfeldt, an Austrian scientist and head of the Max Planck Institute for Behavioural Physiology in Germany. His interest in humans as 'signal carriers' significantly contributed to the field of Human Ethology, including the study of inborn actions.

An inborn action works like this: think of your brain as being programmed like a computer. Your brain is encoded to connect precise reactions with particular stimuli involving inputs and outputs. The stimuli, or input, triggers a reaction, or output. The process is straightforward and simple, requiring no prior experience or learned behaviour.

An example of inborn behaviour is the rapid raising and lowering of the eyebrows as a sign of greeting, a gesture that can be seen around the world. Stamping feet in anger and baring teeth when enraged also seem to be inborn behaviours. It seems that no matter how far humans evolve from their prehistoric relatives, the basic urges and actions remain the same.

Learned gestures

The English zoologist, human behavioural scientist, and author, Desmond Morris, believes that human beings have an abundant variety of actions that, in addition to being genetically inherited, are learned behaviours. Some of these behaviours are discovered, others are absorbed, some are taught, and still others are acquired in a combination of ways.

Discovering actions for yourself

Most people around the world are born with similar hands, arms, and legs, and move and gesture with them in pretty much the same way. An African warrior, a London banker, and a Minnesota farmer with their similar arms, all discover, at some point in their lives, how to fold them across their chests. No one taught them how to take that pose. During the growing up process, as they became familiar with their bodies, they unconsciously discovered they were able to do this. Most of the time, you don't even know how you perform the gesture. When you cross your arms over your chest, which one's on top? See what I mean?

Absorbed actions

Observe a group of teenage girls, watch the guys in the boardroom, or the celebrities on the red carpet and you notice that within each grouping a similar pattern of behaviour exists. Humans are imitative characters, easily influenced by the actions of others, especially if the others are considered to be of a higher status. The higher the status, the more they're copied. Without being aware of it, the people within the individual groups reflect one another's actions, gestures, postures, and expressions.

You absorb most from those you admire.

Trained actions

Some actions have to be learned. For example, say you want to wink. You give it a go and it doesn't quite work. You give it another go. This time you're a little better, still with plenty of room for improvement. Desperate to be an adept winker, you deliberately and doggedly practise until you manage it. You learn how to wink.

Most of you aren't going to join the circus, where somersaulting and walking on your hands is required, but at some time in your lives you shake hands with other people. Having an adept teacher helps. Watch a parent teaching his child how to shake hands properly and you see a trained action being taught. See Chapter 9 for more about different kinds of handshakes.

Refined actions

Several categories of actions influence the many behaviours you perform in your adult life. Some, like crying, are inborn. As an infant, you cried uncontrollably. As a toddler, you wept and shouted. As an adult, you can still let your emotions all hang out or suppress your sobs, depending on local cultural and social influences.

Consider the way you cross your legs. As a child, you discover that sitting with your legs crossed is a comfortable position. You do it without thinking. Then society intervenes. As you mature, the way you cross your legs emulates other members of your sex, nationality, age group, and social class. And you don't even notice this change is happening. (See Figure 2-2.)

Awareness of cultural differences can change your actions, too. With the example of crossing your legs in mind be aware, for example, that showing the soles of your feet is viewed as rude and insulting in many Asian countries, as the soles of your feet, sandals or shoes are considered unclean. If in doubt, point the soles of your feet toward the floor. (For more about cultural differences and body language, see Chapter 15.)

Figure 2-2:
People cross their legs in different ways.

At times, when you're mixing with people you don't know too well, you may feel uncomfortable, without knowing why. The reason is because the others are moving, acting, and gesticulating in a manner different to yours. Even though the differences may be subtle, they're detectable. (See Chapter 15 for more about culture, customs and body language.)

Hearing a Final Word on Non-Verbal Gestures

Charlie Chaplin, Gloria Swanson, and all the other great actors of the silent screen knew how to use their bodies, gestures, and facial expressions to convey messages to their audiences. With the advent of the talkies, the only actors who survived were those who were able to communicate successfully by combining their vocal and physical skills. Many a pretty face fell onto the cutting room floor for want of a decent voice.

Dancers, mimes, and people with speech impairments face a similar challenge of conveying emotion without relying on the spoken word. They rely solely on position, movement, and expression to reveal their inner thoughts, feelings, and attitudes.

You don't have to be a professional performer for your body to reveal, both consciously and subconsciously, your emotions, attitudes, and beliefs. Nor do you have to be a mind-reader to understand the people you interact with. You simply need to be aware of and understand gestures – those you make and those you see. Some are subtle, some are obvious. Some seek to share; others seek to hide. But all are revealing – if you know what to look for.

The remaining parts of this book look at the various types of signals and gestures (researchers have observed and documented almost 1 million of them!) that the body sends and offer advice on how you can use the power of body language to improve your own communications.

Part II
Starting at the Top

The 5th Wave   By Rich Tennant

"They've been that way for over 10 minutes. Larry's either having a staring contest with the customer, or he's afraid to ask for the sale again."

In this part . . .

1 head straight to the top and explore how you can read eyes, lips, and facial expressions. They say the eyes are the windows to the soul, and you'd better believe it. The chapters in this part help you discover how the tilt of your head, the size of your pupils, and the twitch of your lips reveal more than words can say.

Chapter 3

Heading to the Heart of the Matter

. . . .

In This Chapter

▶ Using your head to display power

▶ Nodding your head in agreement

▶ Tilting your head to indicate interest

▶ Discerning the meaning of other head movements

. . . .

*W*hether you hold your head high, cant it in contrition, or drop it in despair, the way you position your head reveals what you think of the person, place, or thing you're encountering. How you place and pose your head indicates whether you're being aggressive, flirtatious, or are bored to distraction.

Head movements have many purposes. They can reveal attitudes, replace the spoken word, and support or challenge what is said. You can steer someone to look or move in a specific direction by using your head to guide her, or you can point with your head when finger pointing would be rude or inappropriate.

Slight head nods, chin thrusts, and sweeping actions emphasise words and phrases. In a meeting, the chairperson nods or her head to indicate who may speak next.

Discover in this chapter how a slight shift in action or angle can make the difference between being perceived as interested or dismissive, thoughtful or arrogant, playful or angry.

Demonstrating Power and Authority

Power is, indeed, a heady thing, and people with power, whether they're aware of it or not, position their heads in ways that reinforce that power. Particular positions of the head correspond to the kind of power you hold.

Lift your head and tilt it backward, and you convey a sense of superiority (and people perceive you as haughty); raise your head and thrust your chin forward, and you send out a 'Don't mess with me!' signal. The following sections explain the variety of messages that head positions signal.

The way you hold your body can cause positive or negative feelings in those around you. Make sure that your head position reflects the response you want.

Signalling superiority

So, you've recently been appointed president of your company, club, or choral society. Had you been paying attention, upon hearing the news you would have noticed that your head lifted when your name was announced. Already, you began to take on the behaviour of a person in a position of authority.

Although you may say that all humans are created equal, when you're in charge, your body sends out signals indicating that you're the one people ought to notice. Sure, you may choose to drop your head in a moment of thought or as a sign of respect, or even to demonstrate a moment of humbleness, but when you want people to pay attention and focus on you, your head rises.

If you find yourself feeling blue, down in the dumps, or just not quite on top of your game, raise your head and hold it in an upright position for a few moments. Notice your mood shifting from low to high. If you're feeling really down, it may take a few extra moments to feel the change. Don't lower your head until you notice the difference in your feelings.

Demonstrating arrogance

A difference exists in a look between assertiveness and arrogance, and that difference reveals itself in the tilt of the head and the jut of the chin. Although assertiveness conveys itself with a raised head, arrogance is signalled by a slight backward tilt of the raised head and a forward thrust of the jaw (see Figure 3-1).

Occasionally, what appears to be arrogance isn't arrogance at all, but camouflaged insecurity. If someone tilts her head away from you slightly, so that she looks downwards over her shoulder, she's put up an invisible barrier between you and her. Although the look of raised head, forward thrusting chin, tilted angle, and downward gaze implies arrogance, the underlying message is one of defensive posturing.

Figure 3-1:
The person on the left is showing arrogance while the person on the right is demonstrating assertiveness.

Alex is a solicitor at a top law firm. He was recently put up for partnership, but was unsuccessful. The partners told him that he came across as arrogant and aggressive. Although I thought these were natural traits in a lawyer, the partners felt that his body language put people off. On first glance, Alex's behaviour can be perceived as arrogant. He often lifts his head, juts out his chin, slightly turns away from you when he speaks, frequently crosses his arms over his chest, and when challenged adds what sounds like a sarcastic laugh to the ends of his sentences. These behaviours create an impression of arrogance and aggressive superiority that make others feel uncomfortable and threatened. What those of us who know him well recognise is that these actions are covering up a lot of insecurity. His lack of body awareness combined with his self-doubt is sending out negative messages. (If you want to read more about how body language impacts on perceptions, have a look at *Persuasion & Influence For Dummies* by Elizabeth Kuhnke (Wiley).)

Displaying aggression

If someone approaches you in an aggressive state you may notice, if you have the time and the courage, that the head is thrust forward from the shoulders as if it were a weapon. In extreme cases, someone who's really angry may use the head as a missile, projecting it forward in a head butt to hit the other person – a not uncommon behaviour among professional soccer players.

George was leisurely driving along a narrow country lane when from behind a speeding BMW came careering around a corner and almost rear-ended him. Experiencing a combination of fear, anger, and moral outrage, George stopped his car, forcing the other driver to brake hard to avoid running into him. The driver leapt out of his car and approached George, who wisely stayed in his. In a flash, George noticed that the other man's face was red with anger, his fists were clenched in front of him, and his head was jutting forward from his shoulders, neck sinews extended, jaw tight, lip snarled, and teeth clenched. Wisely, George recognised the signs of extreme aggression, kept his windows up, locked the doors and called 999.

Showing disapproval

Remember when you were called into the head teacher's office and you knew it wasn't because you had won the citizenship prize? Or, perhaps more recently, when your boss summoned you to inquire why you hadn't met your monthly target? Or that time your tennis partner threw you a look after you hit the ball into the net to lose the final point in the club tennis tournament? We've all been at the receiving end of the disapproving look. My children assure me that often I'm the one giving the look, too.

As with all gestures, the disapproving look involves several actions. In terms of where you place your head, it's positioned with the forehead slanting forward and the head lowered, as shown in Figure 3-2.

The other head position for showing disapproval is with the head held firmly upright over a straight body. The arms are folded, legs crossed, and the eyes probably looking at you with an icy stare.

If you want to indicate that you're disappointed, critical, or disapproving, adopt a still posture with your head firmly positioned in an upright angle looking the other person squarely in the eye as if to say, 'There's no room for argument or excuses here.' Another position you can assume is to lower your head, stare at the floor, and pick at your clothes with your thumb and index finger as if removing an invisible bit of fluff. These positions reveal that you're harbouring unspoken objections.

To read body language accurately, you must observe all the gestures a person is making. The full message lies in the combination of actions, not in a single movement.

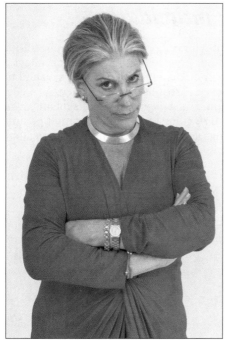

Figure 3-2:
A furrowed
brow and
forward-
tilting
forehead
implies
a critical
attitude.

Conveying rejection

The head shake is the most common way to express a negative reaction. Infants rejecting the breast, bottle, or a spoonful of food turn their heads rapidly from side to side. Anthropologists believe that for adults, the action of turning the head horizontally from left to right with equal emphasis on each side to express rejection, stems from our earliest days.

The head shake has two speeds of delivery:

- ✔ **Fast:** If the listener shakes her head rapidly, she's saying that she disagrees and wants to take over the speaker's role. If, however, she nods up and down quickly, she's indicating that she agrees.

- ✔ **Slow:** A slow back and forth sideways turning indicates the listener's incredulity at what she's just heard. The slow up and down nod, however, implies that the listener is comfortable in her position and doesn't want to take over from the speaker.

Catapulting for intimidation

In any business environment, you're bound to see someone sitting at her desk, hands clasped behind her head, elbows pulled back, chest puffed out. Whoever takes on this pose immediately increases her size and takes on an expansive, self-satisfied or even threatening appearance. As a gesture, this gesture, known as the 'catapult', is a clever way of disguising aggression and intimidation. However, if you're going to sit in the catapult position, make sure that you're not sweating (see Figure 3-3). Underarm sweat smells, shows anxiety and can be off-putting to other people.

Figure 3-3:
Underarm sweating is something to avoid in the catapult position.

Choose your gestures carefully. If your boss calls you into her office to have a word with you, leave your catapult outside unless you're prepared for a counter-attack.

Tossing your head in defiance

A woman frequently tosses her head to show disdain or haughtiness. She flicks her head backwards and gives it a small shake indicating that she has no intention of engaging with the other person, no interest in what's being said, or is unwilling to commit in any way. A person intent on delivering a double-punch gibe holds her head high and throws it back as she lays on the verbal charge.

Beckoning with your head

When you want to attract someone's attention, be it a potential lover, or a helping hand, and a shout or even a wave would be an unsuitable choice, the head beckon is an effective gesture. This head movement is a diagonal back-wards throw and may be repeated several times depending on how urgent your request is.

Touching someone on the head

The head is the most sensitive and vulnerable part of the body: it is where the most important sense organs are stored. The hand is the part of the body that can cause the most harm to another person. The act of touching another person on her head is an intimate gesture, implying trust and a deep bond between the two people. If you touch someone on her head, you're demon-strating your power over her. Seldom, if ever, would you see a student put her hand on the head teacher's head, any more than you'd put your hand on your boss's head. The person in the position of authority, be she taller, older, or wiser than you, has implicit permission to place her hand on your head.

Priests, Rabbis, and other heads of religious organisations place their hand on a supplicant's head as a sign of divine power.

Kissing another person on her head is a way of demonstrating approval and showing a protective attitude. Because the gesture is a one-sided way of kissing someone, it implies that the initiator has a superior position to the receiver.

With child protection laws in place, teachers and other people in authority no longer have permission to touch their charges on the head or anywhere else on the body.

Showing Agreement and Encouragement: The Nod

An almost universal gesture and the most frequent and obvious head movement is the nod. This seemingly simple action has a variety of meanings. In addition to being a sign of affirmation, agreement, acknowledgement, and approval, this up-and-down movement serves as a gesture of recognition, comprehension, encouragement, and understanding.

Body language is an outward manifestation of your feelings and emotions, or, in layperson's terms, your body is reflecting what's going on inside. For example, if you're feeling upbeat and positive your head naturally nods as you speak.

If you want to establish an affirmative environment but you're not feeling quite so perky, nod your head intentionally and lo and behold, you start feeling on top of the world. Simply stated, if you consciously nod your head you create positive feelings. It's all about cause and effect.

Head nodding is catchy. If you nod your head at someone, she usually nods in return. This is true even if the other person doesn't agree with what you're saying. And as for creating rapport, gaining agreement, and getting support, the head nod is your entry point.

Encouraging the speaker to continue

As a listener's gesture, the nod plays an integral part in keeping the conversation going. By using a measured nod, the listener indicates that she's paying attention and doesn't want to take over the speaker's role. This slow, rhythmic nodding encourages the speaker to say more and talk longer. Likewise, by failing to nod your head while listening, the speaker thinks you aren't interested or paying attention. She finds it difficult to continue and quickly ends the conversation.

Start a conversation with someone you know well. As she speaks, nod your head in encouragement. See what effect your head movements have. Then stop nodding all together and observe her reactions.

Generating information through nodding

Research shows that listeners who nod their heads frequently during an interaction can prompt the speaker to generate three to four times more information than when there's no head movement. Experienced interviewers employ the head-nodding technique to obtain additional information and longer discussions, thus making the sessions more effective and productive.

Showing understanding

Although the slow head nod encourages the speaker to continue, shifting gears and speeding up your nodding indicates that you understand what she's saying. The fast head nod has a certain amount of urgency attached to it and shows that you completely support what the speaker's saying, or that you want to interject and take over the speaker's role.

The way you can tell the difference between someone who's interested and encouraging as opposed to someone who wants to take over the conversation is by observing where she's looking. If the person is looking at the speaker she's being supportive. If she's looking away from the speaker, she's indicating that she wants to take over the conversation (unless she's distracted, of course).

If the listener seems to be looking at the speaker supportively, sneak a peep at her eyes. If they're engaged, she's paying attention. If they're dull, she's probably bored or uninterested.

The strength of the nod – the degree of the up-and-down action – communicates the listener's attitude. If she agrees, the head nod is a firm action. A slight nod provides feedback to the speaker letting her know how well her message is understood.

When making a formal presentation, the head nod is a useful gesture to emphasise words and phrases. Use it wisely. Too much repetition reduces the impact of any emphasising technique.

Micro nodding

Often people end their statements with a barely perceptible dip of the head. In a quick motion, the head pulls downward followed by a softer return to the upright position. The action emphasises the speaker's commitment to what has just been said and can be perceived as a slight attack. During his presidency, George W Bush frequently used this gesture, accompanying his words, 'make no mistake about it'.

Displaying Attention and Interest

If you tilt or cock your head, you indicate that you're interested in whatever you're observing. Although men tilt their heads by raising the chin, women prefer the head cock in which the chin is slightly lowered and the head is held at an angle towards the subject of interest.

This section covers all manner of head tilts, and you can see some examples in action in the *Body Language For Dummies* app.

Tilting and canting

Whether you call the action tilting or canting, people and animals incline their heads slightly whenever they hear something that captures their attention. Notice when you perform this gesture that you hold your head at an angle towards whatever's got your interest. The head tilt – or cant – is also used when people are listening attentively.

Although men tilt their heads in an upward movement, mostly as a sign of recognition, women tilt their heads to the side in appeasement and as a playful or flirtatious gesture. When a woman tilts her head she exposes her neck, making herself look more vulnerable and less threatening.

If you're in a social setting and notice a woman in the company of men tilting her head, you can safely bet she's out to gain their attention (see Figure 3-4).

Gestures to assure safety and security

If an adult wants to appear appealing to another adult in order to gain some recompense or advantage she tilts her head to one side and gives a gentle smile and expectant gaze in the other person's direction. Some women, wanting to break down another person's resistance gladly take on the teasing, cajoling behaviours of a precocious young girl. By tilting her head she is reliving the times when she sought comfort, rest, or loving and tender bodily contact as she laid her head against her parent's body. As an adult, she may not necessarily lean into her companion's body, but the gesture alone is enough to stir up protective emotions. With no understanding of what's happening or why, the reluctant feelings that the companion had been harbouring drift away.

Figure 3-4:
A woman
showing
her neck is
showing her
interest.

Because the head tilt can be used to indicate that what you're saying needn't be taken too seriously, make sure that when you're making an important point you keep your head upright.

Fran came home in the wee small hours of the morning after a night out with her girlfriends. Her husband was sitting up in bed, wide awake in a fury. Although she'd done nothing other than have a bit of harmless fun, Fran knew she was in trouble and had to change her husband's mood quickly. She threw herself into her helpless-little-girl behaviour, including wide-open eyes, pouted lips, and canting her head to one side, which she instinctively knew would appeal to her husband's more tender and protective feelings. The gestures worked and after explaining that he had just been worried, and appealing to her to let him know in the future if she was going to be back late, they happily fell to sleep.

If you want to show that what you're saying isn't meant to be taken too seriously, give a short, sharp downward tilt of your head to one side, and add a wink of the eye. People recognise this multi-purpose gesture as both humorous and conspiratorial, as well as being a friendly social acknowledgement.

Who cants the most?

An Italian research project investigating head positions in paintings from the 13th to the 19th centuries, revealed that commissioned portraits of powerful men seldom depict them with their heads canted. Religious and pious figures are frequently portrayed in this attitude. The study also found that female figures are depicted with their heads canted more frequently than male figures.

The head cock

Cocking your head involves a dip of the forehead and a twist of the chin as you incline your head towards another person. This gesture is frequently used as a non-contact greeting and relates back to the days when men would doff or touch their hats in recognition, or tug their forelocks in acknowledgement of another person. Dipping your head is a submissive gesture that can be interpreted as demonstrating subservience.

The head cock is a teasing, cajoling action intended to break down a person's resistance. Women appear appealing and provocative when they employ this gesture, eliciting nurturing and protective feelings from the person they're seeking to entice. Men who resort to the head cock are seeking sympathy or reassurance, or are showing that they're not the tough, ruthless character they believe that society demands them to be. Recall Clark Gable as Rhett Butler in *Gone with the Wind*, cocking his head to those with whom he courted favour, whether it was Mammy, the ladies of southern society or one of his jailors? The overriding effect of the head cock is of the rush of protective and compassionate feelings. Unless, that is, you know that you're being manipulated, in which case you may just feel annoyed.

When you're listening, you unconsciously copy the other person's head movements. The empathy that you share with the speaker is reflected in the shared behaviour.

Sitting tête à tête

People who put their heads closely together are showing that a tie exists between them and no room is available for anyone else. The physical closeness reflects their intellectual and emotional bond. The action is one of exclusion and prevents others from overhearing what they're saying.

The next time you're sitting with your friends having a good gossip or sharing a risqué joke, observe how your heads come close together. When the punch line is delivered, or the dénouement of the story is revealed, see how your head positions change.

Indicating Submissiveness or Worry

Charles Darwin concluded that people lower their heads when they're feeling submissive. The act makes a person look smaller and less threatening. If our intention, conscious or not, is to appear compliant, dipping, tilting, canting, and cocking the head all do the job. Research also shows that self-touching gestures, such as holding your head at the back of your neck and placing your hands on top of your head like a helmet, provide comfort, reassurance, protection, and help to alleviate your stress.

Dipping and ducking

If you've ever walked between two people who are deep in conversation, you may have ducked your head down to keep from invading their space and to apologise for any inconvenience you may have caused.

Some people make a slight involuntary dip of their heads when they approach another person they think is important or if that person's involved in a conversation with someone else.

People who don't care about status distinctions don't usually display submissive gestures. Those who feel they're intruding on important people excuse themselves with a slight dip of the head.

Marsha is an American living in London. She's an active and successful fund raiser for several high-profile aid organisations. In acknowledgement of her contributions to the charity sector, she was invited to attend a reception at Buckingham Palace attended by Queen Elizabeth and other high-ranking members of the Royal family. She was told that when she was introduced to the Queen she was expected to make a formal curtsey. Marsha found that expectation difficult to digest. Although she respects the Queen for the service she has shown to her country, she doesn't acknowledge status differentiations and is loath to demonstrate submissiveness to anyone, even the Queen. Although she didn't perform a full curtsey, out of respect she did give a slight head bow when introduced to the Queen.

Cradling for comfort

The memory from our infancy and childhood of being held and comforted during times of distress lingers and lives in our adult lives. The sensation of having the back of the neck supported creates a sense of security. In times of insecurity, people can often be observed with their hands holding the back of their necks (see Figure 3-5). Subconsciously, they're protecting themselves from real or imagined threats. This gesture provides comfort and reassurance.

Bob attended an all-day company board meeting during which discussions became heated. At one point during the afternoon, he noticed that his chairman sat back in his seat, put his hands behind his head, and began to rub his neck. He then changed positions, moving forward in his chair, rested his elbows on the table, and continued massaging his neck. After a few moments, he clasped his hands on the table, took a deep breath, and addressed the group with new-found focus and purpose. He seemed to have become re-energised by the few moments of self comfort.

Figure 3-5:
The head cradle provides comfort and security; the head clasp acts as a shield.

The head clasp

Wherever the stakes are high, be they on the sporting field, on election night, or on the trading floor of an investment bank, and despair is in the air, you see people clasping their heads as if they're creating a manual crash helmet. The head clasp is a protective gesture in which the hands rise up and cover the top of the head.

Head clasping is a natural response to calamity, real or imagined, and acts as a metaphorical shield, protecting the head from psychological damage.

Showing Boredom

Someone who is bored props her head in her hand. Her eyes droop at half-mast and before you know it she's nodding off (see Figure 3-6). Resting your head in your hand is reminiscent of your childhood, when someone would support your head when you were tired. You rest your head in the palm of your hand because your head feels too heavy to stay upright on its own. Your palm cushions your cheek and your chin drops in a nod. You're usually bored when what you're doing doesn't inspire you or meet your abilities. You may even feel tired and fed up.

Take comfort in knowing that you're not alone if you've ever felt bored. You can recognise the signs of boredom in yourself and others.

Boredom and burnout

According to Ramon Greenwood, senior career counsellor at Common Sense At Work (www.commonsenseatwork.com), critical boredom, in which you're tired of your day-in-day-out job is more dangerous than being bored with a specific part of your work. His research shows that being bored with at least one-half of a person's tasks for any particular job is usual. Being bored by the job itself can lead to burnout. Signs of burnout include fatigue, low morale, fear, despair, absenteeism, hostility (at home as well as at work), increased health problems, and substance abuse – which are all threatening to your health and your career. Boredom and burnout often result over time from bringing more ability to a task than is required. Stated differently, the job only requires half your brain and half your energy.

According to the American Psychological Association, signs of boredom are similar to signs of depression. Common symptoms include changes in sleeping and eating patterns as well as loss of pleasure and purpose. The two groups of people most likely to commit suicide are teenagers and the elderly. Both groups described themselves as bored. This information gives added meaning to the expression 'bored to death'.

Figure 3-6:
A drooped head, glazed eyes and slack facial muscles indicate boredom.

Before determining that someone is bored with what you're saying, look into her eyes. If they're bright and alight, the person who's resting her head in her hand may be thinking. If the eyes are dull and unblinking, she's probably bored.

Showing You're Deep in Thought

Some of the most misinterpreted gestures are those that demonstrate pensiveness or deep thinking. Auguste Rodin's sculpture, 'The Thinker', is the prototype for the thinking position. The subject has his head resting on his hand and is in a forward leaning position.

Placing your hand on your cheek indicates thought, consideration, or some kind of meditation. If your eyes are active and regularly blink, they show that you're considering your options.

The main difference between someone who's thinking and someone who's bored can be detected in the body's energy. A person who's actively engaged in thought shows interest and attentiveness. Her eyes are engaged, she may have one or both hands placed by her head, and her body leans forward.

Resting your head in your hand, out of boredom or interest, requires hand to head contact, which is a reassuring gesture. Whether you're bored or contemplative, you subconsciously comfort yourself with this action, stemming back to childhood. Both when you're bored and when you're thinking, your head may rest in your hand or hands. The way of telling the difference in moods is to look at where your eyes are focused, and where your hands and fingers are placed.

Head resting on hand

When a person's thinking she may bring her hand to her face, put her chin into her palm, or extend her index finger up her cheek while her remaining fingers rest below her mouth. This gesture is particular to the evaluation gesture (discussed in Chapter 9) and indicates that the person is thinking about what to do next.

If the person thinking pulls her body back from the other individual her thinking is critical, cynical, or negative in some way towards the person who's speaking.

When I'm invited to speak at seminars and conferences – particularly in western cultures – I can count on at least a third of the audience to sit with their hands to their heads. Those who are interested and engaged tend to lean forward. Those who sit back with their heads resting in their hands are more of the wait-and-see variety, a bit sceptical and in need of further convincing. (For more about body language in other cultures, turn to Chapter 15.)

Chin stroking

Someone stroking her chin is indicating that she's deep in thought or making an evaluation. In this gesture, a person strokes her chin with her thumb and index finger. The index finger may also stroke the upper lip. If a man has a beard, he may even pull on it.

The 18th century actor, Henry Siddons, in his book *Rhetorical Gestures* says, 'This gesture signifies the wise man making a judgment.'

Chapter 4

Watching Facial Expressions

. . . .

In This Chapter

▶ Communicating your feelings when words are inappropriate

▶ Recognising facial expressions that reinforce the spoken message

▶ Masking emotions

▶ Expressing a range of emotions

. . . .

Face it. No matter what you say, people are going to believe the look on your face rather than what you tell them. Try as you may to hide your feelings, the curl of your lip, the glint in your eye, or the flare of your nostrils gives the game away. Second only to your eyes, your face, when moving, is your most expressive feature.

Facial expressions exert a powerful control over the type and amount of communication between individuals. People make personality and other judgements about each other based on what they see on their faces. Rightly or wrongly, people believe that someone with an attractive face has many other positive attributes.

Sometimes letting your expression do the talking is more appropriate than blurting out what you're thinking or feeling. At other times you may need to reinforce your spoken message with a physical gesture, or express emotions when words fail you. Here's where your face comes in handy.

Communicating Feelings When Words Are Inappropriate

Take a healthy measure of lips, teeth, jaws, cheeks, and you can create yourself a plethora of facial expressions. With more than 44 muscles in your face – 22 per side – you can communicate just about anything you want simply by look alone. And sometimes a look is all you need.

Say that you think the person sitting across from you is attractive, but you'd feel a fool coming out and saying so. The other person may feel a bit threatened or uncomfortable if you expressed your feelings out loud. So, what to do? You establish eye contact and hold it a little longer than usual, you give a little smile, and if you're a woman you may drop your chin a fraction and look up from under your eyebrows. If you're a man, you probably tilt your head back. Not a word's been spoken, yet a frisson is in the air (see Figure 4-1 and the *Body Language For Dummies* app for an example).

Figure 4-1:
Attracted people tend to look at one another, smile and position themselves close together.

The engine behind the expression

The facial nerve (cranial nerve VII) that controls your facial muscles is like a tree. The tap root is located in the brain, and three branches extend from it. The first controls the tearing and salivating process. The second branch is responsible for transmitting taste messages.

The third branch sends facial expressions such as the smile, frown, and squint. Because human facial skin is flexible and responds quickly to brain impulses, most people can express themselves easily without speaking a word.

You may want to send a message telling someone that his behaviour isn't acceptable. A lowered brow, tightened lips, and a slight shake of the head are usually enough to make your point.

A disapproving look may not always be enough. William was a 4-year-old pageboy at his uncle's wedding. William's mother was seated near enough to her son to catch his eye, but not near enough to grab his hand. During the ceremony, William became fractious and began playing with the other young attendants, in spite of his mother's attempts to control his behaviour with her facial signals. No matter how much she frowned, put her index finger to her pursed lips while shaking her head in a definite 'No' gesture, William took no notice. Finally, he turned his head sharply in the direction of his mother, frowned for all he was worth and made a face at her – his little way of saying, 'I know what you want and I'm going to do this my way!'

The next time you disagree with your boss, partner, or associate and believe that it would be inappropriate to say so out loud, you can engage the other person in a bit of ocular one-upmanship. Hold the person's gaze slightly longer than you would normally, with your lips tightly closed. If your timing's right, your expression states your position without saying a word.

Recognising Facial Expressions that Reinforce the Spoken Message

As with all gestures, what your face reveals is going to be believed more than the words you say. Flash your eyebrows in recognition of someone whose company you enjoy, frown when reading your child's school report, smile as a loved one approaches you, and your facial expressions match your verbal message.

Tell your daughter-in-law how happy you are to see her while your facial expression says that you've been sucking on a lemon or you've been frozen in cold water, and don't be surprised if she holds back from you.

Open facial gestures – in which your eyes are engaged, your mouth is relaxed, and your head is tilted with interest – are safe and inviting, whereas closed expressions and gestures – pursed lips, a furrowed brow and squinted eyes – indicate that you're just not prepared to be open (see Figure 4-2). Working in combination with positive language and a well-modulated voice, open facial gestures confirm the spoken message, whereas closed facial gestures can conflict with it. When you're speaking or listening and you want to indicate that you're open to the other person and are prepared to give him a chance, make sure that your facial expressions are open and match your verbal expressions. Conflicting gestures send mixed messages.

Figure 4-2:
Someone
who's not
prepared to
be open.

To develop a well-modulated voice that represents you at your best, start by breathing correctly. Allow yourself to breathe from your abdomen, like a newborn baby. After you've mastered that technique, begin to hum to relax and develop your vocal chords. A well-modulated voice resonates and rises from a firm foundation. (You can read more about the power of the voice in *Persuasion & Influence For Dummies* by Elizabeth Kuhnke (Wiley).)

Myles's girlfriend, Laura, lives near Manchester and Myles lives in London. Because of the distance between the two cities, Laura stays for several days when she visits Myles, who lives at home with his mother, Tina. Tina thinks Laura is a pleasant girl and appreciates the care and attention she's shown Myles. Since they've been dating, Myles's self-confidence has grown and Tina acknowledges that Laura is largely responsible for that. However, Tina doesn't like Laura's over-dependence on Myles and the lack of initiative she demonstrates when she's visiting. Tina initiates the conversations and asks Laura for her help when she's getting dinner on the table. Laura has a bit of a whine in her voice, which Tina also finds annoying. Laura then tells Myles that she doesn't think his mother likes her. Although Tina does like certain aspects of Laura's personality, there are parts that she doesn't like. Tina thought that she was demonstrating openness in the way she engaged with Laura. What she didn't realise was that her facial expressions weren't as open as she believed and Laura was picking up on that.

Suri was scolding her young son, Jordan, for drawing a rainbow on the newly hung wallpaper. Jordan looked scared when his mother first called his name. His lips trembled, and his eyes were wide with fear. After a moment, he relaxed. Although his mother was frowning at him, her mouth looked liked it was smiling. After being told not to draw on the wallpaper again, Jordan skipped off. While Suri was initially annoyed when she saw Jordan's crayon drawing, she also thought it was quite sweet.

Sending out mixed messages through expressions and gestures can be confusing, and serve to diminish the power of the spoken message you are attempting to convey. Figure 4-3 shows an example of a person giving out mixed messages. While the pointed finger and furrowed brow suggest anger, the twinkle around her eyes and the upward curve to the lips indicate that she's not as angry as she may at first seem.

Figure 4-3:
Mixed
messages
diminish the
power of
your spoken
message.

Because of the powerful impressions that non-verbal behaviour can make, choose those gestures that represent the message you want to convey.

Bill Clinton is known for his powers of persuasion. A technique he employs with alacrity is interspersing his remarks with a wide range of facial gestures. During the Labour Party Conference in Blackpool in October 2002, Clinton was called in to convince the non-believers that Britain must support the United States in war against Iraq should the necessity rise. A master of the gesture, Clinton utilised his knowledge of theatre, people and persuasion to act out his feelings. Notably, he used the 'lower lip bite' to create the impression that he connected deeply with his audience and experienced their fear and pain (see Figure 4-4).

Figure 4-4: Chewing on the lower lip while looking at someone who's experiencing pain shows a connection to that person.

When you're not being perceived the way you want to be, consider your facial expressions. If your face is saying one thing and you mean something else, you may have to change your expression. To counteract the message that your non-verbal behaviour projects, readjust your behaviour.

Looking beyond the hang-dog expression

Some people are born looking sombre or sad; they can't help it. Their eyes turn down, their mouths curve south, and their cheeks hang slack, rather like the bulldog whose facial parts all suffer from gravity's pull. The person with a downward facing countenance has a look that spells 'sombre'.

People with sombre expressions can be perceived as unfriendly, thoughtful, or sad. Although they may be telling you how thrilled they are about their latest successful venture, their facial make-up says they're less than happy.

If someone with a sombre expression tells you how excited he is about a project, look to his eyes. If they're engaged and the muscles around the outer edges are pulling upward, you can believe what he says.

People with a perpetually sunny expression can be mistaken as frivolous or less serious. You need to take in the whole person before making a judgement.

Masking Emotions

If you've ever bitten your lips to keep from blurting out sentiments that would undoubtedly cause offence, if you've ever smiled when your heart was breaking, or if you've ever frowned when you've wanted to laugh, you know what masking emotions is all about.

When people want to avoid expressing what's going on inside, they create the opposite facial expression with their pliable facial muscles and skin, and hey presto! they're masking their emotions.

I recently attended a luncheon party and sat across the table from a woman whose mother had died two days previously. Before eating, the guests were asked for a moment of silence in memory of Dottie. I was fond of Dottie and was saddened to hear of her death. I looked at her daughter, whom I didn't know, and as we caught each other's eyes we exchanged poignant smiles. Anyone watching would have seen that we both held our mouths tightly with no showing of teeth – hers slightly pulled to the side, mine more a straight line – our eyebrows tense across our foreheads, and we gave each other slight head nods for fear that doing more would allow the sense of loss to come flooding forth. Although we were doing our best to cover our sadness, a careful observer would have noticed the struggle it took to maintain the mask (see Figure 4-5).

Figure 4-5:
Holding
back an
emotion like
sadness
tightens the
muscles
around your
eyes and
mouth.

After the Falklands War, the then British Prime Minister, Margaret Thatcher, was interviewed on television and asked why a British submarine had been instructed to torpedo the Argentine battleship, the *Belgrano*. Purportedly annoyed that she had to undergo the journalist's questioning, and knowing that it was important for her career that she was seen as informed, calm, and in control, she explained that because the ship was inside the British exclusion zone the action was justifiable. Both she and the journalist knew that was a lie. The truth was that the ship was sailing away from the Falklands and was outside the exclusion zone when attacked. While Mrs Thatcher was making her false reply, her mask fell for a split second and she revealed a brief expression of anger. She gave a quick smile, which anyone looking carefully could detect was false from the lack of engagement in her eyes followed by a momentary flash of anger. Her eyes protruded and her jaw thrust forward. As quickly as the expression appeared, it was replaced by her masked expression.

A jutted jaw and protruding eyes indicate anger or annoyance.

Expressing a Range of Emotions

Whereas words reveal factual data, gestures reveal information about attitudes and emotions, and the range of emotions people experience on a daily basis is vast. From anger to worry, you can count on your face to reflect your feelings.

Showing happiness

If your grandmother was anything like mine, she'd tell you to 'put on your happy face' when meeting someone new because she knew, intuitively, that people respond positively to positive behaviour.

Facial displays of genuine, unadulterated, free-flowing happiness can't be missed (see Figure 4-6). When you're experiencing pure joy, your eyes involuntarily twinkle, the laugh lines at the outside corners of your eyes deepen, your cheeks raise, and as your lips pull up at the sides and separate you expose your pearly white teeth. No one can doubt your joy.

Figure 4-6:
A genuine smile pulls back the mouth and the eyes (left). Insincere people use only their mouths when smiling (right).

Spot the smile

In 1862, the French neurophysiologist Guillaume Duchenne de Boulogne published his studies of facial expressions. De Boulogne used electro diagnostics and electrical stimulation to distinguish between genuine and false smiles. In addition to using the heads of people who had been executed by the guillotine, De Boulogne's principal photographic subject was an old man who had the rare condition of facial anaesthesia. This unfortunate condition made him the perfect subject for the scientist's investigations, because the electrodes used to stimulate the muscles were undoubtedly uncomfortable, if not quite painful.

With a hands-on approach, De Boulogne twisted and pulled face muscles from various angles and positions to discover which muscles controlled which smiles. He identified two kinds of smiles that are controlled by two different muscle sets. The *zygomatic major* muscles, which run down the side of the face, are under your conscious control. These muscles are attached to the corners of the mouth and pull the mouth back, exposing the teeth while pumping up the cheeks. When you want to appear friendly, subordinate, or show how much you're enjoying yourself when the opposite is true, you rely on the zygomatic majors to produce a false smile of fake enjoyment. The *orbicularis oculi* are the muscles that pull the eyes back, make them narrow, and produce laugh lines that radiate from the outside corners of the eyes. The orbicularis oculi act involuntarily and produce a true smile.

Further research by Professor Paul Ekman of the University of California, San Francisco and University of Kentucky professor Dr Wallace V Friesen reveal that the unconscious brain automatically generates genuine smiles. When you experience pleasure, the part of the brain that processes feelings is stimulated, resulting in a smile in which the mouth muscles move, the cheeks lift, the eyes narrow, and the eyebrows slightly dip.

Insincere smiles are easily spotted. You need more than pulled back lips showing off your pearly whites to convince someone that you're feeling happy, pleased, or any other positive emotion. If your eyes aren't engaged with your mouth – that is, if your lips pull back in a smile and your eyes are dull, listless, or averting the other person's gaze – you're sure to be spotted as insincere.

The fake smile, like the one in Figure 4-6, looks manufactured and unnatural.

When you're taking someone's photograph and you want him to smile, find another word – one that elicits a genuine smile – to replace 'Cheese'. The word 'Cheese' pulls back the zygomatic major muscles resulting in a false smile and an artificial-looking photo.

If you're with someone who smiles at you and says he's happy, but a little voice inside tells you that something's amiss, listen to the voice. Then look at the eyes and the cheeks for confirmation. To spot a genuine smile, observe the fleshy part of the eye between the brow and the eyelid. If it moves downwards and the end of the eyebrows dip slightly, the smile is for real.

You can tolerate a lot of awkwardness in another person if he shows by his facial expression that he wants to get along with you. By showing that he's doing his best to be amiable in challenging circumstances – by offering an open smile, eye contact and a tilted head – his behaviour becomes more acceptable than in someone who's disagreeable in both attitude and behaviour.

Cecilia had a noon meeting with a potential new client. Her train into Paddington was delayed and she had to rush to catch her tube. When she exited at the right station, she was unable to find the building. Cecilia prides herself on her punctuality and began to worry that she was going to be late. She saw two men walking briskly toward her. From the pace of their stride, it was clear they were focused on where they were going. Cecilia, appreciating their needs, walked towards them with a mixed look of openness, concern, and confusion on her face, making clear that she was a nice person in need of help. She matched the men's pace, apologised for interrupting them and asked if they were familiar with the area, which they were. When she first approached the men, she noticed a momentary flicker of annoyance cross their faces. She kept her expression open, matched their walking pace so as not to slow them down and thanked them politely and with another smile when they pointed her in the right direction.

Revealing sadness

Look at someone who's feeling blue (see Figure 4-7) and you can see that his facial features are slack and sagging. His eyes are dull and lifeless and the sides of his mouth are probably cast downward. His face seems to have melted or collapsed.

Lips frequently tremble when someone experiences feelings of grief or sorrow. His eyes may become moist, and often a person in this position covers his face with his hand as if blocking out whatever is causing him to feel sad.

Figure 4-7:
Slack, sagging and trembling expressions reveal sadness.

Demonstrating disgust and contempt

Disgust and contempt can be shown in varying degrees, but the general look involves the mouth grimacing while the eyes narrow. The nose wrinkles, the chin drops or lifts a fraction, and the head turns slightly to the side. People showing disgust tend to look downward on the person or object of their contempt. In extreme cases they may lift their upper lip, which in turn makes the nose pull upward (see Figure 4-8).

Chappy and her mother Jean were having a heated political discussion. Not surprisingly, Chappy's views were in direct opposition to those of her mother. Finally, unable to win the argument or to convince her daughter of her misguided judgement, Jean, in a high display of contempt, wrinkled her nose, narrowed her eyes, tightened her lips, and shook her head in disgust as if she had just smelt an over-ripe Gorgonzola (see the *Body Language For Dummies* app for an example).

Signs of contempt are common in the business environment. Looks of disdain and scorn are tossed about the office floor with regularity as when one high-flyer attempts to dispose another.

Nicola is extremely talented at spotting new trends in consumer behaviour. Although her boss admires her perception, she also feels threatened by Nicola's youth, energy, and ability to engage with senior board members. During meetings, Nicola's boss often responds to Nicola's observations and recommendations with pursed lips, a slight narrowing of the eyes, and a small turn of the head away from Nicola, as she attempts to engage with a senior member of the team to dismiss Nicola's contribution.

Figure 4-8:
Looking
downward
on another
person, with
sneering
lips and a
pulled-up
nose, shows
contempt.

Showing anger

You've experienced the emotion, you know the feeling, and you've worn the expression. Anyone in your vicinity recognises the signs. Before the big blow up, you probably stare hard at the source of offence without flinching. Your eyebrows pull down and inward, causing your forehead to furrow. Your lips tighten and turn down at the corners, or open stiffly as if in a frozen shout. You may also grit your teeth together. Some people flare their nostrils when enraged. Finally, if you're incandescent with rage, your face can turn white as the blood drains from the epidermis.

Changing colours

According to British zoologist Desmond Morris, facial colour as a part of the 'Flight or Fight' action system is an indicator of rage level. If someone approaches you menacingly and his face is pale, he's more likely to attack than if his face is red. If the face is red, he's already experienced his deepest rage and has passed the point of attack. Although people think of those whose faces are red with rage as being the perilous ones – and they may easily swing back into a dangerous pale-faced fury – the reddened face is a result of an internal struggle that manifests itself alarmingly in shouts and foul language and is no more worrying than a furiously barking dog. If you've ever been bitten by a dog, you may remember that it wasn't the one who was making a lot of noise who sunk his teeth into you; similarly, the puce-faced, shouting individual is unlikely to be going to do you real physical harm.

If your anger is about to get the better of you, inhale deeply through your nose, breathing deeply into your lower abdomen while keeping your upper chest loose and free of tension. Hold for a count of three, and exhale slowly through your mouth. Deep breathing provides oxygen to the brain enabling you to think clearly. The time it takes for you to breathe and exhale gives you a moment to reflect and calm down.

Recognising surprise and revealing fear

Expressions of surprise and fear are closely connected. In both expressions, the eyes widen and the mouth is opened. The differences are subtle and found primarily in the attitudinal shape and position of the eyebrows, eyes, and mouth. A few other telltale differences can also be picked up.

Surprise!

An expression of surprise, unlike a fearful expression, is open and colourful. From the whites of your eyes and teeth to the redness of the inside of your lips and your mouth, which you expose as your jaw drops, a person can tell when you're genuinely surprised. Granted, not all people open their mouths, but the whites of the eyes show and the eyebrows rise in an arched position.

Justin and Sylvia secretly wed, with only the priest and two attendants present. They hadn't been dating long and few of their friends expected them to last as a couple. When they invited some of their friends to dinner and told them what they'd done, their guests raised their eyebrows and dropped their jaws in surprise, never having expected to hear that news.

When you're surprised or startled, your eyebrows shoot up in an arch and horizontal wrinkles appear across your forehead. The whites of your eyes become more noticeable as you widen your eyes and your jaw drops, leaving your mouth in a slack position (see Figure 4-9).

Figure 4-9:
Looking surprised (left) and fearful (right).

You may notice that someone who has been genuinely surprised covers his mouth with his hand. This is an example of holding back an extreme emotion. Go to Chapter 9 for more information on how revelatory hand movements can be.

Boo!

The telltale signs of a fearful expression are

- ✔ A tensely pulled back open mouth
- ✔ Raised eyelids
- ✔ Exposed whites of eyes

When you're full of fear, your eyebrows rise and pull together in a crooked curve. The centre part of your forehead wrinkles and, while your upper eyelids rise exposing the whites of your eyes, your lower eyelids become tense and rise, too. Finally, your lips tense and may pull back around your open mouth (see Figure 4-9).

Demonstrating interest

When showing interest in what someone is doing or saying, you may find yourself cocking your head in his direction and nodding in agreement. Your eyes widen, taking in the information and your mouth may be slightly opened.

The open position indicates interest. Whether the interest is romantic, intellectual, spiritual, or just plain friendly, the look on the person's face is open. The eyes are engaged, the head may tilt or nod, and the body leans forward as if getting immersed in the subject. No blocks – such as lowered eyebrows, a jutting chin, or a furrowed forehead – stand between you and the person you're interacting with. You lean forward, ready to go, and your expectant face follows.

People nod when they're listening. A slow nod shows that they're taking in what the other person's saying and are prepared to let him continue. A fast nod indicates that although the person may be interested in what the speaker's saying, he feels a sense to hurry things along.

Research into the behavioural similarities within the animal kingdom shows that birds, dogs, and humans among others cock their heads when they're listening attentively. So if you want to know whether your dog or parrot's paying attention, look to the tilt of his head.

When evaluating what you're observing, you may raise one hand to your cheek with your index finger pointing upward and your thumb supporting your chin while your other three fingers curl in on your palm. When decision time arrives, you and your colleagues may find yourselves stroking your chins in a sign of thoughtfulness and contemplation. (Go to Chapter 9 to find out more about what hand gestures mean.)

Chapter 5

The Eyes Have It

In This Chapter

▶ Understanding the power of the held gaze

▶ Avoiding looking at another person

▶ Reading the messages – how eyes tell a tale

*B*ecause much of our face-to-face time with people is spent looking at their faces, the signals they send out with their eyes play a vital part in revealing their thoughts and attitudes. In fact, of all our body language signals, the eyes reveal our thoughts and emotions most accurately: they're placed in the strongest focal position on the body, and because the pupils respond unconsciously to stimuli they can't be artificially manipulated or controlled (well, you can artificially increase pupil size with belladonna but that's another story).

Your eyes are the gateway to the soul and reflect what's going on inside of you. They're also the means of seeing what's going on inside of someone else. Some people instinctively know how to use their eyes to their own advantage, to garner sympathy, convey sexual interest, or to deliver the message, 'Stay away!' With practice, your eyes can speak the messages you mustn't say aloud. This chapter looks at the role that eyes play in communicating your feelings and intentions. You discover how to use your eyes to command attention, display interest, show disapproval, create intimate feelings, and demonstrate dominance. And because communication – even with eyes – is a two-way street, I tell you how to read the eye signals that others give you.

The Power of the Held Gaze

Establishing and maintaining eye contact comfortably with another person can be the basis for successful communication, giving you and the person you're communicating with a feeling of wellbeing and trust. But sometimes, eye contact can be uncomfortable, such as when the other person seems dishonest, untrustworthy, shy or angry. Whether the interaction is comfortable or not has to do, in part, with the way that a person looks, or doesn't look, at you. The intensity and length of time she holds your eye influences the meaning of the gaze. The following sections explain the different attitudes that a held gaze can mean.

Jennifer is a psychiatric doctor working in private practice. A patient of hers, Dorothy, is an elderly woman who was diagnosed schizophrenic when she was in her late teens. Dorothy has managed to live an active life through the use of medication and psychiatric treatment and many of her friends aren't aware of her illness. One behaviour that Jennifer noticed about Dorothy is the way she stares at another person for long periods of time without speaking. The look is difficult to read because of the blankness of the stare. The look is unflinching and can be unnerving to people who aren't aware of the problem.

When a person holds your gaze, she's telling you one of two things: she finds you attractive or interesting, or she may be feeling anger or hostility towards you and is offering you a non-verbal challenge. How do you tell the difference? Look at her pupils: In the first case, the pupils are dilated; in the second, the pupils are constricted. (See Figure 5-1.)

Figure 5-1:
Holding a gaze can demonstrate interest (left) or hostility (right).

Who's watching who?

Some people find establishing and maintaining eye contact difficult and avert their eyes when speaking. Others bore into their listeners with piercing eyes. Because of the connective quality of the eyes – the gateway to the soul as the saying goes – it can be hard to gauge the other person if she refuses to meet your eye. Research shows that when Westerners interact, they look at one another on average 61 per cent of the time. The speaker looks at the listener between 40–60 per cent of the time, and the listener looks at the speaker approximately 75 per cent of the time. People spend approximately 31 per cent of their time mutual gazing. What this tells you is that if someone looks at you more or less than usual, something's going on that's impacting her response.

The average gaze for an individual in western cultures lasts 2.95 seconds and the average mutual gaze is 1.8 seconds. However, in Japan, the Middle East, and some Asian, African and South American cultures, prolonged eye contact is perceived as hostile or discourteous.

To show interest

You can demonstrate interest in what you're doing or saying by fixing your gaze directly on the person or object you're addressing for slightly longer than you may normally do. The length and direction of your gaze tells anyone who's paying attention that you only have eyes for who and what you're looking at. The moment you look at another person, you have given that person your attention. Hold the look for more than two to three seconds and you imply that the person has grabbed your interest and has your permission to look back at you.

Lizzie went to an art fair with her friends, Frank and Peter. Their taste in art – South American contemporary with a twist – was very different from Lizzie's, whose preferences tended toward Monet and John Singer Sargent. Lizzie was uninterested in most of the paintings her friends were admiring. Not wanting to appear bored or dismissive of their taste, Lizzie forced herself to look at the paintings for longer than she would normally have done. Not only did Frank and Peter believe that Lizzie was enjoying the art, she discovered that by giving the work extra 'eye time' she began to appreciate it in a way she previously hadn't. Although she didn't want it in her home, she recognised how other people could value it.

In social situations, focus your gaze on the triangular area between your listener's eyes and mouth. You're perceived as non-threatening and interested.

Pupils, babies, and the art of the deal

Confucius said, 'Look into a person's pupils. He cannot hide himself.' By observing the pupils of another person's eyes, you can tell whether or not she likes what she's looking at. If her pupils resemble warm drops of chocolate, you know that whatever she's responding to is having a positive impact. If they're steely and small, best move away fast! Dilated pupils show a favourable response; constricted pupils don't. Remember, too, that pupils respond to light. They enlarge when the lighting's dim and contract under bright conditions.

Consider these other fun tidbits:

✔ Research shows that most women's eyes dilate to their extreme when looking at images of other mothers and children. The next time you get a chance, observe a mother watching her newborn child.

✔ Newborn babies and young children appear to have larger pupils than adults. When in the company of adults, a child's or an infant's eyes often dilate in an unconscious attempt to look appealing and gain the adult's attention. This phenomenon is one that toy manufacturers (and cartoonists) recognise. To see for yourself, go into a children's store and have a look at the best-selling dolls and cuddly animals: the eyes almost always have oversized pupils.

✔ The ancient Chinese gem traders were expert in watching their buyers' eyes when negotiating prices. If the pupils dilated, the trader knew she was offering too good a deal and had to negotiate harder.

✔ Courtesans and prostitutes were known to make themselves appear more enticing and desirable by putting drops of belladonna in their eyes to dilate their pupils.

✔ It is said that the reason the late Aristotle Onassis wore dark glasses when negotiating business deals was to prevent his eyes from revealing his thoughts. Similarly, professional poker players also wear sunglasses to hide their emotions over a hand of cards.

Of course, without using artificial means, such as the courtesans did, pupil dilation is beyond your control.

Building rapport

When you want to build rapport with someone, research shows that you need to meet that person's gaze between 60–70 per cent of the time. If, for example, Penny likes Tim and wants to do business with him, she should look at him a lot. In response, Tim senses that Penny likes him and likes her in return. They easily look at one another and before you know it the deal's been done!

But what about the shy, timid people who find eye contact difficult? No matter how genuine, honest, and dedicated they are, by struggling to establish and maintain eye contact they send out signals of prevarication and doubt.

Clinton's gaze

People who have met Bill Clinton report that he has a way of looking at a person that makes that individual feel as though not only is she important, but that no one else matters at that point. Like many powerful and successful people, he uses his eyes to engage his listener by letting his gaze scan slowly across the other person's eyes and face as he speaks. The listener feels that no one else is in their vicinity and that she is totally the object of his attention.

Given the choice of working with a person who appears nervous and timid, and who has to make an effort to look at you at all, or someone with engaging eye contact who makes you feel good about yourself, which person do you choose? Research shows that people prefer to work with others with whom they have rapport, or a comfortable relationship. (For more about rapport and how to build it through body language, pick up a copy of *Neuro-linguistic Programming For Dummies* by Romilla Ready and Kate Burton (Wiley) or *Persuasion & Influence For Dummies* by Elizabeth Kuhnke (Wiley).) Even if you feel uncomfortable about making eye contact, making the effort really is worth it. The more you get used to looking another person in the eye, the more confident and trustworthy you appear, and the more rewarding your interactions are likely to be.

Ed regularly has to make formal presentations for his work. Although once into the presentation, he's able to look at his audience – albeit fleetingly – he finds establishing eye contact during his introduction extremely difficult. By watching himself on video replay, he realised how much impact he loses by not making eye contact with his listeners. He recognised that, by failing to establish eye contact with his audience at the very beginning of his presentation, he fails to engage with them and has to work that much harder to gain their attention, interest, and eventual buy-in. To create rapport with his listeners, Ed now establishes eye contact with them before he even begins to speak.

Creating intimate feelings

By letting your gaze wander from the receiver's eyes down the face and below the chin to other parts of the body, you're indicating an interest far removed from the world of business or a friendly 'hello'. In allowing your eyes to wander over your target's face and body, you're showing that you're attracted to that person. If the look is returned, you may be onto a winner. If not, revert to the social gaze or else you may find yourself in big trouble.

When a woman finds someone attractive, she may give that person a sideways glance with dilated pupils. This is referred to look as a 'come hither' look (see

Figure 5-2) because the look is saying, 'Come and get me.' If she doesn't want to be so obvious, she uses the social gaze and keeps her target guessing. (For more information on all the uses and meanings of sideways glances, go to the section 'The sideways glance' later in this chapter.)

Figure 5-2:
The 'come hither' look indicates a sexual interest and draws partners in.

To show disapproval, disagreement, and other not-so-pleasant feelings

Of course, not all gazes are warm and friendly. Often gaze alone can indicate displeasure. Beady little eyes, snake eyes, and shooting daggers with the eyes are sure signs of disapproval or disagreement. If a person holds your gaze for more than two thirds of the time and the pupils are constricted, you can bet you're in disfavour. If, however, you're able to hold the gaze for several seconds longer than you normally would without looking away – an action that would indicate submission – you can send out your own message of disagreement.

Because your pupils contract when you're angry or in a negative mood, the eyes look harsher and less friendly. Fake your smile and backslap all you want, if you're not pleased with what's going on and don't want to give the game away you'd better put on your dark glasses to hide your feelings.

Showing dominance

A dominant person is the one with authority. This person takes command, holds the power, and influences others. The dominant person is in charge.

People in positions of dominance use eye contact confidently. Because they're sure of themselves, their eye movements tend to be slow and smooth. They're comfortable looking at another person for an extended period of time, being careful not to stare, which would just make them look slightly mad or rude.

Gazing is done in two ways: away from and towards. Both types of eye placement can successfully demonstrate dominance. Those in control of the interaction demonstrate their dominance by choosing when and how long to look at the other person. The following sections explain how dominance can be conveyed through the power of the gaze.

If you want to be perceived as dominant, strong, and in control, slightly narrow your eyes (see Figure 5-3). Donald Trump is a master of the beady-eyed glare. So is Anne Robinson in *The Weakest Link*. Throughout his career Clint Eastwood has used this 'visor eyes' posture to great effect, as he did in his recent film, *Million Dollar Baby*. Another master of visor eyes is the latest actor to play James Bond – Daniel Craig.

Figure 5-3:
'Visor eyes'
enable a
person
to come
across as
strong,
dominant
and in
control.

Scenario 1: Being reprimanded

When you want to make a strong point, deliberately avoid eye contact to raise the other person's anxiety levels. If you've ever been reprimanded by an irate boss or disappointed parent, you may recall how the anxiety levels rise when the person speaking refuses to look at you. You know that any moment you're going to get the full force of her glare, you just have to wait to see when.

When I was working as a hostess on a cruise ship, I was called into the Cruise Director's office early one morning. Scotty was a stickler for punctuality and I had been late for an event the night before. I knew I was in for it because I'd heard him shout at my colleagues on other occasions. What I didn't know was how intense the confrontation would be. When I entered his office he was sitting quietly behind his desk, staring out at the ocean with his back turned to me. With barely a glance in my direction, he told me to sit down. Continuing to look out the porthole, he began to berate me not just for the previous night's transgression but for all my other failings as well. Unable to remain quiet and let him blow off some steam, I gave him excuses and argued back. Big mistake. He spun around in his seat and fixed me with a glare so forceful that it felt as if I'd been slapped in the face and punched in the chest. His stare was so intense and he held it for so long that I was unable to meet his eyes. Scotty told me that I'd better watch myself and that he was 'keeping an eye' on me. As he said those words, I looked up to see his eyes boring directly into mine. Not able to sustain the eye contact, I looked away. There was no question at that point who was in the dominant position.

If you find yourself disagreeing with someone and want to make your point, hold the eye contact slightly longer than you would normally. Without saying a word, you leave no doubt that you, too, are feeling dominant and should be taken seriously.

Scenario 2: In conversation

In conversation, the dominant person spends more time looking at the other person when she's talking than when she's listening. Whoever is speaking has control over the interaction. A dominant speaker watches her listeners to make sure that they're paying attention and aren't about to cut in. When the dominant person is in the listening position, however, she conveys her status by reducing the amount of time she spends looking at the speaker indicating that she's not interested in flattering that person and is soon taking back the speaker's role.

The Evil Eye

The prevalent and powerful superstitious belief in the Evil Eye comes from the feeling that people can be damaged by a prolonged stare. Belief in the Evil Eye is strongly held in Mediterranean countries, even among sophisticated people who often carry amulets and other good-luck charms to ward off disasters. Fishermen commonly protect their boats from danger by attaching a pair of artificial eyes to the prows of their vessels as a means of outstaring a potential threat or enemy. This practice began in ancient Egypt and is active in many parts of the world.

Scenario 3: The unflinching stare

You can grab the attention of an adversary by looking her directly in the eye without flinching. Direct eyeball-to-eyeball staring can be deeply threatening. If you've ever played the child's game of stare-you-out, you know that at some point you, or your partner, breaks the contact because maintaining it is just too difficult.

My dear late mother had an uncanny way of looking a person straight in the eye without batting an eyelid when she disapproved of what that person was doing. Her mouth tensed, her eyes narrowed as they tightened around the edges, and her gaze didn't falter. My sister, other selected family members, and I have all experienced the stinging effect of this piercing gaze, lovingly referred to as 'The Look'. It was unflinching, judgemental and could reduce us to responding in one of two ways: we either attempted to stare our mother down, which we never achieved , or else, unable to stand the pressure, we averted our eyes in a downward glance. Either way, Mother won.

If someone's trying to bully you or put you off, look your foe straight in the eye, narrow your eyelids, and focus directly on your target. If other people are around, let your eyes move slowly from one person to the next without blinking. Move your eyes first and let your head follow, keeping your torso still. The effect is unnerving. If you need a role model, Arnold Schwarzenegger in *The Terminator* is your man.

Effective gazes in business situations

If you're uncomfortable looking people directly in the eye and you want to come across as a person to be taken seriously, keep your gaze in the triangular area between the eyes and the centre of the forehead. As long as your eyes remain in that space and you keep control of the interaction, the other person reckons that you're someone who means business. The following are other tricks that come in handy in business situations.

Controlling a bore

Looking a tedious, dull, and mind-numbing bore straight in the eyes without flinching is a highly effective way of stopping her in her tracks. If you fix your eyes directly in the business gaze triangle without a flicker of an eye, you may be amazed at how quickly your bore comes to a halt.

The power lift

If you want to get your message across when you're presenting visual information during a meeting, you have to guide the audience's attention to where you want them to look. A simple way of controlling your listener's attention is to use a pen or pencil. Point to your material and verbalise what you're showing. Then, lift the pen, or pencil, off the page and hold it between your eyes and your listener's (see Figure 5-4). This movement works like a magnet as your listener lifts her head, looks directly at you and, while both hearing and seeing what you're saying, absorbs your message. While you continue to speak, keep the palm of your other hand open.

At last, a way to shorten business meetings!

One study showed that in presentations where visual aids are used, 83 per cent of the information is absorbed visually, 11 per cent through the audio channel, and 6 per cent through the other three senses. A study conducted at The Wharton School of the University of Pennsylvania found that in presentations that relied solely on the spoken word only 10 per cent of the information was retained. In order for a verbal presentation to be effective, key points must be repeated frequently. When a visual element is added to a verbal presentation, the retention rate increases to 50 per cent. The result is that by using visual aids in your presentations, you achieve a 400 per cent increase in efficiency. Further findings showed that when visual aids are used in business meetings, the time of the average meeting is 18.6 minutes as opposed to 25.7 minutes. This equates to a time saving of 28 per cent.

Figure 5-4:
The 'power lift' controls where a person looks during a presentation.

The Wandering Eye: Breaking Eye Contact

Avoiding or breaking eye contact can indicate a variety of things. In many instances, the sign is one of submission or discomfort. Although your instinct may be to run away from unpleasant situations or feelings, fleeing in panic isn't really an option in everyday life because as humans, we aim to cooperate. (Unless, of course, the other person is threatening physical violence, in which case you run in the opposite direction as fast as your legs can take you!) On the other hand, at times avoiding someone's gaze gives you a great deal of strength, appeal, and allure. It's all a matter of whose eyes you're avoiding and how you do it that creates the effect and determines the response. The following are the common reasons why humans avoid eye contact, knowingly or not:

↙ **To 'flee' from an encounter:** Evading someone's glance, gaze, or stare is a defensive, protective action, a form of fleeing from an interaction that stirs up in you a 'fight or flight' response. When you think you're going to lose – whether you're in an argument or trying to gain someone's attention – you unconsciously withdraw from the encounter by pulling your eyes away.

Looking away from another person, avoiding someone's gaze, and averting your eyes makes you look smaller. People who feel uncomfortable unconsciously make rapid and frequent eye movements, indicating that they'd rather scuttle away than stay where they are.

↙ **As a sign of submission:** When you look away from a person who makes you feel ill at ease, you're relinquishing your power and giving it over to that person.

↙ **To avoid confrontation:** As soon as a sign of confrontation appears, anxious people reduce the amount of time they spend looking at the person with whom they're disagreeing. When you're feeling anxious, you avoid looking at another person. Your eyes search for escape routes where you can in effect hide from what's going on rather than seek a solution. When it looks as if trouble's brewing between two people and you sense one of them is going to lose, don't be surprised if you see that person avert her gaze to remove the dominant person from sight.

↙ **As a sign of uncomfortable feelings:** People who are feeling ashamed, embarrassed, or sad, deliberately look away.

↙ **To prompt another person's attention:** Pulling your eyes away from someone can show that you're interested in her. This behaviour is part of the flirtation process and encourages the other person to go after you. If you do withdraw your eyes for this purpose, make sure that you look back frequently.

The following sections discuss the ways that many people avoid or minimise eye contact and explain what these different manoeuvres mean.

The eye shuttle

When you observe someone flicking her eyes back and forth, you can bet that she's subconsciously looking for an escape route. Notice that although her head remains still her eyes move rapidly from side to side. The action allows the person to take in everything that's going on around her and see where she can reposition herself without obviously giving the game away.

Dwight was at a business event where he saw Frank, a man he had met once before and whom he believed may be a potential client, or at least a valuable contact. Focusing on his own agenda, Dwight made a beeline for Frank who was already engaged in conversation with two colleagues. Dwight re-introduced himself and without being invited, joined in the discussion. What he failed to notice were Frank's eyes shuttling back and forth in search of the nearest exit. Although Frank wasn't interested in speaking with Dwight, he was a polite guy and didn't want to embarrass Dwight. While he smiled as Dwight regaled the group with stories and remained where he was standing, his eyes didn't connect with Dwight's as they scanned the room. Frank soon spotted another colleague and disengaged himself from the group, leaving his colleagues to deal with Dwight. Dwight never did do business with Frank, or his friends.

The sideways glance

The sideways glance carries several meanings depending on how the glance is given. It demonstrates interest, uncertainty, or hostility.

When you look at someone out of the corner of your eye and add a slight smile and raise your eyebrows, as shown in Figure 5-5, it would be fair enough for the receiver to think that you're interested in her.

Figure 5-5:
The sideways glance with a smile shows interest.

If someone catches your attention and you want to let her know that you think she's quite cute, look at her out of the corner of your eye and slightly raise your eyebrows. This gesture is mostly used by women and communicates interest.

If you've ever spoken to someone who avoids looking at you while shooting glances out of the corner of her eye, she may well not be very interested in you or what you're saying (see Figure 5-6). It may be time for you to change tack in your conversation, or move on.

Figure 5-6:
The sideways glance away from you can indicate a lack of interest.

People tend to look towards things that interest them, and look away from things that don't. Imagine that you're at a party. Your partner has gone to talk to friends, leaving you with the singularly unpleasant host. Try as you may, unless you're very polite and self-disciplined, your eyes stray in the direction of people or places you find more appealing. The brevity of your glances towards your host signals your lack of interest in her.

If, during a conversation, the listener shoots a glance out of the corner of her eye and combines the action with down-turned eyebrows and a furrowed forehead, you can bet that she's harbouring a critical, dismissive, or hostile attitude.

ANECDOTE

Diana's dipping eyes

Diana, Princess of Wales was exceptionally adept at evoking empathy by dipping her eyes and lowering her head. This gesture is particularly appealing because it makes the eyes appear larger and makes a woman seem innocent and somewhat helpless. Both men and women respond in a protective way as long as they don't think they're being manipulated. Even as a young child, Diana used this gesture to good effect. Although initially she may not have been conscious of what she was doing, experience taught her that when she used her eyes in this fashion she engendered her public's empathy.

The eye dip

Averting your eyes in a downward direction is a deliberate action designed to placate someone in a dominant position as well as an action designed to hide your feelings. In the first instance, by avoiding another person's gaze, you are giving her permission to take the dominant role in the interaction.

Dipping the eyes is also a way of demonstrating the reluctance you may feel from entering into an interaction. By dipping your eyes you're saying, 'If you want to connect with me, you have to make an effort.'

If you think that acting submissively is a weak or negative role to play, reconsider. Acting submissively can often put you in a real position of strength. And it's sometimes the best way to get what you want. Also remember that, in this manoeuvre, you *choose* to relinquish control.

Other Ways Your Eyes Tell a Tale

Because your eyes reveal your thoughts, feelings, and emotions – and you've got loads of them – they move in lots of different ways to give away what's going on internally.

Winkin' and blinkin'

An engaging way to show a fun and friendly attitude is to wink. Winking also intimates that whatever you're talking about doesn't need to be taken too seriously. People who are sharing a secret also share a conspiratorial wink. A wink can carry many messages, so consider the context before deciding on an interpretation.

Not all interactions are fun and friendly though, and one clue is how often the participants blink. On average, people blink between 6 to 8 to 20 times per minute, depending on their state of mind and the activity in which they're engaged.

Blinking longer than usual

If you've ever been in conversation with someone who, while speaking, blocks you out by shutting her eyes longer than she normally would, you know how annoying that action can be. Rather than blinking, these people close their eyes in an unconscious attempt to remove you from their sight. Some people find that closing their eyes helps them to think, focus and concentrate on what they're saying. Or, it can be that they're bored by you or just aren't interested in what you're saying. Perhaps they feel superior to you. Hard to believe, I know, but possible. Whatever the reason, it can be interpreted as rude and off-putting.

I was recently running a workshop on, you guessed it, body language. At one point, one of the participants noted that occasionally I closed my eyes longer than I normally did when I was speaking. Until he pointed this out, I was unaware of the habit. As I reflected, I noted that I would close my eyes fractionally longer than normal when I was thinking and speaking at the same time, such as when I was coming up with an answer to unanticipated questions. Shutting my eyes subconsciously shut out potential distractions. Now that I'm aware of the behaviour, I can consciously control it. I find that, instead of speaking while I'm thinking, looking at the questioner, pausing, and then speaking is a more effective way of communicating with positive impact.

Blinking more often than normal

Many factors influence your blinking rate. When you're excited, you blink more than when you're relaxing in front of the television or concentrating at your computer. The main purpose of blinking is to keep the eye surface moist, clean, and healthy. Under normal conditions, the blinking rate is between six to eight blinks per minute. This can increase by four or five times when you're feeling pressure.

Examples of pressures that can cause rapid blinking include the following:

 ✔ **Normal stress:** Sometimes a high blinking rate doesn't mean anything more than that a person is under pressure.

> ✔ **Lying:** When people lie, their energy increases, and when concocting an answer to a difficult question their thinking process speeds up. However, just to confuse you, sometimes liars slow down their blinking rate.

During the Watergate hearings, President Nixon's rate of blinking increased measurably whenever he was asked a question he didn't want to answer. More recently, during the phone hacking scandal in the UK, in which News Corporation was implicated, Rupert Murdoch (the corporation's chairman and chief executive) demonstrated similar behaviour while undergoing questioning.

Blinking less frequently than normal

When you're speaking and the listener is staring at you in a zombie-like fashion, you're probably boring her to distraction. A sure sign that you've lost her attention is the infrequency of eye blinks and the dull glaze that comes over her eyes.

Lack of blinking can be a sign of boredom, hostility, or indifference to whatever is happening, but it doesn't have to be. Confident people, for example, establish more and longer eye contact than people who are uncertain or are attempting to hide something. Although they blink less, they come across as interested listeners. (To find out more about how confident people use eye contact, refer to the earlier section 'The Power of the Held Gaze'.)

Lack of blinking can cause your cornea – the clear, thin top layer of the eye – to become dehydrated. Your vision becomes blurry and you don't see as well.

Active eyebrows: The Eyebrow Flash

Since ancient times, people have initiated their greetings with the rapid raising and lowering of their eyebrows (see Figure 5-7). Although this action can be so subtle as to be invisible to the naked or untrained eye, the gesture draws attention to the face in order to exchange clear signals of acknowledgement. When you greet another person, you unconsciously raise your eyebrows in recognition.

Except in Japan where the movement is considered rude and has sexual implications (see Chapter 15), the Eyebrow Flash is universal and is even used by monkeys and apes to express recognition and social greeting. People who don't use the Eyebrow Flash when being introduced can be perceived as potentially aggressive.

Figure 5-7:
The Eyebrow Flash is a sign of recognition.

Sit in a hotel lobby or at a bar and Eyebrow Flash everyone who passes by. You find that most people return the Flash and smile. Who knows, they may even come over and talk to you.

Raised eyebrows don't always mean recognition, however. They can also mean the following:

- ✔ **Agreement:** When you agree with what someone is saying, you use the same gesture you use when you greet someone, the Eyebrow Flash.
- ✔ **Surprise and fear:** If you're surprised or scared, your eyebrows rise and stay in that position until the moment has passed.

Widening your eyes

The next time you get the chance, take a look at a baby's eyes. Notice that they're disproportionately large relative to the rest of its face. Unconsciously you respond to large eyes in a protective and nurturing manner. Large eyes make a person look more appealing, as any Hollywood starlet knows. Women create the look of submission by plucking their eyebrows to make the eyes appear larger. They then raise their eyebrows and eyelids, an action that particularly appeals to men. When a woman demonstrates submissiveness by widening her eyes no man in her immediate vicinity stands a chance. His brain releases hormones stimulating his desire to protect and defend her.

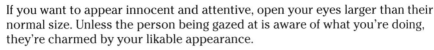

If you want to appear innocent and attentive, open your eyes larger than their normal size. Unless the person being gazed at is aware of what you're doing, they're charmed by your likable appearance.

My daughter Kristina has big green eyes. And she knows how to use them. I have observed her with her beau, her friends – both male and female – her father, her brother and even myself and am amazed and impressed at how she naturally and unconsciously uses her eyes to appeal to people in her life. When she wants help, be it with a project she's working on, her homework or getting her car started on a cold winter's morning, she opens her eyes wide, raises her eyebrows, dips her head, and by gosh, she gets what she wants!

You can make your eyes appear larger by raising your brows and lowering your lids, a technique that Marilyn Monroe used to maximum effect. (Sharon Stone and Kim Cattrall are pretty good at adopting this pose, too.) Most men and some women would, and still do, go weak at the knees when they look at photos of her with her lowered eyelids and raised eyebrows. People respond to this gesture because by maximising the space between the eyelid and the eyebrow the eyes appear larger, giving an innocent, sexy, and mysterious or secretive look.

Flicking, flashing, and fluttering

Fluttering your eyelids is usually associated with flirting, but is also a gesture you may find yourself using when you're on the spot and have to come up with a quick answer. Or, it can simply mean that you've got something in your eye causing an irritation, in which case, you probably rub your eye after fluttering for a moment or two. (Be careful about rubbing your eyes, though, as you may damage them.) Flashing eyes – like Penelope Cruz's in *Vicky Cristina Barcelona* – indicate hot emotions such as anger or resentment although if you flash your eyebrows (refer to the preceding section) you're suggesting agreement or interest.

To flick your eyes over a person or an object shows a modicum of interest which, depending on the response of the person or the amount of curiosity you feel for the object, can move into a longer gaze.

Chapter 6

Mastering Lip Reading

In This Chapter

▶ Recognising how the lips reveal thoughts, feelings, and emotions

▶ Differentiating the smile

'*R*ead my lips,' said President George Bush when running for President in 1988. Although your lips are the doorway to verbalising messages, they're equally adept at revealing emotions, thoughts, and feelings without uttering a word.

In this chapter you discover how the various lip positions, including pursed lips, a pout, and a lop-sided grin, tell the story of what's going on inside.

Revealing Thoughts, Feelings, and Emotions

The lips are made up of a complicated series of muscles running over, under, and around the sides of your mouth (see Figure 6-1). Because the muscles can work independently of one another, they can pull and twist your mouth into all kinds of positions. One side of the mouth can mirror the other so that the whole mouth conveys the same message, as with the turned up sides of your lips in a genuine smile of happiness or the downward turn of your lips when you're sad. Your lips can also pull in opposite ways, one side going up, the other side going down. The upper lip can rise in a sneer. The lower lip can tremble in fear.

The complicated series of muscles that control the lips include the orbicularis oris muscles, which sit at the sides of the mouth. Their function is to pull the lips back and push them forward. The elevators, such as levator labii superior, lift the upper lip, whereas the mentalis, sitting at the tip of your chin, pushes up your lower lip, causing your chin to wrinkle, making you look doubtful or displeased.

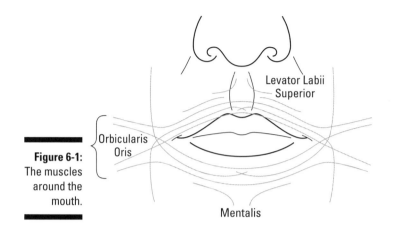

Levator Labii
Superior

Orbicularis
Oris

Figure 6-1:
The muscles
around the
mouth.

Mentalis

The unconscious tension in your lips indicates how you really feel, regardless of what you say. You say you're feeling fine? Then, why are your lips trembling? You say you're happy? Then why are your lips stretched across your mouth like a razor's edge? Whatever emotion you're experiencing – anticipation, pleasure, irritation – you're lips are telling on you (see the *Body Language For Dummies* app for some examples).

Tight lips

Tight lips indicate tension. Tense lips aren't limited to negative emotions, such as anger or annoyance. When you're sexually aroused, your lips become tense, too. All the muscles are working in anticipation.

The moment Amanda was introduced to Simon, she knew that he was the one for her. Not wanting to give her hand away too quickly, she held back her feelings. Amanda said that she always smiled when she saw Simon, and in order to keep a big grin from covering her face, she had to tighten the muscles around her mouth.

Tense and taut, the person with the tight lips is holding back some kind of emotion, be it anger, annoyance, or sexual tension (see Figure 6-2). Perhaps he's pondering a problem, perhaps he's about to kiss you. Whatever the reason, tension is in the air.

Figure 6-2:
Tense lips
reveal that
emotion is
being held
back.

Loose lips

People who are relaxed, sad, or depressed let their lips hang loose. Their lips lack tension. Their expression tells you that they've let go, or, in some cases, given up.

Chewing on lips

When some people feel anxious, they chew on something such as a pencil, a finger, or a lip. Subconsciously, they're reverting back to the breast, which offers comfort. The lip is the easiest object to chew on, because the lip is right there. You don't have to reach for an object and put it between your lips, you don't have to stick your finger in your mouth, you just have to engage your lips with your teeth to find comfort.

The three main lip chewing gestures associated with anxiety are:

- ✔ **Lower lip bite.** The upper teeth bite down on the lower lip. The teeth may rub against the lip, pulling it in and out of the mouth.
- ✔ **Upper lip bite.** The lower teeth protrude forward and catch the upper lip. The teeth may slide back and forth on the lip, in a sucking like manner.
- ✔ **Lip to lip bite.** Both the upper and lower lips come into contact, pulling inwards and resting tightly on the teeth.

In addition to being a sign of anxiety, chewing your lips is also a gesture showing self-restraint – a default mechanism keeping you from saying something that you may later regret.

People who feel embarrassed may chew on their lips as a way of holding onto themselves, even if only by the skin of their teeth!

Maintaining a stiff upper lip

The stiff upper lip is a real facial expression. The upper lip muscle tightens to contain emotion. People who don't want to express their feelings when they've been told bad news or are facing adversity tighten their upper lip to keep their emotions contained rather than letting their emotions spill forth.

Photographs of the disgraced UBS 'rogue trader', Kweku Adoboli, who allegedly lost the bank £1.3 million pounds, show him being taken into custody with his lips tightly clenched. He knew that he was facing massive fines and a prison sentence. His tension was showing.

The concept of maintaining a stiff upper lip, in which sentiments are reined in, dates back to the 1800s and is typical of the English approach to protecting private feelings and keeping emotions private. The stiff upper lip comes in handy when you want to maintain your dignity.

An advantage of the stiff upper lip position is that it can make you look brave. It can also make you look suspicious, as if you're concealing hidden information. As with all gestures, you need to consider the context before leaping to a conclusion about the meaning of an individual gesture or expression.

Holding back your feelings

The phrase 'keep a stiff upper lip' is symbolic of the British, and particularly of the young men educated in the English public school system during the time of the British Empire. 'Do your duty and show no emotion' was the characteristic attitude of that era, although the origins of the phrase can be traced to the USA. Its first printed reference can be found in the *Massachusetts Spy*, June 1815:

'I kept a stiff upper lip, and bought [a] license to sell my goods.'

Although that illustration doesn't explicitly refer to holding back one's feelings, it's similar to other 19th century American references and the meaning is unmistakable. Here's one example, from the *Huron Reflector*, 1830:

'I acknowledge I felt somehow queer about the bows; but I kept a stiff upper lip, and when my turn came, and the Commodore of the P'lice axed [sic] me how I come to be in such company. . .I felt a little better.'

In 1963, PG Woodhouse published a novel called *Stiff Upper Lip, Jeeves* – a quintessential English sentiment.

In more recent times, British heroes have been permitted to demonstrate their emotions in the public arena. Footballers can occasionally be seen crying when they lose, while their fans share and support them in their grief. Before World War II, that kind of behaviour would have been an anathema.

Research conducted by James Gross of Stanford University and Jane Richards of the University of Texas at Austin, suggests that people who fight to conceal their emotions are less able to recall what they see. Tim Dalgliesh, clinical psychologist at the Medical Research Council Cognition and Brain Sciences Unit in Cambridge, believes that keeping emotions under control is not a bad plan. He postulates that you need to keep the balance between memory and emotion, and reasons that it can be beneficial to suppress your emotions in lieu of memory because giving vent to your upset may be worse. So if you're in the middle of your yearly appraisal and your boss is finding nothing good to say about your performance, hold back the outraged shouts and screams. You may not recall the specifics of his sentiments and that may be no bad thing if it means you keep your job.

Pouting for effect

The pout is a very comprehensive gesture, indeed. Whoever's pouting is making it clear that disappointment, displeasure, frustration, or sadness is in the air. The pout also reveals sexual interest, as well as uncertainty and thought.

Whatever the reason for the pout, the facial mechanism is the same. In tandem, you contract your chin muscle and the side muscles – the labial tractors – of your lower lip. Your lips press together, your tongue rises against your palate and your pharynx constricts as it prepares to swallow (see Figure 6-3). Of course, analysing the pout in this rather scientific way makes it seem a difficult expression to achieve, but most people actually find it quite easy – so easy in fact that Hollywood starlets, small children and teenagers have mastered it. 'You just put your lips together and blow' – advice I received one day from an attendant in a ladies' loo who had been observing my feeble efforts to achieve the pout that Victoria Beckham had perfected.

A displeasure pout is one in which the head drops down, eyes tighten, and the forehead crinkles. When the lower lip pushes out, you may be in for a tantrum.

My brother Al's two little daughters, Cathy and Cristina, are fantastic pouters. When they're angry, sad, disappointed, or just pretending to be, they can stick their lower lips out half way down their chins. Sometimes, Al drums his fingertips over their lower lip, telling them that a little man is going to dance on their lips if they're not careful. That's usually enough to make them laugh and end the pouting.

The pursed and pouting lips of a young woman looking at her lover signal sexual invitation. Both the pursed lips of disapproval and the pursed lips indicating sexual arousal are forward moving. What makes the difference is the context they're displayed in.

Frank took a group of friends for lunch, tennis, and swimming at his club. He was particularly attracted to one of his guests, and was hoping to strike up a romantic relationship. When Frank looked at Dagmar, he pursed his lips forward and ever so slightly separated them as if blowing gently in the wind. Later that day, Frank saw Dagmar speaking animatedly with someone else. Disappointed that Dagmar was paying attention to another person, Frank pursed his lips together like an old prune and turned away.

Both men and women's facial lips increase in size and colour when sexually excited.

For more information about the pout, skip to Chapter 13.

Figure 6-3:
The pout
covers a
wide
emotional
range.

Pursing as a sign of disagreement

Pursed lips, in which the lips are puckered in a rounded shape of disagreement, connivance, or calculated thought, send a message of considered dissent (see Figure 6-4). Pursed lips can show that someone's thinking, considering his next move, before he says or does anything. He's holding his thoughts in before letting them out.

One of the signs of disagreement is pursed lips. If you're at a dinner party and your partner is about to spill the beans, a stern pursing of the lips pointed in your partner's direction should stop the flow.

Because pursed lips give a sign of disagreement – and wrinkles the lips, which is aging – you may want to avoid the gesture, unless you want to be known as Old Prune Face.

Figure 6-4:
Pursed, or
'prune lips',
indicate
measured
thinking.

If you're making a proposal or putting forward a suggestion, and your listener meets your ideas with pursed lips, signalling mental resistance, ask him whether he disagrees before continuing your verbal argument. By clearing the air, you make the other person better disposed to understand your position. Equally, he's going to be impressed with your intuitive grasp of his thinking process. (For more about helping people understand your point of view, have a look at *Persuasion & Influence For Dummies* by Elizabeth Kuhnke (Wiley).)

Tensing your lips and biting back your words

When you lock your jaw, your lips tighten. They pull back over your teeth in a closed position. This expression is different from pursed lips because pursed lips push forward.

With tightened lips – whether you're displaying signs of anger, frustration, or demonstrating threatening behaviour – no one can doubt that you're not to be trifled with (see Figure 6-5).

Imagine that you're at your company's Annual General Meeting. In a room full of differing opinions, personal agendas, and subterfuge, the tension rises. Your lips tighten as your jaw locks into position. The tight lips keep the anger from shooting out.

Graeme was invited to attend a meeting at which several of the company's key decision-makers were present. Many of the points and positions that Graeme heard were in direct contrast to his sense of the business. Although with his own team Graeme expressed himself freely and encouraged exchange, in the company meeting, where it was clear that outside contributions weren't welcome, he found himself holding back his thoughts. At one point he observed his own behaviour, noticing that his mouth was in a tense line across his face, with his lips rolled inward and his teeth pressing down on them. The longer he held this position, the more negative he felt.

Figure 6-5:
A locked jaw with tightened lips is a sure sign of negative tension.

Changing thoughts and behaviours

When you're about to move to a different position, be it physically or mentally, your lips come into play. As you end one thought or action and are about to begin another, your lips close, if only fractionally, indicating that you've finished with one thought and are about to begin another.

Observe a person whose mouth is in a tensed position. Note his mouth movements when he experiences a mood shift, expresses an unexpected thought, or abruptly changes his point of view.

Differentiating Smiles

Smiling is universally recognised as a sign of happiness. Smiles come in a wide variety ranging from signalling appeasement to that of the playful child.

Studies conducted by Professors Marvin Hecht and Marianne La France at Boston University indicate that the smile is a submissive signal. People in subordinate roles tend to smile more in the company of those who are more dominant, or in superior roles.

When you're interacting with other people, smile. The impact this gesture has on people's attitudes is amazingly positive and it influences their response to you.

Douglas was stopped for speeding and had to go to the Magistrates' Court to be sentenced. Before going to court he spoke with Al, a lawyer friend, who advised him to smile when offering his apology. Al said that both judge and jury are more inclined to be lenient when the defendant smiles. He also said that as long as the smile is there, whether it's genuine or fake is unimportant. What really matters is that people smile at the right time.

The tight-lipped smile

Stretch your lips in a straight line across your face without exposing your teeth and think of the Mona Lisa, whose smile implies the harbouring of secrets, the restraining of attitude, or the concealment of thoughts. And you know there's no way she's going to make known her mystery to you. That's what's known as the tight-lipped smile.

According to one study, women interpret the tight-lipped smile as a sign of rejection.

Pick up any business magazine and you're greeted by the sealed smile of the professional chief executive. In his cover article, the man promises to reveal his secrets to success. In truth, he tells you nothing you don't already know.

Julia is seldom heard speaking ill of another person. This fact doesn't mean that she doesn't see the full picture of what someone's like, but whatever she thinks, she keeps to herself. She avoids gossiping and sidesteps potentially awkward social interactions with aplomb. Not long ago, I observed her praising the positive attributes, talents, and characteristics of a mutual acquaintance. When someone else in the conversation talked about the less salubrious characteristics of this other person, Julia sealed her lips tightly in a closed mouth smile and said not another word on the subject. Although Julia undoubtedly had similar thoughts, she kept them to herself.

The lop-sided smile

When your muscles pull the sides of your mouth in opposite directions, one side going up and the other going downwards, you've got yourself in a twist. What you're doing is showing opposite emotions on either side of your face and the observer has to figure out what this lop-sided smile is conveying – in Western culture this type of smile can signal sarcasm, embarrassment, and irony.

In a lop-sided smile, one side of your mouth is moving upward in amusement while the other side's pulling down in restraint (see Figure 6-6). Subconsciously, when your mouth seeks this position you're showing both your pleasure and your pain. Harrison Ford and the late Princess of Wales both mastered the gesture of the lop-sided smile. The gesture elicits protective responses in others. The side of the mouth going downward indicates sadness, anxiety, or another negative emotion. The side going upward shows that the person's not angry – had he been, both sides of the mouth would turn down. The gesture is softened by the upward turn of the lip, making the gesture non-threatening.

You may deliberately position your mouth in a lop-sided smile – like Hugh Grant or Paris Hilton – if you want to show your pleasure as well as show your pain. One side of the mouth is saying, 'Yes!' while the other side is saying, 'Better not'.

The drop-jaw smile

This practised smile, in which the lower jaw simply releases downwards, is a favourite of politicians, movie stars, and celebrities (see Figure 6-7). Knowing how contagious laughter is, a person wanting to elicit positive reactions from his adoring public lets his jaw drop, suggesting playfulness and amusement.

Figure 6-6:
The lop-sided smile is compelling because it contains contradiction and mystery.

Figure 6-7:
The drop-jaw smile conveys no hint of appeasement or submissiveness.

Because laughter is more contagious than just smiling, the next time you're in company and want to induce a sense of playfulness in your listeners, apply the drop-jaw smile. By looking unthreatening and as if you're laughing, the others pick up on the feeling too.

Nancy is known for her sense of fun. Her laughter comes from the depths of her being, and can fill a room with joy and hilarity. One night, she and a group of friends were having dinner and drinks at a local restaurant. Nancy's smiling face and cheerful laughter caught the attention of diners at several other tables, all of whom picked up on her laughter and joined in. Eventually, a man from another group approached Nancy and begged her to let them all in on the joke as they were laughing so hard but didn't have a clue what they were laughing about.

The turn-away smile

Turn your head down and away while looking upwards with your lips in a sealed smile, and you can capture the hearts of all who see you. By doing so you look young, playful and secretive – a winning combination.

Most men melt when a woman smiles coyly in their direction and women also aren't immune to the power of the smile that encapsulates both openness and shyness. Parental instincts rise, making the recipient of this smile want to shield and nurture the person gazing at him with this look.

According to Charles Darwin, the action of turning the head away from another person while looking at him and smiling creates a 'hybrid expression', one that is composed of two opposite meanings. The smile signals welcome, whereas the motion of turning away conveys avoidance. The tension that's created by these two opposing actions is irresistibly appealing and more powerful than its individual parts.

The closed-lip grin

The closed-lip grin is a restraining or concealing gesture, hiding bad teeth or covering up information. In the closed-lip grin, you hold your lips together. Your pearly whites stay hidden and your feelings remain private except to the people who noticed that, although the corners of your mouth seem to be smiling, your teeth aren't showing. A closed-lip smile is a concealing gesture used by playful children, politicians, and anyone else who's hiding something.

Someone who's teasing or being playful with another person may give the closed-lip grin. Someone else may give the closed-lip grin as a means of showing that although he's happy to speak with you, he's not telling you everything.

Mandy and Steve recently sold their house and were happily prepared to say who had bought their property. When someone asked them how much they had sold for, Mandy's lips sealed shut. She smiled in the closed-lip gesture, and looked at Steve as if to say, 'Mind the hatches! Too much information!'

Keeping your teeth covered when you're smiling indicates that you're keeping something in (see 'The tight-lipped smile' earlier in this chapter.)

The full-blown grin

When you give a full-blown grin, you know that you've given your face a good work out. The person at the receiving end smiles with you, radiating in the sunshine of your smile, as Stevie Wonder may say.

The muscles around your eyes crease and crinkle, and your teeth go on display as the sides of your lips stretch towards the tip of your ears. Your head pulls back, even if ever so slightly and, bingo!, you've sent out the feel-good factor.

When you're watching someone smile, note the direction the head goes in. A forward tilt indicates humbleness. A backward tilt tells you that the person's pleased and proud (see Figure 6-8).

Figure 6-8:
Full-blown
smiles
indicating
humbleness
(left) and
pride (right).

Remembering that Laughter's the Best Medicine

Laughter and smiles usually go together hand in hand. Some laughs burble up from the bottom of the vocal mechanism, and burst forth with abandon, like the belly laugh. Others get stuck in your throat, or up your back sinus passages. Some land in your chest and all that escapes are little bits of blowing air pushing through your nose like short trumpet blasts. If it weren't for your shaking shoulders and smile spread across your face, people wouldn't know that you were laughing.

Whatever kind of laugh you've got – a giggle, a snort, a snicker, or a good old-fashioned hee-haw – the depth of the sound, where the sound is placed and how much of it you allow to come out, indicate your mood and feelings.

A person who laughs from his boots is willing to release. He's not afraid to hold back. When he laughs, the world laughs with him.

Simon was at a family reunion, watching his two daughters playing with their cousins. Whether it was the sunshine, the pleasure of being together with his family, the naughty joke his father-in-law told him, or the three pints of beer he'd drunk, he threw his head back, opened his mouth wide, and jiggled from his boots to his shoulders as peals of laughter burst forth from his lips. His wife and her parents got caught up in Simon's laughter, and ended up laughing so hard that tears streamed out of their eyes.

Sometimes laughing is inappropriate, but impossible to restrain.

Frederika was kneeling in church, supposedly praying, when her mobile phone vibrated in her jacket pocket. She carefully removed it, so as not to be seen by her father, who was sitting one seat away from her. Frederika opened the text message from her friend, who had sent her a joke. Frederika read it silently to herself until she got to the unexpected punch line, at which point a snort of laughter escaped from her nose before she could stop it. Her father cast her a disapproving look, which made Frederika's laughter increase. She finally had to hold her lips shut and squeeze her nose to keep any more sound escaping from her mouth.

Part III
The Trunk: Limbs and Roots

The 5th Wave   By Rich Tennant

"I don't know, Mona — sometimes I get the feeling you're afraid to get close."

In this part . . .

Here I travel down the body visiting those parts that reflect inner states and create impressions by the way they move and position themselves. How you dress, the way you stand, cross your arms, bite your nails, shake hands with someone – all give an insight into your attitudes, feelings and, indeed, the sort of person you are.

Chapter 7

Taking It From the Torso

. . . .

In This Chapter

▶ Recognising how your body speaks for you

▶ Finding ways to change your attitude

▶ Exploring the effects of posture

. . . .

The stance you adopt and the way you position your body reveals how you feel about yourself and others. Slumping into your hips, drooping your shoulders, and letting your stomach hang out isn't a particularly pleasing picture and reflects a poor self image. The person who approaches you with head held high, an open chest, and a firm stride is the one who gains your attention.

In this chapter you find out how to get your muscles working with your attitude, to show the world just who you are.

Gaining Insights into the Impact of Posture

How you use and abuse your body determines how you feel about yourself and how others perceive you. Jobs are won and lost, reputations made and destroyed, relationships dissolved and cemented based on how the people involved present themselves.

Walk down the high street on a busy day and observe people passing by. Watch for those who appear to feel good about themselves. You notice that they move with ease. Their gestures are open and welcoming, with shoulders back and heads held high.

Keep watching people pass by and notice how the ones who don't seem comfortable with themselves move. Their heads are probably tucked into shoulders, arms folded across chests, and they move at a dreary pace. They look a sad and sorry lot. People who don't feel good about themselves hide in their clothes, their postures droop, and you have little hope of getting a genuine smile from them (see Figure 7-1).

Figure 7-1:
Depressed
posture
collapses in
on itself.

Your posture, gestures, and expressions reveal how you feel about yourself and determine how others relate to you.

Not only can you determine how others perceive you by the way you hold your body, you can also determine your own frame of mind. The way you present yourself reflects and influences your mood and attitude.

Evaluating what your own posture says about you

If you spend too much time slouching with a deadpan expression on your face and slumped shoulders, you're going to appear inert and ineffectual. If, on the other hand, you hold yourself upright with an alert expression on your face, you look energised and ready for action.

To determine what your own posture reveals about your self-image or mood, follow these steps:

1. **Stand in front of a full length mirror and take a good, long look at yourself.**

   Observe how you're standing, the position of your head, and the look on your face. What is the message you're conveying?

2. **Turn away for a moment. This time decide how you want to be perceived.**

   Dominant, submissive, bored, angry, surprised? The list goes on. Carefully consider how you can convey that attitude by the way you stand and breathe, and by the look on your face.

3. **Turn back towards the mirror, having adopted the image you want to portray.**

   What do you notice? What are the differences and similarities between your first and second postures?

By being aware of the messages that your stance, gestures, and expressions send out you can consciously determine how you're perceived. With time and practice, you automatically adopt the appropriate pose for the attitude you want to reveal.

Should you find yourself in a downbeat, miserable mood that you want to get out of, do the following:

- Inhale from your abdomen.
- Gently open your chest as if it were a treasured keepsake.
- Allow your head to lift from the base of your neck like a balloon tied to a string on a sunny day.
- Observe your surroundings.
- Continue to breathe gently, like an infant at rest.
- Settle into the moment.

If I'm not mistaken, by now you have a gentle smile playing around your lips, and the outer corners of your eyes may even be creasing with enjoyment.

It's okay to not feel good about your body as long as you act as if you do. Why? Because, as I tell my clients, 'The way you act is the way you are.' If you act with a positive frame of mind, you feel that way. People want to spend time with you. When you enjoy yourself as you are, you make it easy for others to be in your company. And you may even find that by acting as if you feel good about yourself, you find that you actually do.

Showing intensity of feelings

People who are extremely agitated, exceptionally despondent, or enormously cheerful reflect these moods, in part, by the way they hold their bodies. When your feelings are intense, it's like putting an exclamation mark at the end of a sentence. Intensity calls attention to itself. For moments of deep despair, your muscles relax, your body collapses on itself, and you look like a forlorn rag doll. When you're filled with passion and excitement, your muscles tighten, your sinews become taut, and your movements are forceful and concentrated. (See Figure 7-2 and the *Body Language For Dummies* app.)

Take yourself back to a time when your feelings were working at full tilt. Freeze frame that image of yourself. What do you observe? You see that your muscles are working in equal proportion to your feelings, mood, and attitude.

Signs of emotion being acted out intensely are

- Fist-slamming
- Sharp finger pointing/waving/wagging
- Slouching
- Stomping
- Passionate hugging
- Uncontrollable crying
- Collapsing from exhaustion

As you read the words, you may recognise the feeling. Act out the gesture and the feeling intensifies. Add sound to the action, and the feeling becomes even stronger.

People nodding in agreement, as well as those shaking their heads in disagreement, often vocalise a humming sound. Someone who's annoyed may slam her fist and make a grunting sound as the fist hits the surface.

If you're feeling tired and worn out, you may sigh as your body collapses in on itself. If you're feeling energised, you may make a short, sharp sound of enjoyment. If you want to intimidate someone, a low growl in the back of your throat shows that you're prepared to stand up and defend yourself. For more about the impact of sound and body language on communication, pick up a copy of *Persuasion & Influence For Dummies* by Elizabeth Kunhke (Wiley).

Figure 7-2:
People
showing
opposite
emotional
intensity.

At a tennis tournament, my daughter Kristina and I were invited to sit in the
sponsor's box. Not only was the seating close enough to observe and enjoy
every gesture Rafael Nadal made, we were in prime seats for hearing every
thwack and grunt as he and his opponent, Andy Roddick, put their full body
force into their swings. As the strokes became stronger, the sounds became
louder and the feelings intensified. We sat forward in our seats and when
Nadal eventually won the point, his supporters momentarily lifted themselves
from their seats, their hands moving upwards in jubilation as they cheered
and clapped. Roddick's camp, on the other hand, dejectedly sat down and
backwards in their seats and let out a little grunt-like sigh. Roddick eventually
went on to win the game.

If you're cuddling with your honey and want to let him or her know just how
much you're enjoying the experience, make a gentle purr or sigh as you
snuggle in closer.

Alex was being groomed for partnership at a large city law firm. Although considered to be a bright and capable lawyer, Alex had some unresolved anger issues relating towards his hot-tempered, domineering mother. During a practice role play for his interview, I purposely interrupted him while he was answering a question I'd posed. Angry with the interruption and without thought, he rose from his seat and clenched his fists while his facial muscles pulled his lips to a tight thin line. I had no doubt in my mind that Alex didn't like being interrupted. We looked at his actions and decided together that alternative behaviour choices would have worked more to his favour.

Revealing personality and character

Are you King of the Jungle or Misty Milk Maid? Do you see yourself as a winner or a loser? How you hold your body, whether your body is upright and crisp or downtrodden and limp, shows the world who you think you are.

Think of yourself as an iceberg like the one in Figure 7-3. Below the water line is what makes you tick. This inner core contains your sense of self and is the base from which your actions arise. Here you find your values and beliefs, your drivers and motivators, and your strengths and unique selling points (USPs). Above the water line is your outer self, what other people see. The way you gesture, the way you carry yourself, your manners and mannerisms, plus how you choose to dress, reflect how you feel about yourself and all that's going on below the water line.

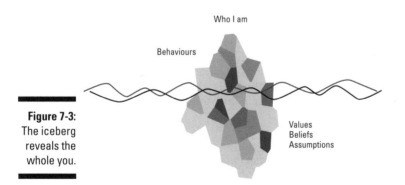

Figure 7-3:
The iceberg reveals the whole you.

If your self-perception is that of a strong, forceful, and dynamic Master of Mayfair, your body is upright, your stride purposeful and your gestures focused and contained. Think of Michael Douglas in the film *Wall Street*. If you see yourself more as a simple, quiet, country lawyer – along the lines of

Tom Hanks or James Stewart – your body may be more relaxed, your way of moving a bit easier, and your gestures more fluid. Whereas if you're Jack the Lad from southeast London, your body may strut and swagger, and your head movements appear quick and sharp.

If your character has some aspects that you don't like, change your attitude. As your attitude changes, so do your actions.

Knowing the Three Main Types of Posture

Although you have a repertoire of different postures you can adopt, you tend to prefer one to the others. You may prefer to sit, others may prefer to stand, whereas still others are quite happy to spend their time lying down. You can become so associated with one particular posture that people who know you well can recognise you from a distance by the way you use your body. Your posture is a clue to who you are and opens the door to understanding your character and personality. For example, the person who holds herself erectly has a different temperament from a habitual sloucher (see Figure 7-4).

The three main types of postures are:

✔ Standing

✔ Sitting (including squatting and kneeling)

✔ Reclining

Within this limited list, you can display your mood and temperament by the way you hold yourself and position your head, arms, and legs. People who slouch give the impression of being dull, uninterested, or lacking in confidence. People who hold themselves upright appear to be engaged, energised, and alert.

Every body has a past

According to research by the American anthropologist Ray Birdwhistell, a person's posture reflects her past. People who have experienced prolonged depression may slouch and sag into their bodies, whereas people who have a positive outlook tend to hold themselves upright.

Figure 7-4:
The person on the right appears engaged while the person on the left seems somnambulant.

Standing

Some people are happy to stand. This position enables them to think and move more quickly than if they had to pull themselves out of a chair or get out of bed.

At cocktail parties and other similar events, people tend to stand. This enables them to walk towards someone they want to engage with and move away from someone they'd rather not get cornered by.

Because moving toward and away from someone or something is easier from the standing position, this position is considered to be more active than sitting or lying down.

Participants at meetings frequently stand. The reason for this is that people think more quickly and come to decisions more expediently than they do when given the chance to sit. This is the Let's Go position.

Kate attended a client meeting at an advertising agency in Denmark. When it was time for her and her client to brainstorm some ideas, they went to the Stand Up Room, which was designed for quick thinking and decision making. In the middle of the room was a tall stone table, provided for people to lean on and take notes. The table was the only furniture in the room. What Kate found was that, although it wasn't her preferred environment, she was able to make quick decisions and firm commitments.

Sitting

The seated position can be a less energised position than standing. Because your body is bent in the middle, you may well collapse over your waist or flop back into your chair like a wilted flower if you're feeling a bit tired. Sitting is a more relaxed position than standing. The pressure is taken off your legs and feet and your buttocks take the weight.

Sitting postures convey different states of being depending on how your arms, legs, and head are positioned.

If you're tired you may unconsciously lean back into a chair, letting your legs and arms hang loose with your head tilted backwards. This is a sure sign that you're feeling worn out. At other times you sit upright, ready for action. Your back is straight, you're leaning forward, and you look like you mean business.

If you go into your boss's office and you notice her body's hunched over her desk, wait to be invited before speaking. Her body language is telling you she doesn't want to be interrupted. If she raises a hand with the palm facing towards you, turn and leave. If, however, she beckons you in by turning her palm toward herself and wiggling her fingers, you may enter.

Although a relaxed sitting position aids thinking and reflection, be careful not to hold the pose for too long. You end up feeling drained and dejected.

The sitting erect position shows that you're focused in the here and now and that you're ready to take a decision or progress an action.

Libby was a focused student, obtaining a First as an undergraduate and further honours as she gained her Masters Degree. She made a point of sitting in the front row during lectures, knowing that there she stood no chance of nodding off or demonstrating any signs of boredom or lack of interest. She says that by placing herself in the front row she was better able to concentrate on what the lecturer was saying.

Lying down

If you want to take some time for quiet contemplation, relaxation, and reflection, you may find yourself wanting to lie down. This is the position for getting in touch with your feelings and is a submissive pose. You don't find the Prime Minister taking this position at a press conference.

As Human Resources director of a large firm, John found himself getting quite agitated before budget reviews, knowing that the partners would challenge him on his training and development expenditures. One quiet afternoon he found himself sitting with his feet on his desk, leaning so far back in his chair that he was almost prone. He felt clear headed, relaxed, and able to sort his feelings from facts. After he made up his mind how he was going to address the partners at the review, and felt confident in his choices, he sat upright in his chair and purposefully wrote his notes.

Changing Attitudes by Changing Posture

If you find yourself in a mood you don't like, change your posture. By changing the position of your body, your frame of mind changes, too. If you find yourself in an enjoyable mood, notice the position of your body as well as your gestures and expressions. By being self-aware, you can keep the behaviours you like and eliminate those that you don't.

If you find yourself feeling glum and your slumped shoulders are revealing attitudes you may not want to share with just anybody, physically change your posture and see what happens.

Plant your feet squarely underneath your knees, your knees under your hips, pull up from the waist, and open your chest as if you see it as a loved book. Let your head rise from your neck and shoulders, floating like a balloon on a string while your arms and hands reach forward as if to embrace

- ✔ A bouquet of your favourite flowers
- ✔ A lover
- ✔ Someone you don't like but have to go through this gesture with regardless

You may have noticed some changes in the way your body moved, according to how you felt about what you were embracing. You may have felt mood changes, too.

Whistling happy tunes

In Rogers and Hammerstein's musical, *The King and I*, Anna, an English widow, with her young son, moves to Siam (now Thailand) to serve as teacher to the King's 26 children. Although somewhat overwhelmed at the prospect, and feeling less than confident, she knew that were she to show her fear, she'd lose her authority and the respect of the King. When they were about to embark, her son asked if she were afraid and, if so, how could she go through with this adventure. She said that although she was scared, she would act as if she were brave. In the song 'I Whistle a Happy Tune', she sings, 'While shivering in my shoes, I strike a careless pose, and whistle a happy tune, and no one ever knows I'm afraid.' She knew that if she projected the image she wanted to create, people would respond to her accordingly, and all would be well. And it was. She gained the respect of the King, the admiration of his courtiers, and the love of his children.

In addition to changing your posture, you can also use visualisation to galvanise your spirits. To do so, visualise yourself at your most confident. What do you look like? How does your voice sound? What feelings are you experiencing? Notice what's going on around you. If other people are there, what are they doing? How are they reacting to you? Make your visualisation as real as you can. See yourself smiling, your eyes engaged, claiming your space, demonstrating likability, and moving with purpose. Having created this picture of yourself in your mind, you can replicate it any time you're feeling self-conscious, insecure, or lacking in confidence. For further information about visualisation techniques, I suggest that you refer to *Neuro-linguistic Programming For Dummies* by Kate Burton and Romilla Ready and *Building Confidence For Dummies* by Kate Burton and Brinley Platts (both published by Wiley). You can also find out more about visualising yourself as you want to be in my (Elizabeth Kuhnke) book, *Persuasion & Influence For Dummies* (Wiley).

Confident people don't always feel confident. They simply act as if they are.

Using Posture to Aid Communication

I'm not saying that you can tell 100 per cent, exactly, precisely, and without a doubt all the details of what someone is thinking by looking at her posture. What I *am* saying is that you can tell a lot about people's mood, attitude, and state of mind by observing how they hold their bodies. Observing and registering what you notice about how people move and position themselves gives you an insight into how best to communicate with them.

Look what's talking

Albert Mehrabian, Professor Emeritus of Psychology, University of California, Los Angeles and author of the seminal study of non-verbal communication, *Silent Messages*, is an authority on communication. His findings about the relative importance of verbal and non-verbal messages showed that the way a message is delivered is believed more than the words, when inconsistency exists between the words themselves and the delivery. His findings have become known as the 7 per cent, 38 per cent, 55 per cent rule. Mehrabian concludes that three elements are involved in any face-to-face communication: the words, the tone of voice, and the body language. According to Mehrabian, these three elements account differently for understanding the emotional meaning behind the message. Words account for 7 per cent of the message, voice tone for 38 per cent, and body language for 55 per cent. Note, however, that this research only applies to face-to-face communication of feelings and attitudes.

Before beginning an encounter with another person, observe her posture to help you determine how best to engage with her.

Showing high and low status through postural positions

If you think of people in authority, you think of them in elevated terms. They don't have to be tall to show that they're top of the pecking order, they just have to carry themselves as if they were. Open and confident posture is the norm for individuals in high status positions. Conversely, people with lower status demonstrate their position by acting in a deferential manner. Their posture is closed and protective. (See Figure 7-5.)

Indira works for a large city firm. When she was put up for promotion, the male partners struggled when making their decision. Although Indira's capabilities were acknowledged as superb, something in her demeanour made them uncomfortable and uncertain. When Indira and I worked on her personal impact, she explained that she had been raised to show deference to people in positions of authority. Because of the hierarchical nature of the firm, she saw the partners as authority figures and behaved as she'd been taught. Her shoulders were slightly hunched, her chest somewhat rolled in, and her head slightly bowed. After practising specifically targeted exercises, Indira's posture changed, as did her self-perception. She now stands upright, makes eye contact comfortably, and moves with authority. And, she was made a partner.

The next time you're at an event where people are informally standing and talking in groups, watch the body language to discover who's in and who's out. The people who stand with their weight on one foot are the outsiders, and the ones who lean in with their heads tilted slightly forward are the insiders.

Following are a few random bits of info about posture as a sign of status:

✔ When a person deliberately defers to you, they are showing low-status behaviour.

✔ In many Eastern countries, bowing is expected as a sign of respect.

✔ In the military, a sign of respect is to stand to attention.

✔ You're more likely to hold your hands on hips in the presence of individuals whose status is equal to or lower than yours. In front of someone whose status is higher than yours, your body language is symmetrical.

Leaning forward to show interest and liking

According to Professor Albert Mehrabian of UCLA, people who like each other tend to lean in towards one another. The more you like someone, the more your body inclines in her direction. The forward lean is a sign of intimacy and affection.

By leaning towards another person, you're sharing space with her and showing that you want to be close. Accomplished interviewers understand the power of getting physically close to the person they're interviewing. After they've created a rapport with the person, they lean towards her to show trust. By appropriately moving into another person's personal space, you're demonstrating that you like her.

Debbie and Jonathan have been married for 16 years. They're still physically affectionate with one another and are comfortable cuddling and touching one another. Their friends frequently remark how much physical contact they make and how much in love they seem to be. One Sunday, Debbie and Jonathan had a group of friends to lunch. As Jonathan opened a bottle of champagne, the liquid spurted from the bottle, making a mess over the counter and floor, wasting half the bottle of bubbly. Debbie immediately rushed to Jonathan and leaned into his chest, giving him a hug with one arm, as she cleaned up the counter with the dishtowel in her other.

Although facial expressions give more information about emotions, posture shows the degree of intensity.

If you carefully observe a group of individuals interacting, you can tell their degree of attention, involvement, relative status, and how they feel about one another by the way each one positions her body in relation to the others. People who are actively participating in the exchange lean towards one another. Those who are reflecting on what's going on pull back. The opposite of the forward lean is the backward lean, which indicates fear and displeasure. Someone who's not interested or is bored with the conversation may slump and look in another direction. (See Figure 7-6.)

If someone is really angry, not only does she scowl, she leans forward as well. If someone is filled with happiness, she smiles as her body moves forward. In both cases, it seems as if both people want to get further into the emotion. The expressions on the face reveal the emotion. The lean of the body reveals the intensity of the feeling.

Figure 7-6:
Note who's actively participating in this conversation between three people and who's pulling back.

Stand upright with your feet hip width apart, put your hands on your hips, lean forward and frown. Now stand in the same position, slightly leaning back and smile. Just by this slight change of posture and facial expression you have conveyed two very different moods.

When you're at a meeting that's lost your interest, sit forward in your seat and rest your elbows on the table while you look at the speaker. This posture both helps your energy rise and you to feel more engaged.

Dicken was preparing for a job interview. He was feeling conflicted about the interview because he was leaving his current job, not having progressed as far in his career there as he'd wanted to. During a practice session, he leant back in his chair, letting his chest droop and his head sink into his shoulders. When he saw himself on video, he realised the negative signals he was giving out. I encouraged him to sit towards the front of the chair and lean forward, letting his elbows rest on the table. When he saw himself again, he observed how much more interested, engaged, and likable he seemed.

Shrugging Signals

A child avoiding telling you the truth adopts the wide-eyed, head-pulled-back 'What? Who me?' look as she raises her shoulders in disbelief. The student who's called on by the lecturer to summarise the chapter that hasn't been read raises her shoulders in submissive apology. The person who wants to show a complete lack of interest gives a disdainful lift of the shoulders as she turns her head away. A submissive gesture, the shrug absolves the shrugger of any responsibility and indicates apology, disbelief, and lack of interest.

What makes a shrug?

According to English zoologist Desmond Morris the shrug is made up of five elements, four of which are key to understanding the gesture. He labels these four elements *key elements* because they can, on their own, convey the message. The key elements for a shrug are:

1. **Hunched shoulders.** The shoulders are raised and lowered. Both shoulders are not required to convey the shrug. One shoulder hunching up on its own while the other remains still is an equally valid shrug.

2. **Hands twisted into the palms up position.** The palms of the hands face upward in an open position. A shrug can be successfully transmitted through the upward turning of one or both hands.

3. **Lowered mouth corners.** The head and body remain still as the corners of the mouth turn down.

4. **Raised eyebrows.** Like the full bodied shrug, an upward jerk of the eyebrows can convey astonishment, indifference, and bewilderment.

Any of these four individual gestures, taken on their own and in context, can be perceived as a shrug.

The one other element that goes into a full shrug is an *amplifier*, or supporting element. The amplifier in a full shrug is tilting the head to one side. This type of element taken on its own can't accurately transmit the message. It has to work in combination with one or more key elements to convey the point.

A number of different shrugging styles depend on the attitude being conveyed and the individual performing the gesture. People from Mediterranean and Latin countries use their gestures freely, whereas Anglo-Saxons and Asians are more restricted in their use of physical movement. See Chapter 15 for more about body language across cultures.

Signalling lack of knowledge

You're at your first meeting of the day, feeling confident that you can answer any question your boss may throw your way. And then the unanticipated comes and you freeze like a deer panicking in the headlights. You don't want to show your ignorance so you control your gestures. A well-trained observer, however, would spot the nano-second, micro-movement of your shoulders as your head momentarily drops into your rising shoulders like a turtle sucking its head into its shell.

An elderly couple approached Guy in London to ask him directions to Buckingham Palace. English was not their mother tongue and they struggled to understand Guy as he gave them detailed directions. Looking at them as he spoke, Guy was able to tell that they didn't understand what he was saying. They raised their shoulders and hands in bewilderment as they tilted their heads as if that would help them understand him better. By speaking slowly, using simple terms, pointing in the right direction, and counting out his fingers how long it would take them to get there – if they didn't get lost – he hoped that they understood him correctly. The final lift of the old woman's shoulders indicated that perhaps they had their doubts.

Showing unwillingness to get involved

In addition to conveying misunderstanding, lack of knowledge, and apology, the shrug can also indicate an unwillingness to get involved. Because of the submissive actions that make up a shrug – head pulled down into the shoulders, open forward-facing palms serving as a shield, raised eyebrows, and a tilted head – the action indicates that you don't want to be drawn in.

Raising your shoulders is a defensive behaviour designed to protect your neck, one of your body's most vulnerable parts. By holding your open palms in front of you you're showing that, although you have nothing to conceal, you're also setting up a barrier between you and another person.

Rory is a secondary school chemistry teacher. Inevitably, at the end of lessons a mess of test tubes, beakers, and other related items wait to be cleaned and put away in their proper place. When he asks his students who's responsible for the mess, without fail they raise their shoulders, palms, and eyebrows as they turn away from Rory, signalling their denial of any responsibility.

If you want to indicate that you want to remain neutral and uninvolved, raise your hand to shoulder height with your palm facing outwards and slightly shrug both shoulders.

Implying a submissive apology

Because the elements in the shrug – hunched shoulders, open palms, raised eye brows, and so on – are all submissive, the shrug is the perfect gesture to use when offering an apology.

A man of few words and the grand gesture, John had been in a foul temper for most of the day. Although Louise is usually quite patient and accepts her husband's moodiness, by late afternoon she was so frustrated that she burst into tears. Realising that he'd been out-of-sorts and treating Louise unfairly, John left the house, returning shortly with a large bouquet of tulips, Louise's favourite flowers. Offering them to her, he apologised without ever saying the words, 'I'm sorry'. The lift of his shoulders, his raised eyebrows, his slightly turned down mouth, and his dropped head as he presented the flowers to Louise conveyed his apology.

Although this exercise doesn't convey emotion, mood, or attitude, the shrugging gesture may bring you some relief when you're feeling tense or tired. Raise your shoulders up towards your ears and tighten them as much as you can. Hold that position for three to five seconds, and then release. Roll your shoulders in circles both backwards and forwards to complete the tension release. To avoid injuring yourself when doing this exercise, be careful not to overdo the tightening.

Chapter 8

Arming Yourself

. . . .

In This Chapter

▶ Shutting people out

▶ Letting someone in

▶ Disguising anxiety

▶ Sending signals through bodily contact

. . . .

*W*hether you're crossing your arms as a protective shield or opening them as a sign of welcome, the way you position your arms tells an astute observer how you're feeling.

Certain postures elicit certain moods. Crossed arms hold your feelings in and keep other people's out. They show that you've set up roadblocks beyond which no person dares travel. Stay with this position for too long and you find yourself feeling shut off and negative. Unless, of course, you're cold, in which case holding your arms across your chest keeping the warmth in and the cold out makes perfect sense.

As for contact, touching can be a great tonic as long as you know who, when, where, and how. Get touching right and the person you touch feels engaged and connected; get it wrong and prepare yourself for a sharp smack.

This chapter shows you how you can read arms signals, appear self-controlled, and increase your influence through physical contact.

Building Defensive Barriers

Any gesture that protects your body from an assault – be it real or imagined – is a defensive barrier. Ducking your head, averting your body, even tightening your lips and narrowing your eyes, are all examples of defensive behaviours. As opposed to open gestures that welcome others in, these behaviours protect you and keep others out.

Arms crossed on your chest

When you were a small child and feeling threatened and insecure, you may have hidden behind your mother's skirts or a solid piece of furniture. As you reached pre-school age, you may have created your own barrier by folding your arms tightly across your chest. During your teen years, you probably relaxed your grip and added crossed legs to the equation in order to appear more cool and less obvious.

The crossed-arm position is common throughout the world and communicates a defensive stance (see Figure 8-1). Not only does it serve as a protective guard against a possible attack, crossed arms also represent an inflexible position that tells you that this person's not budging. If a woman finds a man attractive, for example, she keeps her arms in an open position, but she crosses her arms over her chest with men she finds aggressive or unappealing.

You may also cross your arms over your chest if you're feeling anxious, or are lacking confidence. Crossing arms is a common position to adopt when you're among strangers and is often seen in lifts, public meetings, when waiting to board an airplane, or anywhere that you may feel insecure, apprehensive, or intimidated.

People who say that they cross their arms over their chests because the gesture feels comfortable are right. Any gesture that matches the corresponding attitude feels comfortable. So, if someone feels negative, self-protective, or in any way uneasy, even if he's not consciously aware of these feelings, it is quite common for that person to cross his arms. If he feels relaxed and is enjoying himself, he adopts an opened-arm position that reflects his attitude.

The meaning of the message is in the receiver. Studies show that people react negatively to the crossed-arm position. Even if you're comfortable with your arms crossed over your chest, people observing you are going to interpret your attitude as defensive. So, unless you want to show that you disagree or don't want to engage, find other positions for your arms.

Blocking out information

Two groups of volunteers were asked to participate in an American research project in which the participants attended a series of lectures. The purpose of the project was to examine the effects of the crossed-arm position on retention of information and attitude toward the lecturer. The first group was instructed to sit in a casual, relaxed position, with their arms and legs in an open position. The second group was told to fold their arms tightly across their chests during the lectures. The study showed that the group with the folded arms had a more negative view of both the lectures and the lecturer and retained 38 per cent less information than the group that sat with their arms and legs uncrossed.

Figure 8-1:
The crossed
arm position
is a
protective
one.

If you adopt the crossed arm position when you're in a group of people, you soon notice other members of the group adopting the same pose. Although influencing people into assuming this position is easy, you may discover that you have difficulty in achieving open communication when the majority of the group has adopted this stance.

Most people adopt the arms-crossed position when they disagree with what's going on around them, as illustrated during a recent public meeting in our village. A landowner applied to the local council to turn his farm into a golf course. The villagers were divided in opinion over this change of land use and a public hearing was held. Those in favour of the change sat on one side of the room while those against the proposal sat on the other. At the start of the meeting, many of those who opposed the plan sat with their arms crossed over their chests. As the supporters spoke in favour of the proposal, more and more of the opponents crossed their arms. When the time came for those who opposed the plan to speak, the supporters crossed their arms. As the meeting progressed and people became more adamant and agitated, almost the entire gathering sat with their arms tightly folded across their chests. No constructive discussions took place at that meeting and the individuals present left feeling disgruntled.

An attitude can lead to a gesture or posture that reflects the emotion. As long as you maintain that pose, the attitude remains. Therefore, to get someone to change from a crossed-arm position, give him something to do or hold. Then he has to unlock his arms and lean towards you. This breaks his negative posture and creates a more open body position, which in turn leads to a more open attitude.

Gripped crossed arms

A sure sign of restrained anxiety and apprehension is when the arms are folded across the chest and the hands are tightly gripping the upper arms. The person appears to be fortifying himself against adversity and holding on for dear life. People waiting in the doctor's or dentist's reception room can often be seen in this position, as can inexperienced air travellers who adopt the posture as the plane takes off and lands, indicating that they are in need of comfort or reassurance.

Depending on their level of concern, they may grip their arms so tightly that their fingers and knuckles turn white.

Crossed arms and clenched fists

Cross your arms and clench your fists, and you look as if you're heading towards a fight. This position demonstrates hostility as well as defensiveness, and can lead to aggressive behaviour. Don't be surprised if your jaw clenches and your face goes red too – individual gestures work in combination with others to convey attitudes.

If someone crosses his arms and clenches his fists when you're speaking to him, open your arms and expose your palms in a non-threatening, submissive position. This posture has a calming effect and the other person is more likely to drop his aggressive stance and discuss things in a more reasonable manner.

The crossed-arms, clenched-fists posture is a sign of control and authority. Police officers who cross their arms tend to clench their fists as well to indicate that they're the boss and aren't to be trifled with. Interestingly, people who carry weapons seldom cross their arms because they already feel protected by their weapon.

Crossed arms and thumbs up

A typical pose that superior type, up-and-coming young men adopt when engaging with their manager in the work environment is to stand with their arms crossed over their chests with their thumbs pointing upwards (see Figure 8-2). This position demonstrates both apprehension and confidence. Their uneasiness is conveyed through the crossed arms while the thumbs up position shows self-confidence and a sense of 'coolness' and control.

When you first meet a group of people, you can demonstrate your status and superiority by not folding your arms. Shake hands firmly, stand at the appropriate distance, and keep your hands by your sides or in the power position with one hand resting in the other at waist height.

Richard was recently promoted to partner in a prestigious city law firm. Although considered to be extremely talented and an asset to the firm, he also has the reputation of being somewhat brash and arrogant. After shaking hands with the firm's senior partner at a social event for the newly promoted lawyers, Richard folded his arms with both thumbs pointing upward and engaged his boss in conversation. As he spoke, he used his thumbs to gesture. This pose showed that while he was seemingly full of self-confidence, he also felt the need for some protection.

Figure 8-2: Crossed arms with thumbs up is typical of young, high-flying males.

Because of the structure of women's upper torsos, they cross their arms lower on the body than men do. Girls entering puberty tend to adopt this protective position more frequently than more mature females.

Touching yourself: Hugs, strokes, and more

The way you touch yourself gives observers clues as to how you're feeling. Most self-touching movements provide comfort and are the unconscious, mimed gestures of another person's touch, as if you've divided yourself into two people: the one who is providing the comfort, and the receiver of the touch. Some of the more common include the following:

- **Hugging or stroking yourself:** When you were a child feeling distressed or upset, your parents, or whoever was looking after you, would hold you in their arms to comfort you. Now that you're an adult, when you feel self-conscious and insecure, and no one's there to reassure you, or it would be inappropriate to seek solace from another person, you hug or stroke yourself to provide your own comfort and reassurance. The most common self-touching actions are rubbing your neck, stroking your arms, or fondling your face (see Figure 8-3).

- **Half-hugs:** Because, when you cross both arms across your body, you show that you're feeling afraid or defensive, you may adopt the half-hug position instead. In this position, one arm crosses your body and holds or touches the other arm, creating a partial barrier. Women typically use this gesture more than men.

- **The fig leaf:** Men hold hands with themselves in a barrier position to make themselves feel secure. Covering their 'crown jewels' they subconsciously protect themselves from a potential full frontal attack (see Figure 8-3). Look at the line-up of soccer players during a penalty kick and see where they place their hands and arms – as well they should!

The next time you see someone who's feeling lonely, dejected, or in any way vulnerable, notice how he positions his hands. You see that he holds his hands in the fig-leaf position in an attempt to create feelings of comfort and reassurance.

Placing objects in front of yourself

By placing a coffee cup, a clipboard, or any other object between yourself and another person, you are setting up a protective barrier. These barriers are a subconscious effort to conceal any nervousness or insecurity you may be experiencing, whether you're aware of the feeling or not.

Figure 8-3:
The fig leaf position makes a person feel more secure, while stroking is comforting.

During a role play with a client in which she had to enter her boss's office, sit across the table from him, and make a recommendation that she knew he wouldn't like, Lynne clutched a pad of paper in front of her, clasping it tightly to her chest. Although she said that she had to carry the pad for taking notes, the way she held it clearly indicated that she was feeling insecure and threatened. So strong were her subconscious feelings that not even seeing herself on video convinced her that a different posture would create a stronger, more authoritative and professional appearance.

If you're at a function where drinks are being served and you're feeling insecure, hold your glass or cup in front of you with both hands. This action creates a subtle barrier, behind which you can seek refuge. As you look around the room, you are likely to see that almost everyone else is standing in the same position, indicating that you're not alone in your feelings.

Giving the cold shoulder

As you are undoubtedly a kind and thoughtful person who would never purposely insult anyone, this section is probably superfluous to your requirements. However, should you ever feel the need to display indifference or aloofness with the intention of giving someone a quick, sharp jab to his ego, turn your shoulder towards him, creating a barrier between yourself and your object of contempt. With a look of disdain, a downward turn of the mouth, and the briefest of glances, the gesture leaves the recipient in no doubt of your feelings of scorn and derision towards him.

Conveying Friendliness and Honesty

Open arms indicate a receptive, friendly, and honest attitude. This position says that you've got nothing to hide and are approachable and amenable. It draws people to you, making them feel comfortable and at ease in your company. By leaving your body exposed, you're indicating that you're receptive to whatever comes your way.

Go to any sporting event and watch the players. The moment the winner sinks his final putt, crosses the finish line, or scores the winning goal his arms open with the thrill of victory. The losers cross their arms in front of their bodies or let them hang dejectedly by their sides.

Every summer my son, Max, and I visit his godmother, Libby, who is my dearest lifelong friend. As Libby lives in Oregon and we live in England, we seldom see one another more than once a year. The moment Libby sees us exit the customs hall, she flings her arms open before folding us in her embrace. Her open arms are like a welcoming beacon indicating her joy at seeing us.

If you want to persuade someone to your viewpoint, hold your arms in an open position. Open arms indicate a confident, constructive attitude and create a positive impression. You're perceived as sincere, direct, and trustworthy, as long as your other gestures are equally open and forthright. (For more about body language and persuasion refer to *Persuasion & Influence For Dummies* by Elizabeth Kuhnke (Wiley).)

Gestures of the rich, famous, and royal

During the Middle Ages people viewed royalty as all powerful, a perception that extended to the belief that people who suffered from the glandular disease, scrofula, commonly referred to as 'the King's evil', could be cured by the monarch's touch.

Just because someone is continually in the public eye doesn't mean that he's comfortable being on show. Celebrities, politicians, and members of royal families have subtle gestures intended to demonstrate how cool, calm, and collected they're feeling when inside everything's screaming, 'Get me out of here!'

The most common gestures you see public personalities adopt involve gestures where an arm crosses over the body. Instead of folding both arms in an obvious protective barrier or grasping hold of one arm, the person touches a personal object on himself such as a watch, shirt cuff, or ring. The gesture has no purpose other than to disguise nervousness. Here are a few other gestures you may have noticed:

✔ **Holding a handbag:** The Queen is rarely seen in public without her handbag. Yet unlike most women, queens and celebrities carry little if anything in their handbags. They have other people to do that for them. The accessory simply serves as a complement to her outfit and as a means of keeping distance between herself and others. Holding the bag over her arm immediately sets up a protective barrier between herself and her public. When she's feeling nervous or insecure, the Queen can hide behind a handbag and fiddle with its contents.

✔ **Playing with a pocket:** Prince Charles has devised a way of slipping his right hand into his jacket pocket that's intended to give an impression of a relaxed attitude. The astute observer realises that what he's really doing is hiding feelings or holding back an impulse. Firstly, he turns up the flap of his pocket. He then fingers the flap before he finally places his hand inside. He often leaves his thumb protruding so that his entire hand is not hidden. Leaving the thumb out of the pocket is a 'macho' gesture as demonstrated by tough guys who hook their thumbs over their belts or shove their hands into their trouser pockets leaving the thumbs exposed.

✔ **Fiddling with cufflinks:** Another gesture particular to Prince Charles is the cuff-link fiddle. During public walk-abouts he frequently adjusts his cuff links as he moves towards his destination. This gesture allows his arms to cross in front of his body and serves no purpose other than to give himself a sense of security. Tony Blair, the former Prime Minister, would often adjust his cuffs before speaking in public. Roger Moore, when playing James Bond, also adjusted his cuffs before facing an adversary. These gestures are defence mechanisms, designed to reduce anxiety.

✔ **Tidying a tie:** Men in public view often straighten their ties as they move from one spot to another. This is particularly true when a man is about to make a formal speech or is simply preparing for what's coming next. This gesture is a symbolic way of making sure that everything's in place and nothing's on show that shouldn't be. For example, when David Cameron gets out of a car wearing a jacket and tie he often straightens his tie as he walks towards his destination. This is his way of preparing himself for what's coming next, making sure that what's already looking good stays that way, and displacing any anxiety he may feel.

Touching to Convey Messages

The thing about touching is that it means many things to different people. Touching is a great way to offer comfort, create a bond, and increase your influence. Some people use the gesture as a sign of reassurance, support, and encouragement. Others use it as a signal that they want to interrupt you. Touching frequently occurs when someone's expressing excitement or is feeling festive. You also see people touch one another when there's a disaster or when they're listening to another person's troubles.

The act of touching isn't straightforward. Touch in an appropriate way and you come across as a caring, sharing kind of person. Touch incorrectly and you're perceived as an untrustworthy sleaze. Like most things, it's not what you do, it's how you do it. So heed this advice:

- ✔ **When to touch:** Neither the United States nor Britain are societies that encourage a vast amount of touching between individuals. People tend to relate a touch to a sexual advance when the intention may simply be to show support, express sympathy, or demonstrate tender feelings. Different people respond differently to touching. Some people are natural touchers and freely give, and comfortably receive, hugs and kisses. For others, unsolicited touching is an anathema and is to be avoided at all costs. If in doubt, don't touch.

  Before touching another person, pay attention to the kinds of contact he feels comfortable with. Until you know someone well, proceed with caution.

- ✔ **Where to touch:** A great deal of research has been conducted about where you're allowed to put your hands on another person and where you better not touch. The findings consistently conclude that your opposite-sex friends have more leeway about where they can place their hands on you than your same-sex friends. Unless, that is, you're gay or lesbian, in which case the opposite is true. Mothers are allowed more leeway, but not fathers.

- ✔ **Where not to touch:** Different cultures have different rules about touching. For example, what you may consider to be an affectionate gesture, such as patting a child on the head or ruffling a friend's hair, is highly insulting in Thailand. (See Chapter 15 for more about touching in different cultures.)

- ✔ **How long to touch:** Most parents instinctively know long they may touch their children. For example, during a child's infancy both parents are comfortable bathing and changing the child. As the child grows older, the father leaves these activities to the mother. This occurs slightly earlier for his daughter than for his son. Eventually, too, the mother leaves her child to bathe alone (and hopes he does a good job of it).

If you're having a conversation with someone who you find appealing, allow your hand to touch his slightly while you speak. Also, when you're introduced and shake hands you may let your hand rest slightly longer in his than you normally would do. If you're uninterested in or are repulsed by the person, your touch is brief and uncommitted.

Touching plays an important part in superstitious rituals. The tradition of touching wood after making a boasting statement stems from the ancient act of touching the sacred oak to appease the god Thor. Touching iron for good luck comes from the archaic belief that iron holds magical and supernatural powers.

Creating a bond

Consciously make physical contact with someone and you immediately establish a connection between the two of you. Parents touch their children, lovers touch their partners, and doctors touch their patients. The power of touch is binding.

Engaging with other people through physical contact is something at which politicians and business people with sophisticated political skills are particularly adept. The double-handed handshake is a favourite of anyone seeking to connect with another person (see Figure 8-4). By using your right hand for shaking and your left hand for touching the other person's hand, lower arm, or elbow, you demonstrate your desire to bond with that person.

The next time you shake hands with someone you've just been introduced to, lightly touch him on his hand or elbow with your left hand as you repeat his name. This creates a positive, memorable impression by making that person feel valued. Plus, repeating the person's name helps you to remember it.

Touching between individuals of equal rank and status occurs regularly. Patting a friend on the back, giving a chum a hug, or squeezing a colleague on the arm, are gestures that convey friendship and camaraderie.

At Hugo's annual rugby dinner the players were jostling about, punching one another on the arm, slapping each other on the back, and draping their arms over each other's shoulders. The young men were comfortable with this level of reciprocal touching between equals. When the coaches spoke to the players they were seen patting the team members on the back, initiating handshakes, and occasionally squeezing their upper arms. At no time did any of the players touch their coaches in a similar fashion. Unconsciously, the players were exercising their symbolic right to impose themselves on one another. In contrast, they demonstrated respect for their coaches' authority by treating them in a different manner.

Figure 8-4:
Offering a double-handed handshake establishes a bond and superiority.

Get your timing right when touching another person. Holding the touch for longer than three seconds makes the other person wonder what your intentions are.

The person doing the touching in a double-handed handshake is the top dog, although when the other person touches back, they're each demonstrating their sense of personal superiority. For this reason, save the double-handed handshake and the touching with your non-shaking hand for people of equal or lower status to you. You may be perceived as overly ambitious or familiar if you touch someone with a higher status this way.

The longer the touch, the more intense the message. If you know the person you're speaking to well and you have a good rapport, you can feel comfortable touching that person at length. If you don't know someone very well, you're both likely to feel uncomfortable touching. Think of times when you've accidentally brushed up against a stranger or someone you didn't know very well. You probably pulled away quite quickly.

Demonstrating dominance

Something to remember about touching is that it's a hierarchical gesture. The person who initiates the touch holds the authority. The doctor touches the patient, the teacher touches the student, and the priest touches the parishioner. For a person of lower status to initiate touch with someone holding a higher position is considered impertinent.

At his annual summer office party, Paul, the chairman of the company, circulated among his staff, placing his hand on the shoulders of many of the younger men and giving the female employees a squeeze on the upper arm in greeting. Not one of the staff members responded in a similar way. Whether they were aware of it or not, they knew it would be inappropriate and impertinent to reciprocate the touch.

Your gender determines, to a large extent, what your touch means. A male boss who touches his female secretary, does so as a sign of power and control. Woe betide the female subordinate who touches her male manager or the female boss who touches her male employee. Whereas a man's touch is perceived as paternal and powerful, a woman's touch is interpreted as a prelude to intimacy with sexual intent. Even in today's world of supposed gender equality, men struggle with the concept of women and power.

Avoid touching work colleagues. Because of laws governing behaviour in the work place, you can receive a formal complaint for making a gesture that may be interpreted as inappropriate physical contact.

Research suggests that men perceive women as 'uptight' when they complain about men presumptuously touching them. Female students and women working in restaurants, offices, and factories are used to being touched by their male superiors and they're expected not to interpret these gestures as sexual advances. The research also shows that men may interpret a woman's touch as conveying sexual intent, whether this is the case or not. The findings demonstrate that if touching implies power or intimacy, and women are considered by men to be status inferiors, a woman's touch is read as an intimate gesture, because power is not a reasonable interpretation. Sad but, according to the research, true.

Unless the people who are touching one another are of equal status, the person who is in a higher position is the one who, in theory, initiates the contact. A flagrant disregard for this practice occurred in 1992 when Queen Elizabeth II was visiting Australia. Without considering the potential implications and reactions, Paul Keating, the Australian Prime Minister at that time, put his arm around the Queen's waist in an effort to guide her as she walked among the crowds. British traditionalists were appalled at his behaviour. The Australians didn't understand what the palaver was all about. And as for the Queen, we never knew what she thought. More recently, the Queen and Michelle Obama have been seen hugging one another, and walking with their arms around each other's waists. The Queen appeared both maternal and frail while the First Lady appeared comforting and supportive.

Reinforcing the message

Touch is a powerful gesture. Depending how you administer it, it can be a sign of love, support, anger, or frustration.

Say you're arguing with another person. The tension rises, cruel words are said, and before you know it you're slapped across the face. This is an extreme example of reinforcing a negative message. The gesture supports what's been said and is a physical sign of anger, frustration, and desire to inflict pain.

Your little girl falls down and scrapes her knee. As she cries, you cradle her in your arms and stroke her hurt leg to soothe and comfort her. Here, the touch is a calming and placating action meant to reassure and to console.

In both cases, the touch reinforced the message. The type of touch determined the type of message being reinforced.

Savvy sales people, marketers, and advertisers understand the importance of appealing to as many senses as possible, including the sense of touch, when selling to the buying public. You *see* the product and your visual sense is stimulated. You *hear* the product, like the snap, crackle, and pop of breakfast cereal or the roar of a powerful engine, and your auditory senses are stirred. And when you *touch* the product, whether soft carpet or smooth leather, your kinaesthetic response reinforces the message that this product is something that you like the feel of.

I recently bought some new carpeting for my home. Before I made my final decision, I walked on the different samples to feel which felt best beneath my bare feet. Because I often lie on my bedroom floor when I'm speaking on the phone, I lay down on the carpeting sample in the showroom. Both the saleswoman and my contractor were quite surprised by my behaviour, which made perfect sense to me.

If you want to appeal to someone, appeal to all his senses.

The mother of the senses

An embryo, rocking in its mother's amniotic fluids, is sensitive to touch. At 9 weeks old, its fingers bend in a gripping motion when its palm is touched. At 12 weeks, its fingers and thumb can make a fist. When the embryo's foot is touched on its back or its sole, its toes curl in and fan out.

If you think about it, your skin is your biggest organ. It wraps itself over, under, and all around inside you. Skin is your oldest and most sensitive organ, too. Before you were able to hear or speak you could feel. Your sense of touch began in the womb.

If you're giving advice or information to another person, you may touch him on the hand, arm, or shoulder to deepen your connection and reinforce your message.

Before touching another person, you need to establish a connection with him. You wouldn't touch a stranger any more than you'd invite a stranger to touch you. In a relationship between two or more people, the dominant person, or the one holding authority, implicitly has the permission to touch.

Notice people travelling in a crowded tube or train. Most draw into themselves to keep from touching the people sitting or standing next to them.

Jo went out to lunch with her friend Caroline who was having problems with her boyfriend. At one point during their conversation, Caroline was on the verge of tears. Instinctively, Jo reached out and gently touched Caroline's hand. She let her hand rest there until Caroline composed herself. Jo's touch felt reassuring and had a calming effect. By combining this gesture with a forward lean and speaking sympathetically, Jo was able to help Caroline relax and see things from a more peaceful perspective.

Inappropriately touching another person can be perceived as rude, threatening, and intrusive.

Increasing your influence

Out of your five senses (sight, smell, sound, taste, and touch), your sense of touch is your oldest and most responsive. Your body reacts viscerally to touch, leaning into the hand offering comfort (see Figure 8-5) and pulling away from the hand that harms.

If you touch someone on the arm or shoulder when you're asking him a favour, he may well agree. Grab someone by the arm to get his attention and he probably pulls away.

So, how can you tell if someone welcomes touch or is adverse to it? Observe how he relates to other people and objects. People who touch themselves, such as rubbing or stroking their faces, hands, arms, and legs, respond to touch and would probably, all things considered, respond positively to your touch. A person who avoids self-contact and doesn't fiddle with figurines is telling you to keep your hands to yourself.

Wendy wanted her son Todd to agree to follow her into the estate agency business. She hoped that her son would find himself a profitable career selling homes and properties. Todd needed convincing. He felt he didn't have the necessary skills and doubted his ability to close a deal. During their discussion, Wendy leaned forward and touched Todd's arm as a gesture of reassurance and gentle persuasion. Her touch felt comforting and Todd's body became less tense. His facial expression softened and eventually Todd agreed to Wendy's plan.

Figure 8-5:
Touching
can be
comforting
and
encouraging.

Embracing during greetings and departures

The next time you're at an airport, watch how friends and family members hug when they're arriving and when they're departing. What you notice is that when people hug upon arrival they maintain the embrace longer than upon departure. When they first see one another, the hug is intense and the embrace strong. The people are welcoming and bringing one another into their most personal space. The departure hug is shorter and less passionate. It's almost as though by the time the people are saying good-bye, they're having to let each other go.

Part of my duties as on-board hostess for Holland American Cruise Lines was to stand at the gangplank for meeting and greeting of the passengers. At the same spot, a week later, we'd be saying our goodbyes. When the passengers first arrived there was little touching if any between us, as I welcomed them on board. I may have briefly shaken the hands of some. I definitely used my hands to guide others. By the end of the cruise, it was a different story. Embraces, hugs, and heartfelt handshakes – we were new best friends united. Having spent days at sea together, we had established enough of a relationship to comfortably touch one another. Some I even gave an extra little squeeze.

If someone pats you on the back when you're hugging him, he's giving you a signal that 'enough is enough' and he's ready to be let go of.

Chapter 9

It's in the Palm of Your Hand

In This Chapter

▶ Discovering how hand positions indicate attitudes

▶ Making your fingers do the talking

▶ Feeling for different handshakes

▶ Displacement activities

Scientific research shows that more nerve connections exist between the hands and the brain than between any other parts of the body. Unconsciously, your hands reveal your attitude towards another person, place, or situation. By the way you position your hands, rub your palms, and fiddle with your fingers, you're telling anyone who's paying attention what you're really feeling.

Watch how your hands move spontaneously in greetings, farewells, and as you cement an agreement. Before you know it, your hands illustrate a point you're making and are effective in demonstrating both your sincerity as well as your annoyance. Whether you're expressing love, anger, joy, or frustration, your hands hold the message.

In this chapter, you discover how you can use your hands to support the spoken word and add substance to your message. You find out how to position your hands to convey authority and dominance as well as demonstrate openness and submission. You see how other people reinforce what they mean by the way they mimic the actions or situations they're describing. You discover how to read a person by the way she shakes hands, and finally, you discover the telltale signals that the hands and fingers unconsciously reveal when you think no one is watching.

Up or Down: Reading Palms

Numerous experiments have been conducted to record how people respond to hand gestures. Research has shown that when a speaker uses the palm-up position, the vast majority of the listeners react positively to what's being said. When the speaker delivers the same message with the palm facing downward the positive response rate drops significantly. And when the speaker points her finger directly at the listener, the positive response becomes practically non-existent. The listener reacts negatively toward the speaker, tunes out what she's saying and makes personal judgements about her.

The open palm

The open hand is an ancient sign of trustworthiness. It's a positive position and is helpful for establishing rapport with another person, and is also a submissive, non-threatening gesture. The next time you walk past a pleading street beggar, look at how her hand is positioned. Chances are the palm is facing upwards.

Showing honesty

If you want a simple way to tell whether someone is being open and honest with you, look at where her palms are facing. If one or both of the palms are facing up, this gesture is a pretty good sign that you're hearing the truth (see Figure 9-1). When people hold their hands in a front facing open position, the words that would match this position would be along the lines of, 'Honestly, I mean what I'm saying. You can absolutely trust that I'm telling you the truth.'

Oh, sure, con artists, professional liars, and used car dealers know the tricks and use the open palm gesture when trying to convince you that they're genuine and sincere. But you're able to detect that something's not quite right because other gestures of honesty, such as open facial expressions, calm breathing, and a relaxed stance, are missing. Alarm bells ring as your instincts cry out, 'Wait a minute. This person's a fraud!'

Making a connection

You often wave to someone you know when seeing her from a distance. Your palm is in the open position, facing front, rhythmically moving from side to side. This is a similar gesture to the one you use when waving goodbye. When you wave, you're almost reaching out towards that person with a desire to touch her.

A good way to make contact with a large group of people is to hold out one or both of your hands with your fingers spread apart and your palms facing upwards. This gesture, shown in Figure 9-2, acts like a magnet and pulls people towards you.

Figure 9-1:
The open palm indicates honesty and trustworthiness.

Figure 9-2:
The raised open palm draws your audience in.

Saluting through time

Historians are uncertain about the origins of the Hand Salute. It probably dates back to late Roman times when assassinations were not uncommon. If a citizen wanted to see a public official, he was required to approach with his right hand raised to demonstrate that he didn't hold a weapon. A similar gesture developed for armoured knights who raised their visors with the right hand when meeting a fellow comrade.

The practice of offering a Hand Salute gradually became a way of showing respect. In early American history, it wasn't uncommon for a man to remove his hat in greeting. By the 1820s, the gesture was modified to simply touching the hat.

Traditionally, the British military saluted by taking their hats off as a sign of respect. In the early 1800s, the Coldstream Guards amended that gesture. Because of the wear and tear on the hats by constant removal and replacing, the soldiers were instructed to clap their hands to their hats and bow as they passed by their superiors. Other regiments quickly adopted this procedure.

By the mid 19th century, the Army salute took the form of an open hand, tightly closed fingers, palm to the front, the gesture that remains today.

The Naval salute is markedly different from the 'Open Hand' British Army salute, in that the palm of the hand points downward towards the shoulder. This gesture can be traced back to the days of sailing ships, when the ship's timber was sealed with tar and pitch to protect it from the seawater. To preserve their hands, officers wore white gloves. As it was considered highly undignified to show a dirty palm when saluting, the hand was turned to a 90-degree angle.

When you want to establish a sense of trust and honesty, let your hands remain visible. Otherwise, you may look like you're hiding something. (For more information on what hidden hands mean, go to the later section 'Hiding your hands'.)

You can also use open-hand gestures to connect with your listeners, helping them to grasp an idea that you're explaining or showing them that you value their opinions:

- ✔ Say that you want to plant a thought into someone's mind without verbally force-feeding the idea. Bend your elbows at a 90-degree angle and hold out both your hands side by side, as if you're showing her the large size of a fish you've caught. Then slowly beat your open hands rhythmically up and down and watch the light bulb turn on as the listener sees the picture.

- ✔ The next time you're speaking and you want to hear what someone else has to say, turn towards that person with your palm open and extended in her direction. The gesture is as though you're giving her a gift. By handing her the chance to speak, she feels acknowledged and that you're interested in what she has to say (see Figure 9-3).

Figure 9-3:
Gesturing toward another person acknowledges her and demonstrates your interest.

✔ Watch someone who wants you to come on board with her way of thinking. See if she holds both hands in front with her, palms facing her body as if she's embracing another person. If you find yourself using this gesture when you speak, you may also be attempting to grasp your own suggestion or idea.

The downward facing palm

Turn your hand over with your palm facing downwards and Bingo!, you're projecting power and authority (see Figure 9-4). This position is used for giving orders where no room exists for discussion. Gesturing with your palm facing downwards says, 'I'm in control here. Do as I say!'

You have to be careful when using this gesture, especially if your fingers are tightly closed because of its association with dominance and tyranny. Think of the Third Reich and the Nazi salute if you're in doubt. Hitler purposely selected this gesture. He instinctively understood the intimidation it conveyed.

If you want to calm down a tense situation or ask for quiet, hold out both your palms slightly pointed downwards with your fingers slightly separated and gently beat them up and down. Make sure that your fingers are relaxed or you may just be fanning the flames of the fire!

Figure 9-4:
The down-
ward
facing palm
conveys
dominance
and control.

Closed-palm, finger-pointed

Close your palm into a fist, point your index finger, and look out, world!
You've just created a symbolic club for beating into submission anyone
who's listening (see Figure 9-5).

Think back to a time when someone – a parent, teacher, or boss – pointed
a finger at you and shook it for all it was worth. Don't be surprised if the
memory makes you cringe. You know just how threatening and aggressive
this gesture feels. That's because it comes from our primate ancestors who
shake their 'fists' before pummelling their opposition into submission with a
right over-arm blow. Ouch!

While you're remembering annoying gestures you'd rather forget, what about
the one where the speaker beats her pointed finger in time to what she's
saying. Again, this action makes you feel as if you're being beaten with a
sharp stick. It may make you feel like a naughty child being reprimanded.

Figure 9-5:
The closed-palm, pointed-finger is threatening and aggressive.

The finger wag moves rhythmically sideways, back and forth like a metronome. Another annoying gesture, this action is a silent 'telling off' and reminds you of just how badly behaved you are.

The finger jab, the wag's closest cousin, is like a stabbing motion and is quite intimidating. Not one of the most conciliatory of gestures, use it at your peril.

If you habitually point and beat your finger when speaking, make a conscious effort to practise the palm-up and palm-down, fingers-loose positions. You find that you can create a positive impact on people and a relaxed atmosphere.

Hands Up!

Second only to your face, your hands are your most visually expressive feature and can be equated to your voice because they talk so much. They serve as a substitution for words as well as supporting the spoken word by illustrating and amplifying what you're saying. For example, when you're giving directions to someone who's lost, you most likely use your hands to get her back on the right path. When you're emphasising a point, your hands move in time with your words. When you're describing a shape or a particular scene, your hands create a visual picture of what you're saying. These kinds of hand gestures make complicated explanations more comprehensible.

Hiding your hands

When you conceal your hands by putting them behind your back or shoving them in your pockets, these actions are like keeping your mouth shut. What your hands are saying is, 'I don't want to talk!'

Take yourself back to your childhood. You've just been caught with your hand in the biscuit tin. You quickly pull it out and stick it behind your back while saying, 'No! Honestly! I didn't take anything!' And all the time your hand stays hidden.

Fast forward to your life now. You've been out on the town with your pals, you arrive home as the sun is rising, and your parent/spouse/partner asks you where you've been. Rather than owning up to whatever minor, or major, indiscretion you may have got into, if you're a man you most likely shove your hands into your pockets or cross your arms with your hands tucked neatly away while coming up with a good excuse. If you're a woman, you busy your hands with a flurry of activities. Either way, your palms stay hidden.

Many (many!) years ago when my husband Karl was starting off in sales, he was told to watch the customers' hands when they were giving reasons why they couldn't buy his product. What he noticed was that when people were being honest with him, they used their hands freely and often exposed their palms. He also noticed that when someone was being less than truthful, her hand movements were reduced and kept more concealed.

The hand rub: Good for you or good for me?

When you rub your palms together, you're signalling a positive expectation. How quickly you rub them indicates who's going to benefit. The slow palm rub can appear devious or crafty and may leave you feeling a little uneasy. You can bet that whatever positive result may happen is going to happen for anyone but you. The quick hand rub indicates excitement, pleasure, and enthusiasm. If someone is offering you an opportunity and is rubbing her hands together quickly as she speaks, you can feel assured that her proposal is good for you.

Consider these examples:

- ✔ A friend tells you how excited she is about a holiday she's about to take, a promotion she's been given, or a fabulous idea she's just had. She may well quickly rub her palms together with a big smile on her face.

  Once upon a time I lived and worked in Las Vegas, Nevada. No, I wasn't a showgirl! However, I occasionally went to the casinos and observed the gamblers. Something I noticed at the craps table was that people throwing the dice inevitably rubbed them together quickly before throwing them. This action, along with the look of concentrated anticipation on their faces, indicated that they were expecting something positive to happen. Most of the time something positive did happen, but for the casino, not the gambler.

- ✔ The car salesman or real estate agent sits you down and asks whether you're ready to pull out your cheque book, rubbing her hands slowly together as she does so. Meaning? Buyer beware!

- ✔ After taking all your relevant details about the purchase you want to make, the sales person rubs her palms together quickly and says, 'I've got just the thing for you!' Here the message is that she expects the results to be to *your* advantage. And if it works out for you, it probably works out for her. Everyone wins in this case!

The folded hand

You may think that folding your hands together is a positive gesture because it looks contained and controlled. But look again. Studies show that rather that demonstrating confidence, this gesture actually reveals frustration or hostility and signals that the person is holding a negative attitude. By folding your hands, you're indicating that you're holding something in them that you don't want to let out.

Sure, some people may say that they're just comfortable with their hands folded in front of their waists, resting on a table, or in the fig leaf position protecting their private parts. And they may be. But because, like most gestures, this one is unconscious, you can be sure that more is going on than pure comfort.

The next time you're in a meeting and the speaker refuses to give anyone else a chance to talk, watch the hand positions of the rest of the group. They're likely to be in folded positions until someone finally interrupts, at which time the hands open as the person begins to speak.

If you're speaking with someone whose hands are clenched, you can bet that she's holding annoyance, negativity, or frustration. Do whatever you can to get her to unlock her fingers to expose her palms, including giving her something to hold or a task to perform. The longer her hands stay put in the closed position the longer, the hostile attitude remains.

Hands clenched

Think back to a time when you were really scared, nervous, or holding back a strong negative emotion. Chances are that you were clenching your hands for all you were worth and your knuckles were a bright white: the stronger the emotion, the tighter the clench. In addition to the strength of the clench, you can also take meaning from where the clenched hands are placed.

In front of the face

Studies indicate that the higher the hands are held in the clenched position the stronger the negative mood (see Figure 9-6). So, if your boss is sitting with her elbows resting on her desk and her hands are clenched in front of her face, she's probably going to be difficult to handle. By putting her hands near her mouth, she's indicating that she's holding back what she would like to say. Be careful not to push her too far. She just may unclench those hands and let the words fly out!

Anne is a fast-thinking, focused, and determined businesswoman. She has numerous projects on the go at one time, all of which require her attention. She values her staff enormously and makes a point of having a few minutes of personal conversation with them all during the week. Most of them know that although she's genuinely interested in their wellbeing, she also likes people to get to the point and not go into too much detail. Nigel has worked for Anne for 16 years and likes to have a chat and a gossip. He frequently comes into Anne's office to do just that. The moment she sees him coming, Anne puts her elbows on her desk and clenches her hands in front of her face, as though she's putting up a barrier to keep him from getting too close and to keep her from blurting out something she may later regret. Although Nigel doesn't seem to read the signals, Anne's secretary knows that gesture is a sure sign of her frustration and annoyance. In order to shield Anne and protect Nigel's feelings, she allows Nigel a few minutes of Anne's time before coming up with reasons why Anne has to end the conversation.

In the mid position

Say that you're working at your desk, frantically beavering away to meet a deadline and someone comes in for a chat. Although you're quite annoyed about being interrupted, you want to appear cordial and welcoming. You stop what you're doing, fold your hands on your desk in front of you, and ask, 'How may I help you?' Folding your hands and keeping them at this mid position signals that although you're irritated you're not yet ready to explode.

If the interloper is paying attention, she sees that by holding your hands in a clenched position you're holding back a negative emotion. If she's smart, she suggests coming back at a more convenient time.

Figure 9-6:
Hands in the clenched raised position indicate negativity.

The fig leaf

A lot of people stand with their hands folded in front of their private parts. This position tells you that they're comfortable standing like that or that they don't know what to do with their hands. They're probably subconsciously feeling threatened and looking for a position that offers protection. By putting their hands in front of their most vulnerable parts, they feel comfortable because they're covered. And, now their hands have something to do. Don't be fooled into thinking that this is a naturally confident position. The reason the position's comfortable is because it acts like a shield.

Letting the Fingers Do the Talking

If you look at the way people use their hands when they're speaking, you can see that they often look like they're holding onto their words. These actions are based on the precision and power grips, which are the two ways you can hold onto an object. (See the *Body Language For Dummies* app for some examples.)

Your hands and fingers also grab themselves when you're feeling under pressure, frustrated, or conversely, when you want to demonstrate control or authority. Even as I'm searching for the right way to convey this message, I'm resting my elbows on my desk while I grip my palms in front of my face, watching the knuckles turn white. Finding no answer there, I put my fingers to my mouth. Again, no luck. Shift to resting my chin in my palms as I search for inspiration. Even Henry, my dog, can tell by the way I'm using my hands that a struggle is going on here.

The precision grip

Hold something small between your thumb and fingertips. It can be a pen, a needle, or a delicate piece of fabric. This is the precision grip, shown in Figure 9-7, which allows you to hold and manipulate an object precisely.

Now, when you're speaking and want to say something accurately or delicately press your fingers and thumb together in a similar position with your palm facing towards you. Presto! Your listener understands that you're reinforcing what you're saying with great precision and accuracy.

Figure 9-7:
The precision grip demonstrates exactness.

To focus your listener's attention and be seen as authoritative, place your index finger against your thumb in the 'okay' gesture with your palm facing outward and your fingers softly rounded. This way you avoid intimidating your audience and you're likely to be perceived as thoughtful and goal oriented. This gesture is a favourite of modern politicians. Gosh, what a surprise!

In some countries, the okay signal is considered rude. Before making any definite gesture, find out what is acceptable behaviour and what may cause offence. (You can read more about the use of the okay signal in Chapter 15.)

When you ask a question or are feeling uncertain about a point you're making or responding to, you may well find that your thumb and index finger are almost – but not quite – touching (see Figure 9-8). Funny how that happens, as if the fingers know that the answer isn't quite there. When the fingers do come together in a definite grip, the action is as if they've grabbed the information and are holding onto it.

Figure 9-8:
The thumb and forefinger not quite touching shows hesitancy or uncertainty.

The power grip

People who want to be perceived as strong, serious, and forceful use their whole fist to make a point (see Figure 9-9). This action is as if they are holding onto a strap on a fast-moving bus or hammering a nail into a block of wood.

You can use this gesture effectively in two ways. If you choose to deliver your message in a mild mannered way, leave your fingers bent, not fully closed. If, however, you mean business and are taking no prisoners, close your fingers into a fist and watch the fur fly.

Watch a public speaker or politician who deliberately wants to show just how much conviction and determination she has. Wow! Look at that tightly closed fist pumping up and down as if beating a big bass drum. Makes you wonder whether more than a bit of showmanship is going on.

Figure 9-9:
The power grip demonstrates conviction and determination.

A similar gesture is the air punch, where you beat the air with a tightly closed fist to give force to a strong statement. This gesture is also the one you can use when your team scores, your proposal is accepted, or you win the lottery.

To show power but with a little less force than you would use in a tightly held power grip, let your fingers and thumb curl inwards as if they are loosely grasping an object. This is a way of getting people to take your message seriously without having to act out with an abundance of force.

If you're speaking to an audience and want to establish authority, let your fingers and thumb curve inwards as if they're almost but not quite holding an invisible object. You'll be perceived as in control and sure of what you're doing.

The power chop

Sometimes when you speak, you may feel so passionate that you find yourself using your hand like a weapon, jabbing, punching, or chopping. Hopefully, you're just hitting empty air rather than a person or an object.

Your listener had better take you seriously when you use these gestures because they're a sure sign that whatever you're feeling is pretty strong and you aren't going to accept any arguments or contradictions. In other words, you mean business!

To demonstrate real forcefulness when you're speaking and to underline your determination to swash-buckle your way through the obstacle course, turn your hand into a symbolic axe blade by positioning it sideways with your fingers held closely together. Now, make strong downward chopping movements. Your hand and arm start acting like a meat cleaver and woe betide the person who gets in your way. UK Deputy Prime Minister Nick Clegg is particularly adept at using this gesture when making his points.

The scissors or double-chop motion is a great one to use when you're rejecting or disagreeing with what someone else is saying. Cross both your forearms in front of your body and make outward cutting motions with your hands. You're indicating that you don't want to hear any more by cutting off the conversation.

When my teenage son Max was doing his best to convince me why he should be allowed to travel the world on his own, I wasn't about to be swayed. His passionate arguments were countered with my motherly wisdom. Not only did my words say, 'No', everything I was doing was rejecting his proposal. It was when I combined the double-chop motion with the finger shake that my daughter Kristina came in with the conciliatory palms down, gently beating gesture that reduced the tension and created a modicum of calmness.

The steeple

In his studies of body movements, Ray Birdwhistell noted that confident, superior types of people whose gestures tend to be minimal or restricted 'steeple' their fingers to demonstrate their confident attitude. You can achieve this position by letting your finger tips lightly touch like the steeple on a building.

This gesture is also called the 'power position' because people often use it in a superior/subordinate interaction. Lawyers, accountants, and anyone in a position of authority frequently give instructions or advice with their fingers in this position.

✔ **The raised steeple:** When the fingers are raised in front of the chest, the speaker is giving thoughts or opinions. (See Figure 9-10.)

Use the raised steeple position judiciously. Taken to extremes, it can convey an arrogant 'know-it-all' attitude. If you tilt your head backwards when taking this position, don't be surprised if you're perceived as smug or arrogant.

✔ **The lowered steeple:** When you're listening you may find your fingers in the lowered steeple position (see Figure 9-10). You look interested and ready to respond when you put your hands together like this. Women tend to use this position more often than the raised steeple.

Figure 9-10:
The lowered steeple indicates a listening attitude; the raised steeple indicates thoughtful authority.

Gripping hands, wrists, and arms

If you want to project superiority and confidence, put your hands behind your back and grip one hand with the other. Look at prominent male members of royal families around the world. Observe senior military personnel, police officers patrolling their beats, or the headmaster of your local school striding through the corridors. They all adopt this position of authority. They are showing no fear of exposing their vulnerable necks, hearts, or stomachs to potential threats and hazards.

The next time you're in a stressful or uncomfortable situation, adopt the palm-in-palm-behind-the-back stance. Note how your feelings change from frustrated, insecure, or angry to relaxed and confident.

As the grip moves up the arm, though, the meaning changes. You can bet that if someone is gripping her wrist behind her back rather than just her hand she's holding back frustration. This gesture is a way of maintaining self-control, as if the hand is holding the wrist or arm to keep it from hitting out. The farther up the back the hand goes the greater the level of frustration. By the time the hand reaches the upper arm this person may have moved from frustration to anger. This gesture is also a sign of nervousness and is an attempt at self-control.

Gesturing with your thumbs

Gestures associated with the thumb convey dominance, superiority, and in some cases aggression so you won't find it surprising that in palmistry the thumb denotes strength of character and ego. If you've ever heard the expression 'under the thumb' you know the implication is that the person with the thumb is the one in control. Woe betide the person under the thumb, as according to ancient Roman history the thumb turned down served as a sign of imminent death.

- ✔ **Thumbs up:** The thumb up position generally denotes agreement. But be careful using this gesture as in some cultures doing so is perceived as rude and highly offensive. (See Chapter 15 for more on this.)

- ✔ **Thumbs protruding from a person's pockets:** This gesture demonstrates dominance and self-assuredness. Although both men and women use this gesture, the woman is rare who adopts the position of holding her jacket lapel with the thumb exposed, whereas men often do.

- ✔ **Gesturing towards another person with your thumb:** When you use your thumb to point towards someone else, you're being dismissive, disrespectful, or ridiculing the other person, especially if the gesture is accompanied by a sneer, a downward glance and a toss of your head (see Figure 9-11).

Andrew had the unfortunate habit of ridiculing Jane, his wife, in front of their friends. When they were in company he would often refer to her as 'the little woman' gesturing in her direction with a closed fist, using his thumb as a pointer. Although Jane told him how irritating she found this gesture, as well as the accompanying remarks, Andrew took no notice. He did notice, however, when after several years of rude and disrespectful behaviour, Jane divorced him.

Figure 9-11: Thumb gesturing towards another person is rude.

Analysing Handshakes

Shaking hands upon meeting is a tradition that creates a bond of solidarity. Our ancestors in their caves greeted one another with outstretched arms and exposed palms to show they were free of clubs and other life-threatening weapons. Scuttle along to the Roman period, where it was common to carry concealed daggers up ones sleeve. Hence, two men would grab each other's lower arms as a means of greeting and to check out the other's intentions.

As the handshake evolved it became a gesture to cement agreements, offer a welcome, and bid someone farewell. Therefore, make sure that when you shake hands the gesture is open, congenial, and positive.

Deciding who reaches out first

Although shaking hands when meeting another person for the first time is customary, in some instances making the first move may not be appropriate. For example, if you've forced the meeting or the other person is uncomfortable in your presence it would be inappropriate for you to extend your hand as a sign of trust and welcome. Yet if you consider the person you're meeting to be your equal and you're both glad to see one another, you simultaneously extend your hands in greeting.

When you show up at a customer's without having been invited wait to see if she extends her hand in welcome. If you put your hand out first, she may feel forced to shake your hand, creating a negative feeling. If no handshake is forthcoming, give a small nod of your head instead.

Because some people aren't sure whether or not to shake a woman's hand in a business context, the woman should extend her hand first to show that she's comfortable to shake hands (see Figure 9-12). That way avoids wondering and fumbling.

Figure 9-12:
A woman offering her hand first shows she's in charge.

Conveying attitude

Some people shake hands as if they're Attila the Hun about to put you in your place. Others remain passive and detached, barely offering you a fingertip. Still others present you with a cold, clammy hand reminiscent of a wet mackerel. How people shake hands tells you a lot about them, their attitude, and their feelings about the person they're about to touch.

University of Alabama professor William Chaplin and his students examined the relationship between personality and styles of handshakes. They found that extroverted and emotionally expressive people are inclined to shake hands firmly whereas neurotic and shy people don't. They also found that women who have an open attitude to new experiences use a firm handshake.

The bone cruncher

Before you can stuff your hand in your pocket, the Bone Cruncher is there, turning your knuckles into pulverised bone. These people seem to have an overly aggressive attitude to compensate for their ineffectualness. The Bone Cruncher is to be avoided when it comes to shaking hands because you can do little to counter the action.

To avoid a potentially painful handshake, both men and women should avoid wearing rings on their right hands in a business context.

If you think that your hand has been purposely crunched, say 'Wow! That's one strong grip and it really hurt!' You're letting the person know that you're onto her game. This has even more impact if other people are present observing the interaction. She's unlikely to play that trick again.

George lacks social skills and is unaware of how much pressure he puts into his handshakes. He unconsciously makes up for his social ineptness by putting an extra hard squeeze into his grasp. Women find it especially uncomfortable to shake hands with George. He squeezes their hands so forcefully that women have sometimes walked away from having shaken hands with George sporting red welts where their rings have cut into their fingers. One friend mused, 'If he does that shaking hands, I wonder what happens when he kisses you?'

The wet fish

If you've ever been presented with a totally limp hand to shake, you know how unconnected it feels when your hands meet. People who refuse to commit to a handshake tend to be self-important and aloof. Granted, surgeons and concert pianists need to guard their fingers and are known for their soft handshakes. And people who have to do a lot of shaking also offer a relaxed hand in order to protect their fingers.

Some people offer the uncommitted handshake for other reasons. Some women think that it's appealing to present themselves as submissive to both men and women (see Figure 9-13). Very strong people sometimes offer a soft handshake as a way of highlighting their physical power. If a person's lacking in confidence, she also holds back from making a connection.

Bonnie comes from Dallas, Texas, and works for a large investment firm in London. Her working environment is predominantly male. Although she's highly accomplished, her boss and peers perceive her as being quite submissive. One of the reasons for this is because of the way she shakes hands. Regardless of the million pound deals she regularly lands, she still highlights her femininity by offering a soft handshake, as she was taught to do growing up in the southern USA. Her male clients and colleagues speak with veiled respect about the Southern Belle and her wily ways, while her female colleagues from northern England watch in wonder.

Figure 9-13:
A soft handshake can be appealing. Note how other body parts reflect the softness.

The power shake

At times you may want to show that you have the upper hand, meaning that you're strong and in control. You can do this by making sure that your hand faces down in the handshake. Although your palm doesn't have to be completely turned over so that it faces directly downward, the slight turning shows that you're in charge (see Figure 9-14).

Figure 9-14:
The palm that faces down holds the authority.

Even if you unconsciously place your hand in the top position, you have the automatic advantage. This is because the hand down position is associated with dominance and control whereas the upward facing palm conveys compliance and passivity. Even if you and the receiver are unaware of your hand positions, you feel more dominant and the other person feels more submissive.

The double-hander

The double-hander is a favourite in the corporate and political arena. Through this particular handshake, the initiator aims to portray sincerity, honesty, and a deep feeling for the receiver. By using it, you increase the amount of physical contact and by restricting the receiver's right hand you gain control of the interaction. Because the double-hander is like a mini hug, choose your receiver carefully. Ideally, this handshake should only be used where a personal relationship already exists.

If someone thrusts her hand towards you, palm facing downwards, and grabs your hand in hers putting you in a submissive position with little chance of balancing the equation, what do you do? Allow the power player to take your hand with your palm facing upwards. Then, before she knows what you're up to, put your left hand on top of her right to create a double-hander. From this position you're able to straighten the handshake and gain control subtly and effectively.

When you use the two-handed handshake, the left hand conveys two points worth noting. Firstly, it reveals the intensity of feeling you're demonstrating towards the receiver. The higher up the arm your left hand goes, as shown in Figure 9-15, the deeper the level of intimacy you want to show. This is a complex movement in that the gesture shows both the degree of connection you have with the receiver as well as the amount of control you're exerting. The second point is that your left hand invades the receiver's personal space. Unless the receiver has positive feelings for you, this gesture can lead to feelings of suspicion and mistrust. If in doubt, don't use it; especially on your boss.

Figure 9-15: Intimacy and control increase as the left hand moves up the arm.

The leach

Some people just don't know when to let go. They grab your hand, shake it, and then hang on until you want to pry their fingers off. This is a subtle way of demonstrating control. By prolonging the contact, they're engaging you for longer than you may have wanted. Interestingly, you'll probably allow the contact to remain until you can think of a good reason to pull away; such as, 'Excuse me, I have to go now' even though you may have just arrived!

The space invader

Whether you're pulling someone into your territory when shaking hands or you're invading her space by plunging your arm into her terrain, a power play is taking place and you hold the power (see Figure 9-16).

In the first instance, you propel your arm forward, forcefully grip the receiver's extended hand, and simultaneously go into a quick reverse thrust, yanking her into your space and huddling over the handshake until you're ready to let it go. If you pull someone into your personal space, you create a handshake on your terms. You're in charge.

Be aware of the amount of force you apply or you may find the other person falling on top of you as you pull her in. That's what you call getting the relationship off on the wrong foot!

If you invade the other person's territory, you extend your arm fully, forcing the other person to retreat back into her domain. Her arm ends up in a cramped position while your extended arm fills her space.

Figure 9-16:
Space invaders demand power and control.

The firm shake

If you want to create a sense of mutual respect and equality, make sure that when you shake hands with another person both your palms are in the vertical position, your fingers are wrapped around one another's hands and that you apply the same amount of pressure. Your hands should meet in no-man's land, halfway between your space and the other person's.

Taking the left side advantage

The next time you look at a photograph of two leaders standing next to one another, see if one looks more dominant than the other (see Figure 9-14). Chances are that you perceive the person on the left side of the picture to have the edge.

If the photograph shows them shaking hands you can easily see that the hand of the person on the left is in the upper position, making her appear more powerful and in control. Savvy politicians are aware of the impact this body position makes and jockey to place themselves to the right of their colleague, or adversary, in order to come out on the left in the photo.

To gain the left side advantage to make yourself appear as if you're calling the shots, position yourself to the right of the other person. If you want to increase your power play, place your left hand on your colleague's back while shaking hands. Although the other person may feel annoyed by your obvious power play, you can smile warmly, knowing that you've got the advantage.

Displacing Your Energy

If you ever noticed yourself drumming your fingers, pulling your earlobe, touching your face, or scratching your head when you haven't got an itch, you're experiencing displacement activities. Displacement activities are easy to spot because they are the small, inconsequential gestures you make when you're feeling inner turmoil or frustration.

People who are experiencing frustration or internal conflict often feel the need to take action. If they struggle to find an appropriate action to address the source of annoyance, they fill the void with meaningless activities to keep themselves busy.

Drumming for relief

If you're in a meeting and someone's drumming her fingers on the table, pay attention. This person is telling you something. Bored, frustrated, or even irritated; the percussionist is impatient.

Stephen works for an international law firm. He recently found out that his colleagues call him 'Thumper' because of his constant finger drumming during meetings. Stephen reveals his state of mind by the tempo of his finger tapping. When he's bored, he drums the four fingers of his right hand in quick succession. When he's thoughtfully considering a suggestion, he quietly taps his middle finger. When he's prepared to conclude the meeting, he knocks his knuckles on the table. Without saying a word, his colleagues know what Stephen's thinking.

Fiddling for comfort

Notice what you do the next time you feel anxious. Chances are that you'll fiddle with an object. You may jangle your keys, twist a ring on your finger, or adjust your clothes. You may also touch yourself by picking at your nails, tugging your earlobe, rubbing your cheek, or running your fingers through your hair. The purpose of these actions is to ease any nervousness you may be feeling.

When people are feeling anxious, they focus their excess energy onto themselves as a way of providing temporary relief. These actions are sometimes referred to as 'adaptors' because they help you adapt to your internal tension. Adaptive behaviours are mainly focused on the head and the face. Unconsciously you may find yourself stroking your face, running your fingers over your lips, or rubbing the back of your neck when you're feeling upset. These hand gestures are reminiscent of those your mother may have used to comfort you when you were a child.

Hand to nose

When your hand goes to your nose, you know a falsehood is going on inside. Whether you're telling a deliberate lie (as if), having a dishonest thought, pretending to be brave when you're totally terrified, or simply feeling a moment of self-doubt, the hand going to your nose is the signal.

As I was walking my dog Henry, thinking about my day's challenges, I began to notice that each time I moved from one thought to the next my hand made a definite movement. I particularly noticed when I wiped my nose, a sign of falsehood and doubt. Granted, it was cold, my body was warm, and my nose was running, so I had to wipe it. But at the time I had been thinking that I'd be able to meet a deadline when, in fact, I seriously doubted that I would.

The act of self-touching signals a need for reassurance. Rubbing the nose, giving it a quick wipe, or a simple scratch are responses to the tingling sensation caused by heightened blood flow to the nose when you're feeling stressed.

To tell if someone's feeling under pressure, observe her hand to face gestures.

Hand to cheek

The hand to cheek gesture indicates boredom, disinterest, and fatigue (see Figure 9-17). Resting your hand on your cheek is like resting your hand on your pillow. Before you know it, you may be nodding off into dreamland. In meetings, lectures, and restaurants you see people resting their heads on their hands as negative feelings creep in.

Figure 9-17: Hand-to-face gestures reveal evaluations, disinterest and boredom.

If you're speaking in a public forum and you notice that heads are resting in hands, change what you're doing. The change catches their attention and saves you the embarrassment of heads collapsing into hands in an embarrassing heap.

Biting fingernails

If you ever work in intelligence, you're told to observe people's mannerisms. Mannerisms are a sure sign to a person's state of being and are more difficult to disguise than facial features. Mannerisms are so entrenched that eliminating them is hard, whereas facial features can be fairly easily changed. During any assessment of another person, look to her hands to see what they're like.

Doctors examine a patient's fingernails with the same amount of care and attention as they look at the face and the eyes. Any irregularity, including shape and colour, is evidence of physical poor health and psychological stress and anxiety.

Nails bitten or picked to the quick lead to brachyonychia, a condition in which the width of the nail plate and nail bed is greater than the length. If any of the nails, especially the thumb, have been sucked they may show teeth markings. These are signals that someone is experiencing extreme tension. You start to doubt that she confines her stress behaviours to nail-biting alone. From the look of Gordon Brown's fingernails, Britain's former Prime Minister is a regular nail bitter.

Hand to chin

The chin resting on the top of the hand is a sign of thinking: The person's pondering something. The thumb under the chin with the index finger pointing up the side of the face signals that an evaluation is being made. She's listened and now she's making an assessment (see Figure 9-17).

Recent photographs of Hilary Rodham Clinton show her posing in the evaluation posture, with her chin resting on her thumb and her index finger pointing up her chin. The pose indicates that she's weighing up the merits of the argument.

Chapter 10

Standing Your Ground

. . . .

In This Chapter

▶ Finding the right stance for your attitude

▶ Showing how you really feel

▶ Revealing information without meaning to

. . . .

*A*t certain times in your life, you've had to take a stance and make a firm decision. You probably planted your feet firmly on the ground and got on with what you had to do. At other times you've been able to take it easy, wandering from one pillar to another post.

You've stamped your foot in anger – or known someone who has – you've rubbed your ankle up against another's as well as your own, and you've stood with your weight on one leg in boredom, as well as bouncing on your toes in excitement.

In this chapter, I look at the different types of stance you adopt depending on your mood and circumstances. You also discover what the swinging foot is saying, as well as the pointed toe.

Showing Commitment and Attitude through Your Stance

The foundation for any stance is to stand with your feet evenly placed under your hips and with your weight equally distributed between them. What you choose to do with that foundation depends on what you want to show and how you want to be perceived. How you hold yourself reflects the effects of life experiences as well as social position.

You can spot status by the way a person stands. The Queen doesn't slump, at least, not in public. The petty officer stands to attention when his superior enters the room. The servant bows at his master's will.

The person who slouches, who lets his head droop, his shoulders hunch, and his feet turn inwards shows submission, a lack of commitment and indicates that he's withdrawing, or holding back. Conversely, people who place their weight evenly between their legs, with their feet firmly planted under them, look confident and self-assured, providing the other body parts are working in harmony with the feet and legs. When standing in this position, don't be surprised if you find yourself holding your head high, with your chest open and stomach in. Presto! You're standing like a winner.

If you want to assess a person's attitude, look at how he's standing. Most people make the majority of their important decisions when both of their feet are on the ground. If you want to be perceived as powerful, influential, and in control, stand with your legs slightly apart with your weight evenly distributed between them (see Figure 10-1).

Figure 10-1:
Evenly placed weight provides a firm foundation.

Straddle stance

The straddle stance is a stable position and the one most favoured by those who are showing dominance. It requires that your legs are straight, and that your feet are placed wide apart with your weight equally distributed between them.

With their higher centre of gravity, men adopt the straddle stance more frequently than women. Their height notwithstanding, men also adopt this position more frequently in the company of other people when they're using their posture as a means of communication.

The expressions 'Having your feet on the ground' and 'Standing on your own two feet' refer to the ancient Chinese custom of binding women's feet. This custom was mostly reserved for royalty and meant that the women whose feet had been bound were unable to stand on their own two feet without causing pain.

Macho messages

A resolutely immovable posture, in which someone has planted his feet so firmly that there's no room for budging, tells you that he's standing his ground (see Figure 10-2). He's also showing you who's boss by filling more space and covertly presenting his bits.

Figure 10-2:
The straddle stance strongly conveys messages of dominance and power.

During his last year at junior school, Tommy, aged twelve, was in the school's winning rugby team. At the celebration party after the match, a group of boys stood in a circle, talking among themselves. As proud winners, each one of them had adopted the straddle stance, demonstrating his commonality and team spirit. Even at such a young age the boys were showing their machismo and their solidarity.

If you're feeling defeated and want to change your mood, adopt the straddle stance, with your head held high and your shoulders back. By adopting this powerful position, you can create the matching feeling.

The codpiece

In 1482, the codpiece came into being after Edward IV imposed a law forbidding men below the rank of Lord to wear short doublets that exposed their genitalia. Men, unwilling to be inconvenienced by sewing up the doublet's crotch seam, turned to the codpiece as a solution.

Originally designed as a triangular piece of fabric tied at the three corners, or stitched at the bottom angle and tied at the top two angles, the codpiece fitted over the gap in the front of the hose. Men quickly realised that this new fashion served as an artificial enhancement to what may be lacking in size or stature.

Developing from a flat piece of fabric, the codpiece transmogrified into bombastic shapes. The family jewels at first rested in pouches from which they easily protruded. Over the course of a century, padding was added to the pouches until they were finally discarded in favour of large, padded shapes of unfathomable dimensions serving no function other than enhancement. These were tied onto the hose or shirt, leaving the 'items of value' to reside behind the ostentatious shapes.

During the reign of Henry VIII, the codpiece progressed into a loaf shape, after which it turned into an elongated oval that temptingly peeped out from the puffy folds of the Elizabethan trunk hose. Made of highly decorated and eye-catching material, the codpiece served as a status symbol; the more flamboyant the piece, the higher the status.

In the 1550s, the male members of the Spanish court, flushed with viral pride over their successes in the New World, sported codpieces resembling permanent erections.

As men's fashion changed in the late 1500s, the codpiece became obscured by the voluminous folds of the trunk hose. However, this item did not completely disappear and can be seen in Jacobean portraits in early 17th century England.

In 1975 Eldridge Cleaver, the former leader of the Black Panthers (an Afro-American civil rights organisation) made a foray into the fashion world as a designer of men's underwear. The distinguishing feature of his design was an enormous codpiece-like set of genitalia. His reasoning was that clothes hide a person's sexuality and he wanted to get sex back into the open. Many rock stars and fetishists continue to wear codpieces for that reason.

Threatening signs

Throughout history and across cultures, phallic displays have been considered signs of dominance. By standing with his legs apart, a man unashamedly shows his crotch to anyone who's looking, declaring himself to be The Terminator. Exposing himself this way, even though he may be fully covered, demonstrates that as far as he's concerned, he's the boss.

You can tell if two people are ready to fight, or are merely summing up each other in a friendly way. If they stand face to face with their feet apart, their hands on their hips, or their fingers and thumbs tucked into their belt loops or the tops of their pockets, they probably don't like one another very much and are looking for trouble. If, however, their bodies are turned slightly away from one another, they're simply sizing each other up in a friendly interchange.

A dominant male baboon exposes and flaunts his erect penis as a signal to the other male baboons of his power and position. Men in New Guinea proclaim their position in the community by the size and decorative features of their penis sheaths. European males in the 15th and 16th centuries wore codpieces as a sign of virility and status (see the sidebar 'The codpiece' for details).

In the most recent version of the James Bond film, *Casino Royale,* the British actor, Daniel Craig, strides out of the ocean wearing a swimsuit that unashamedly draws the eye to his crotch. The light blue colour of the swimwear, combined with Craig's ice blue eyes and his well-endowed and highly toned body, highlights the character's strength and power.

Parallel stance

The parallel stance (shown in Figure 10-3) is a subordinate position where the legs are straight and the feet are placed closely together. You may well take this position if you are called up in front of the headmaster, reporting to your commanding officer, or standing in front of a judge, awaiting sentence.

Feet placed closely together reduce the foundation for standing and make the stance more precarious. You can easily push someone over from this position if you were to catch him off guard. People who aren't sure about their position on a subject unconsciously adopt the parallel stance. Standing with their legs closely placed together they're indicating that they feel hesitant or tentative. A wider stance provides a broader and firmer foundation. It is much harder to unbalance a person who's standing with his legs separated (refer to the preceding section 'Straddle stance').

When Max received his school's Naval Cadet of the Year Award, he had to march across the quad, outfitted in full dress uniform. His stride was firm and his legs moved crisply. His shoulders were back and upright. When he reached his commanding officer, he smartly placed his feet together and kept his position held high. By standing to attention, with his legs straight and his feet closely placed together, in front of his commanding officer, he was demonstrating both his respect and his subservience.

Buttress stance

Built against or projecting from a wall, buttresses are architectural structures designed to support or reinforce the wall to which they are attached. In a more general sense, the word suggests support, as in one person buttressing another person's arguments.

In the buttress stance, you place most of your weight on a straight supporting leg, allowing your other leg to serve as a buttress. This non-weightbearing leg can be straight or bent. Whichever it is, the foot most likely points away from where the rest of the body is facing.

TRY THIS

Taking a stance

To experience the contrasting sensations, attitudes and impressions that result from standing in the straddle and parallel positions do the following exercise.

This exercise requires a full-length mirror.

1. Stand in front of the mirror and adopt the parallel stance.

2. Hold that position for sixty seconds.

3. Observe yourself closely and identify the feelings, thoughts, and attitudes you experience as you stand in this position.

What message could your posture be conveying? How might others perceive you by your posture? How could your response to others' reactions affect your self-perception?

Repeat this exercise, this time standing in the straddle stance. Ask yourself the same questions as in the previous exercise. What differences do you notice?

Although people adopting the buttress stance say they're just resting comfortably, this position signals that the person wants to get away (see Figure 10-4). The stance bears a close resemblance to the act of walking. Just before moving, you shift your weight to one leg in order that the other is free to take a step. Although you may not choose to move from the buttress stance, your legs are positioned so that they easily can. This position gives a cleverly disguised message, saying that you want to go.

If you see someone repeatedly shifting his weight from one foot to the other while in conversation with you, he's signalling that he's ready to take leave of your company.

If you notice someone standing with one leg serving as a buttress, take a look at the direction in which the toe of his buttress foot is pointing. The direction the foot takes frequently points to the object the person is thinking about. It may be pointed in the direction of someone who's caught his eye, but it most often points in the direction of his escape route.

Figure 10-4:
The buttress stance shows that you want to move.

Scissor stance

Think of your legs as if they were the two blades of a pair of scissors. Cross one over the other, keeping your knees straight and you're in the classic scissors stance. This is an obvious defensive gesture, because the person is doing his best to protect his most precious parts without resorting to putting his hands over his jewels. (For physiological reasons, women find it easier to adopt the tightly closed scissors position than men do.)

Preening and posing

From the Middle Ages to the middle of the 19th century, men of elevated position and high social status adopted a stance that conveniently displayed the inner part of the leg – one of the body's erotic zones. Gentlemen and posers would bear their weight on one leg, presenting the other with the inner thigh facing. The fashion designs that saw men's dress move from hose to tight breeches accessorised with fine shoes, permitted and encouraged men to indulge their desire to preen and pose, showing off their legs and their masculinity. Today, red-carpet celebrities know how to position their legs to display them to their best advantage, turning their feet outward to reveal their inner thighs, the softer and most erogenous part of their legs.

When one leg is crossed over the other and one of the two knees is bent, the position is called the 'bent blade stance'. Someone standing in the scissors stance or the bent blade stance is demonstrating his immobility. The feet are placed in such a way that a speedy departure is impossible without legs and feet struggling to uncoil themselves.

Crossed legs, especially in the standing position, relay varying messages:

- ✔ **Negativity, defensiveness and insecurity:** Crossing your legs is a defensive position. The gesture often accompanies the crossed arm position, reinforcing the barrier. If legs only are crossed, the suggestion of defensive or negative feelings is less strong than crossed arms.

- ✔ **Commitment and immobility:** A person standing with his legs crossed when in conversation is showing that he's committed to the interaction and has no intention of leaving.

- ✔ **Submission:** The crossed leg position comes across as submissive because the stance conveys no sign of impatience.

- ✔ **Vulnerability:** Standing in a position from which you can't easily move makes you appear vulnerable (see Figure 10-5). When women take this stance, they often dip their heads and look up from under their brows, adding to the impression of defencelessness.

Figure 10-5:
The scissor position can make a person look appealingly vulnerable.

If someone tells you that he's standing with his legs and arms crossed because he's cold, see how his hands and legs are positioned. Someone who's really cold tucks his hands into his armpits, or hugs himself. His legs are stiff, straight, and pushed tightly against each other.

In a gathering of people, those who don't know one another well tend to stand slightly apart from each other, with their arms and legs in a crossed position. Their jackets are likely to be buttoned as well, giving a complete picture of people who are feeling submissive or defensive because they are symbolically denying access to themselves.

Entwining your legs

Some gestures are particular to men and others are particular to women. The leg twine in which the top of one foot locks itself around the other leg is used almost exclusively by women. This position highlights insecurity and resembles a tortoise in retreat.

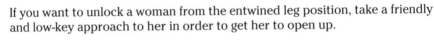

If you want to unlock a woman from the entwined leg position, take a friendly and low-key approach to her in order to get her to open up.

Fran was asked by her History of Art university lecturer to stand in front of the lecture hall and discuss the latest assignment. Being uncertain of what was expected of her, she stood in front of the class of 120 students, with one foot drawn up behind her supporting leg and pressed against her calf. Although she was confident about her knowledge of the material, she felt shy and timid speaking in front of such a large group of people, many of whom she didn't know. When she realised how she was standing, she placed both feet firmly under her and found that she felt more confident and secure, and was able to speak with authority and assurance.

Research shows that the body reflects the mind's state. Studies show that people meeting in a group for the first time usually stand with their arms and legs in the crossed position. As rapport develops and they become more comfortable with one another, they release the closed pose and open up their bodies. The procedure follows a predictable pattern that entails uncrossing their legs first and placing their feet in the parallel pose. The arms and hands unfold, and become animate. When the people feel comfortable and at ease, they move from the parallel stance to an open position in which the feet are slightly apart and facing the other person. Similarly, indicators of someone who has withdrawn from the conversation are crossed arms and legs. A person sitting in this position is unlikely to be convinced by anything you may say or do.

Reflecting Your Feelings by the Way You Position Your Feet

Because your feet are the farthest point from your brain, your grey matter has less control over them than it does, say, over your hands or facial expressions. You're less aware of where your feet are facing and what they're doing than you are of your eyes, which are about as close to your brain as they can get.

Pointing towards the desired place

Humans evolved with two legs, the purpose of which is to move forward towards what you want and move away from what you don't want. The direction in which your feet point tells the observer where you want to go. We've all experienced talking to someone you know who would rather be anyplace else than with you. While his face is smiling and his head nodding, his feet are pointing away from you (see Figure 10-6).

When the feet, head, and torso are pointing in the same direction you're showing an open, or dominant, attitude.

Figure 10-6: The woman is indicating that she'd like to leave, while the man wants to hold her attention.

Your feet act as pointers, signalling where your mind is going. Like a magnet, they point in the direction of someone who appeals to you.

Ros is a vivacious, attractive woman who men flock to. At a recent party, she was flanked by a group of three men who struggled to take their eyes off her. Each man stood with his front foot pointed toward her, silently indicating his interest. Her feet shifted from man to man, reeling each of them in like a fish on the line until she shifted her foot position towards her next target. All the time, her face was smiling and her body was in an open position, demonstrating her ingenuousness and warmth.

If you want to show someone that you find him attractive, point your foot in his direction. When you're interested in a particular conversation, or another person, place one foot forward towards the person, shortening the distance between the two of you. If you're not interested in the person, or in what he's saying, keep your feet back. If you're seated, and are speaking with another person who holds no interest for you, pull your feet back under your chair.

If you're in conversation with another person and notice that he doesn't seem entirely engaged with you, look at where his feet are pointing.

Wolfgang and Daniela were at a party. It was late and Wolfie was tired, bored and wanted to be in his own bed watching television. While he and Daniela were saying their good-byes, Wolfie couldn't understand why he was having so much difficulty in getting Daniela to leave. Had Wolfie looked, he would have seen that while they were saying goodbye to their host, Daniela's feet remained pointed in the host's direction, whereas Wolfie's feet were heading towards the door.

Fidgeting feet

Fidgeting feet are a good indicator of someone's impatience threshold. The feet say they want to flee and so are forced to fidget until the time comes to walk or run. If you're standing, you may repeatedly tap your foot to indicate your impatience. If you're sitting with your legs crossed, you may twitch the hanging foot up and down, or back and forth.

To appear calm on the outside when everything inside's in a panic, breathe from your abdomen, adjust your stance and let your feet take root.

Signs of holding back

Studies of body language by Gerard Nierenberg and Henry Calero, in which they paid particular attention to the participant's ankles, showed a high rate of individuals locking their ankles when holding back information.

In-flight airline personnel are trained to spot passengers who would like service and who are too shy to ask for it. Apprehensive travellers sit with their ankles locked, especially during take-off. When being offered refreshments from the cabin staff, these same individuals tend to unlock their ankles and move toward the edge of their seats. If, however, the ankles remain in the locked position, the crew are alerted to the fact that the person may really want something, even though he may be saying 'No'. The crew member responds by asking if the passenger is sure that he doesn't want something. Asking the passenger in this manner has an opening-up effect on that person.

Further studies into patients in a dental surgery showed that, of 150 male patients observed, 128 immediately locked their ankles when they sat in the dentist's chair. These men tended to grip the chair's armrests or clench their hands together around their groin area. Of the 150 women analysed, only 90 initially sat with their ankles crossed. Women, too, clench their hands, but they tend to rest them on their mid-section.

If a person sits in the waiting room with his ankles uncrossed, he's probably there for a routine dental check-up that he knows won't take too long and won't be particularly painful. If, due to extensive dental work, the patient has to make a number of visits to the dentist, that person becomes more comfortable in the dentist's chair after four or five visits, and doesn't lock his ankles.

Research with law enforcement and government bodies reveals that most people being interviewed knot their ankles at the start of the interview. The reason for this is as likely to be based on fear as on guilt.

Defendants sitting outside a courtroom waiting for their hearing are three times more likely than the plaintiffs to have their ankles tightly crossed and tucked under their chairs in an attempt to control their emotions.

Nierenberg's and Calero's research into the human resources profession revealed that most interviewees lock their ankles at some point during an interview, indicating that the person being interviewed is holding back an emotion or attitude. Using appropriate questioning techniques during a negotiation in which one party locks his ankles, the questioner can get the other to open up and reveal valuable information.

Finally, Nierenberg's and Calero's research showed that patients who were being wheeled into an operating room with their ankles crossed and their hands clenched, tended not to have reconciled themselves to the unavoidable.

Knotted ankles

Whether you're sitting or standing, if you've knotted or twisted your ankles together, the sign you're giving is that you're locked in and not budging. Locked ankles reflect a closed, insecure, or a negative attitude, suggesting ambiguity, or revealing a lack of confidence. Knotted ankles are definitely not a sign of someone who's feeling confident and in command.

People who say they're comfortable sitting with their ankles tightly crossed probably are. Their bodies are reflecting their mental state, and there's no tension between the two. Whether they confess that they're comfortable because their actions are reflecting their attitude – which according to the signs may be nervous, anxious, or defensive – depends on how comfortable they are in admitting their emotional state.

To appear more open, confident, and approachable, uncross your ankles.

When Shaun first began running training sessions, he was quite nervous standing in front of a large group, many of whom he didn't know personally. When he watched himself on videotape, he discovered that he was standing with his ankles crossed in front of him. As he moved across the stage, like a figure skater, he would push off with one foot, crossing one leg behind, or in front of, the other. As a result of seeing himself in action, Shaun was able to adjust his behaviour. Now when he walks across the stage he moves with purpose, placing one foot in front of the other.

Observe the differences in how men and women sit in the crossed ankle position. Men often clench their fists, resting them on their knees, or tightly grip the arms of the chair. Their legs are splayed, exposing their open crotch. Women tend to hold their knees together, with their feet often placed to one side, their hands resting in their laps side by side, or with one placed on top of the other.

The Army expression 'keeping your heels locked' means that, if a matter is not your personal concern, you aren't to disclose what you don't have to.

Twitching, flicking, or going in circles

If you suspect someone of lying to you, or holding back information, look at his feet. Research on deception reveals that a person who's asked to lie shows more signs of fraud below the waist than above. Are his feet twitching, flicking, or going around in circles?

Hand and eye movements are under conscious control. Because they are close to your brain and a main source of communication, you're more aware of what they're doing than you are of your legs and feet which, no matter how short you are, are still quite far from your brain.

Letting the feet do the talking

Research by Paul Ekman and William Friesen on deception behaviours, shows that when a person lies he produces more ruse signals in the lower part of his body than in the upper part. Because people are more aware of what their hands and eyes are doing they can consciously control their actions. Although the legs and feet are also under conscious control, they are mostly ignored and often out of sight. They are therefore a more accurate source of information. Videotaped recordings of people lying were shown to other people who were asked to determine if the people on the tape were lying, or telling the truth. The evaluators answered more correctly when they were able to see the lower part of the body. The findings showed that liars pay more attention to what their hands, arms and faces are doing because they know that that's where people look. Because their lower extremities are out of the way, liars forget about them and are betrayed by miniature muscle movements in their legs and feet.

Leaking information isn't restricted to deception. For example, people showing interest in another person use their bodies to reveal what their minds are thinking and their mouths mustn't tell. Say that a man is speaking to a woman he finds particularly attractive. He's very likely to stand with one foot pointing toward her with his legs apart exposing his groin area, and holding his arms in a splayed position to make himself look larger and fill more space. If the woman doesn't find him attractive and wants to give him the brush-off, she holds her legs together, faces her body away from him, folds her arms, and makes herself appear as small as possible. No one says a word, yet the visual messages tell the story.

Walking Styles

Some people slump and drag their feet. Others add a lively bounce to their step. Still others swagger, shuffle, or career along a path. However a person walks, he's being true to his internal rhythms, feelings and emotions. Or, he's presenting an image of what he wants you to believe. Watching people walk can tell you a lot about their health, attitude, and general state of being.

How you walk reflects your mental state. Vivacious, healthy, and energetic people walk faster than people who are elderly, ill, or infirm. The energetic walker swings his arms high, both in front and behind, sometimes giving the appearance of marching. For the most part, young people have more muscle flexibility than older people and can move faster, giving the appearance of energy and excitement.

If you find yourself feeling depressed and dragging your feet as you walk along, increase your tempo. A quicker pace increases your energy and lifts your spirits.

The exaggerated walking style adopted by military personnel deliberately conveys the image of dynamism and forceful vitality.

Chapter 11

Playing with Props

. . . .

In This Chapter

▶ Projecting your self-image

▶ Putting glasses to good use

▶ Performing the rituals – smoking, make-up, and dressing

. . . .

*E*very moment of every day, you project an image of yourself just as other people project images of themselves. People use a plethora of props, such as items of clothing, pens, glasses, smoking paraphernalia, and make-up to create an image. Mention props to an actress and her eyes come alive. She knows that these inanimate objects are her friends. Props can create an image behind which you can hide or through which you can reveal your character.

As you observe someone and the way in which she accessorises herself, you can figure out what that person's like. Your success rate depends on your level of sensitivity, and your ability to recognise and interpret what other people's choice of props, or accessories, is revealing.

In this chapter, I look at how the way you handle your props reflects your thoughts, mood, and attitude. I also consider the choices of props, and how you use them to create a perception. Finally, I consider the power behind the prop.

Using Accessories to Reflect Mental States

How people use their accessories – glasses, pens, briefcases, and handbags, for example – indicate how they're feeling. The pen clicker at a meeting, the nervous traveller riffling through her bag, and the starlet hiding behind her sunglasses all tell you through the way they play with their props how they're feeling inside.

The girl props her sunglasses on her head, her brother wears his cap backwards on his head, their father perches his reading glasses far down his nose as he examines his children's behaviour, and the elder brother at the sink nosily snaps a dishtowel. Coy, defiant, domineering, annoyed; each person is telling you their state of mind.

Regardless of the purpose for which props are designed (glasses for reading and protecting our eyes from the sun, briefcases and handbags for holding personal and work items, and pens and pencils for writing), how you handle them reflects your mental state. You put things near and in your mouth when you feel in need of reassurance – chewing on fingers, pencils, and arms of glasses for example. You check your briefcase and handbag repeatedly to set your mind at rest. You throw things in annoyance. Your moods are revealed in the way you handle your props.

Showing inner turmoil

According to zoologist Desmond Morris, putting objects in or near the mouth is reminiscent of an infant seeking comfort at its mother's breast. Any gesture, no matter how small, in which you place an object against your lips or mouth (see Figure 11-1), is an attempt to relive the sense of security you felt as a suckling babe, and is a sign that you need reassuring. In other words, chewing on the arms of your glasses, chomping on a pencil, and sucking on a cigarette indicate that all is not at peace in your world.

Some tension-relieving activities you may observe include:

- ✔ **Adjusting clothes:** This action indicates that the person is feeling uncomfortable. If you see someone making adjustments to her clothes when none are needed, you're correct in thinking that the person's feeling tense.

- ✔ **Biting fingernails and cuticles:** This action is similar to the sucking behaviour of infants and provides reassurance. The action is also related to the gesture of putting your hand in front of your mouth to hold back a thought or an emotion.

- ✔ **Playing with objects:** Jingling change in pockets, clicking a pen, or fiddling with jewellery are deflecting signals indicating nervousness. Touching the objects provides sensory reassurance, similar to holding a favourite toy when you were a child.

- ✔ **Running fingers through hair:** When you're feeling tense and agitated, you may find that your hand goes to your head and your fingers run along your scalp. This gesture is a comforting gesture, reminiscent of the hair ruffles, or strokes you received as a child.

✔ **Shaking a shoe.** Nervous energy building up like a pressure cooker has to come out somewhere. Although you may look calm in your upper torso, if you're nervous, anxious, or excited, a jiggling foot gives your game away.

✔ **Smoking.** As a sucking gesture, smoking provides comfort associated with being nourished.

You can see these tension-relieving activities in action on the *Body Language For Dummies* app.

Figure 11-1:
Sucking on an object signals a need for reassurance.

Pausing for thought

When you need to take time to think something through, you may find yourself rolling a pen between your fingers, taking a sip from your coffee cup, or doodling in your notebook. These behaviours provide comforting sensory stimulation. Sipping and chewing actions provide the reassurance you found as a suckling infant. Behaviours that involve a form of stroking are comforting.

When you see someone remove her glasses slowly and deliberately, and repeatedly wiping the lenses (when her glasses aren't particularly dirty), you may be right in thinking that she's stalling for time. If she then sucks or chews on the earpiece, she's unconsciously indicating that she's seeking reassurance.

Studies conducted by Gerard I Nierenberg and Henry H Calero, pioneers in the study of non-verbal behaviour, show that some people deliberately remove and clean their glasses as many as five times an hour. Video recordings of intense negotiation sessions show this gesture happening frequently. The people performing this gesture usually wanted to stall for time while considering whether they would ask a question, request clarification, or raise more opposition. Nierenberg and Calero also discovered that a person sucking on the earpiece of her glasses during negotiations subconsciously implies that some form of nourishment, likely to be in the form of more information, is required.

If you have a tendency to speak first and listen later, put something into your mouth to keep you quiet. This can be the earpiece of the frame of your glasses, a pencil, or a glass of water. This action gives you time to think about what you're going to say before blurting out something that you may later regret.

Through the Looking Glasses

Glasses can enhance the eyes, framing them provocatively. They can hide the eyes when the lenses are tinted. They can open the doorway to communication, and they can act as a road block. Some people wear glasses with non-prescription lenses for these reasons. They don't need them to improve their vision; they wear them to project an image.

Because of the number of people who wear glasses, this section on the signs to watch for can help you see things more clearly.

Stalling for time

Someone wanting to gain time before making a decision takes her glasses off, cleans the lenses, and puts them back on again. Others take their glasses off and suck on the arm's earpiece. This latter gesture frequently appears at the close of a negotiating session when someone's been asked for a decision. When the person puts her glasses back on, at this point she's indicating that she needs or wants more information. When someone takes her glasses off and cleans the lenses immediately after asking for a decision, the best thing to do is hold your fire.

Scrutinising the situation

If someone peers over the tops of her glasses at you, don't be surprised if you feel scrutinised. Peering down on another person conveys a critical or judgemental attitude. The glasses underscore or highlight the action.

The act of looking down on another person is intimidating, aggressive, and indicates intense feelings. The person being looked at is put in a lower, subservient position to the person doing the looking (see Figure 11-2).

Figure 11-2:
Peering down on people can make them feel uncomfortable.

If you wear glasses and want to pin someone down without climbing on top of her, drop your glasses onto the lower bridge of your nose and peer over them long and hard. This is a guaranteed way of making the person you're looking at feel scrutinised and on the line.

Because of the design of granny glasses which many people use for reading, you naturally look over the top of them when you lift your eye from the page. This inadvertent gesture elicits negative responses, which may not have been your intention.

Simon is a smart, thoughtful, and sensitive man. He was surprised to discover when he received feedback on his interpersonal skills that his colleagues and subordinates perceived him as stand-offish. When I looked at what he was doing that had led to this perception, one action I noticed was that, when he speaks to people, rather than removing his reading glasses, he looks over them. This sets up a barrier between himself and the person he's speaking to. Because he doesn't need glasses for long distance, he found that when he took his reading glasses off he was able to see the person he was speaking to more clearly. At his next appraisal, he was described as open and accessible. I like to think that taking his glasses off contributed to people's new perceptions of him.

Controlling the conversation

You can use your glasses to control a conversation. Think of yourself as a conductor. When you want the attention to be on what you're saying, put your glasses on. When you want to demonstrate that you're listening, take them off. To indicate that the conversation is over, fold your glasses and put them away.

Showing resistance

Some people take their glasses off quickly in a flash of annoyance, or slowly with much deliberation. Both of these gestures are sure signs of resistance to what is occurring. Someone rejecting a proposal may throw her glasses onto her desk.

To relieve the emotional tension, you need to change your approach so that the other person puts her glasses back on. Then the two of you together can see the situation more clearly.

Appearing cool

Sunglasses belong in the sun, not in nightclubs and meetings. Their original purpose was to protect your eyes by blocking out light. Some celebrities and wannabes use sunglasses to keep other people from getting too close to them, and others say they wear them to protect their eyes from flashing light-bulbs. Your eyes are one of your primary means of communication. Speaking to someone who's wearing sunglasses is a bit like speaking to the Wizard of Oz. You can hear the person, but you can't see them.

Wearing sunglasses on your head creates the impression of being cool, in the groove, and youthful. Parking your sunglasses on your head gives the appearance of having a huge pair of doe-like eyes with enticingly enlarged pupils, mimicking the positive effect that babies and cuddly toys with big painted eyes have on a person.

Spectacles at the office

Studies show that people wearing glasses in a business context, whether male or female, are perceived as intelligent, knowledgeable, conservative, and genuine.

The heavier the frames of the glasses, the more frequently these descriptions were reported. Business leaders who wear glasses tend to choose heavy frames, which may be why, in a business context, glasses can be seen as power props.

Highly decorated frames that make a fashion statement are not taken seriously in a business environment. Glasses with oversized lenses, such as those favoured by Elton John in his early days, overly decorated, coloured frames, or any frame that has rhinestone-encrusted branding, says that you're more interested in fashion than business. In an office environment, such glasses can quickly and drastically reduce your credibility.

Frameless glasses, or those with thin, spindly frames, hold less authority than heavier framed glasses. Because they make the wearer appear more accessible than heavy frames, frameless versions may be preferable for social situations, or when you want to portray a 'good guy' image. Wear your heavier frames when you're presenting the year-end financial results, when looking serious, knowledgeable, and in control is important.

Contact lenses make the pupils of your eyes appear large and appealing, moist, and dilated. Your eyes look softer and more sensual, which, although appropriate for a social situation, may not be appropriate in a business context.

The perception of women who wear both glasses and make-up (discussed in the later section 'Making It Up as You Go Along') is that they're smart, self-assured, urbane and outgoing.

Holy Smokes

Despite health warnings and government bans on smoking in public places, you can still find puffers hanging outside office blocks and night clubs as well as walking along the streets and driving in their cars. And whatever your views about smoking, understanding the signals that people send by the way they smoke is useful. Smoking gestures follow a predictable pattern. Gestures associated with smoking vary from the way people open the pack, to how they inhale and exhale, and to the way they flick the ash off the end of the cigarette and stub it out. What tells an onlooker about the smoker's attitude and state of mind is not the ritual itself, but how the smoker performs it.

Smoking and sexual displays

The act of smoking is highly sexual in nature. The similarities between sex and smoking are most dominantly displayed in the sucking action. In addition, the actions of preparing for having a smoke and having sex can be compared in terms of foreplay. The person smoking a cigarette reaches for the pack, takes out the cigarette, lights it, inhales, and then releases the smoke. The person having sex reaches for her partner, unbuttons his shirt, fondles and kisses him, and you can figure out the rest.

Although both men and women smoke, they have different habits around their habit. For instance, men and women hold their cigarettes differently. A woman holds her cigarette higher in the air with her wrist bent back, displaying the soft skin. Her body is open, accentuating her chest. In this provocative position, the cigarette takes on the appearance of a small phallus that the woman slips between her lips and seductively sucks.

When men smoke, they hold their wrists straight, pointing upward like an erect phallus. After they've taken a puff, they tend to drop their smoking hand below chest level, closing their bodies off, putting them into a protective position. Some men also hold their cigarettes by pinching them between their index finger and thumb. The cigarette is hidden inside the palm, conveying an image of secretiveness and seduction.

In spite of health concerns and the dangers of smoking, the rituals involved continue to be an acceptable form of courtship. The man offers to light a woman's cigarette. The woman cups her hand around the man's as she drags deeply on her cigarette, gazing into his eyes slightly longer than she would normally.

Women who smoke can be perceived as being submissive. The message a female smoker gives is that she can be persuaded to do things that aren't good for her. Male smokers are perceived as risk takers and therefore exciting.

Ways of smoking

You can find different types of smokers and different ways of smoking. Some people take long, deep inhalations while others take short, quick puffs. Some flick the tip of their cigarettes even when there's no ash, while others leave the ash to dangle. Some people smoke their cigarettes right down to the filter; others put them out after only a drag or two. By watching how someone manages this prop, you can draw some conclusions about her mental state.

- ✔ **Deeply inhaling:** The deep inhale acts as a sedative. The action relaxes the smoker and is her way of responding to stress. If you notice a smoker drawing in deeply, you can rightfully presume that this person's feeling the pressure.

- ✔ **Quick puffing:** By puffing quickly, the smoker is stimulating her brain. Her awareness becomes heightened and she feels ready for action. This person may frequently pick her cigarette up and put it down rather than holding on to it for a prolonged time.

- ✔ **Exhalation:** The speed of the exhalation indicates the intensity of the movement. If a person exhales quickly with the smoke going upwards, she's feeling quite positive. If she blows out quickly facing downwards, her feelings are negative. Slower exhales indicate a more considered feeling.

- ✔ **Flicking, tapping, and twisting:** These nervous gestures indicate agitation, anxiety, and insecurity.

- ✔ **Putting the cigarette out:** A person who stubs her cigarette out firmly, grinding it into the ashtray, is showing that she's made up her mind and is ready to go. If she takes her time putting out the cigarette, she's not ready to act.

Speciality smokers

Cigarettes are easily accessible if you're over 16 and have the money to pay for them. More sophisticated forms of tobacco, such as fine cigars and superior pipe tobacco, are reserved for specialist shops and cost substantially higher prices than cigarettes. People who smoke cigars demonstrate a superior attitude and have particular shapes and sizes that they prefer. Pipe smokers are also selective about their preferred kinds of tobacco and pipe styles.

Cigar smokers

Because of the size and cost of cigars, they're associated with success and superiority. High-flying business executives, gangland bosses, and people in prominent positions can often be seen wielding a cigar. They're associated with good fortune, which is why people often celebrate the birth of a child, a successful business accomplishment or a streak of good luck by puffing on a fine Havana.

Some cigar smokers buy one and keep it for luck, with the intention of smoking it when they meet with success. The expression 'close, but no cigar' said after a narrow escape, comes from this tradition.

Comedians like George Burns and Groucho Marx made the cigar a major part of their persona and relied on it in their comic timing. Both would hold their cigars slightly away from their bodies, look at their cigar before drawing on it, tilt their heads upward as they exhaled a puff of smoke, and then deliver their punch lines.

Famous cigar-smoking public figures include Winston Churchill, King Edward VII, and Sigmund Freud, all highly successful and dominant men. When Freud was challenged about the phallic shape of his cigar, he is purported to have replied, 'Sometimes a cigar is just a cigar.'

Pipe smokers

Pipe smoking is associated with Oxford dons and elderly uncles and connotes stability, intelligence, and wisdom. Pipe smoking involves many rituals that require the smoker's attention. By concentrating on the acts associated with smoking a pipe such as cleaning, filling, and tamping the pipe, smokers can focus on the pipe and not the people around them. Like many objects, the pipe has functions other than just what it was specifically designed for.

Pipe smokers often chew on their unlit pipes. The act of putting something their mouths harks back to infancy and the reassurance they felt when suckling on a breast or a bottle.

Where smoking began

Because of the potency of tobacco, it has long been associated with a male rite of passage, stemming from the pre-Columbian era in America. Although small amounts of nicotine were found in some Old World plants such as belladonna, early habitual tobacco use seems to be limited to the Americas. Experts believe that the tobacco plant in its current form began growing in the Americas around 6000 BC. During the 19th century, it was common for men to retire to the 'smoking room' after dinner to discuss important matters.

Stress and smoking

Studies show that smoking tobacco increases stress rather alleviating it. Psychologist Andy Parrott, PhD., of the University of East London found that stress levels in smokers increase as they develop a regular smoking habit. His research also shows that when people stop smoking (that is, break the habit) their stress levels reduce. When smokers are denied nicotine, they experience tension and irritability. When they smoke, that state is reversed.

Addicted smokers feel stressed when they're not smoking, and their mood is normal when they're smoking. In other words, for smokers to feel normal, they must always be puffing on a cigarette. When smokers quit, they may experience bad moods for the first few weeks. Once the body is completely free of nicotine, the moods even out as the craving for the drug, and the accompanying stress levels that come with it, reduce.

Because pipe smokers hold their pipes in front of themselves, and often cross their other arm across their bodies, the pipe serves as a mini shield, protecting the smoker from anyone else.

In addition, a pipe can be used as a pointer to direct someone's attention and a baton to beat out the rhythm of the speaker's words.

Marco, a university professor, is a pipe smoker. He has a collection of pipes from which he chooses, depending on his mood and how he wants to be perceived. He frequently carries an unlit pipe into his lectures, where he uses the pipe as an extension of himself. When gesturing towards a student or an item on a slide, he points with his pipe. When confronted with a question that requires some thought, he tamps the tobacco in the bowl of his pipe. He lights the pipe, takes several puffs, and blows the smoke upwards before looking at the person who posed the question. Marco uses his pipe as an extension of himself for indicating where he wants his audience's attention to focus, as well as using the pipe as a screen behind which he can hide.

Making It Up as You Go Along

One of the benefits of being a woman is that she can enhance her image by applying make-up without drawing undue attention to herself, whereas a man certainly would do if he were to apply make-up as part of his daily routine. Whether going out on a Saturday night or coming into work Monday morning, the woman who has taken the time to apply her make-up appropriately is going to get noticed.

Not for women only

Archaeological finds in the Iranian geographical plateau have revealed that approximately 10,000 years ago both men and women were avid wearers of make-up. Early examples of facial cosmetics were made from colourful stones as well as animal skin, shells, bones, and teeth. Men and women of the Kermani tribe in Iran used white powder made of lead or silver as a foundation, highlighting their cheeks with a red powder made from the hematite stone.

Both men and women wore make-up with enthusiasm. Men applied their cosmetics with such care that it was often difficult to tell them apart from the women. Surena, the 5th-century BC Iranian chieftain known for his bravery and fearlessness, used to decorate his face for battle with such finesse that even his enemies were surprised.

Although it is well documented that men regularly wore make-up, little proof existed that the same was true for women until masks and statues were discovered in Khuzestan. These masks had eyebrows that were elongated and painted black. The lips and cheeks had a rose tint and a painted line extended from below the eyes to the eyebrow.

As personal adornment became more important, water, which the early cave-dwellers used for viewing themselves, was no longer a satisfactory solution. The Iranians discovered a material that, when melted, shaped, polished, and formed into sheets, accurately reflected a person's likeness. These early mirrors were also highly decorated, often with beautiful mythological images.

Make-up at the office

Studies consistently show that business women who wear make-up advance further and faster in their careers than women who don't (perhaps because, sadly, men are still doing most of the promoting). This is not to say that a woman should apply her make-up with a trowel for the office environment. Save that for the clubs, discos, and a hot night out. Make-up is meant to enhance a woman's image and to be applied in such a way that the wearer looks healthy, not overdone.

Making up for play

At times, a guy and a gal want to put on the Ritz, strut their stuff, and show the world what they're made of. Most women, and a few men, apply make-up to enhance what they've already got. They exaggerate their leisure-time look, making their lips more prominent, their eyes emphasised, and their clothes and accessories geared towards fun and frivolity.

Clothing: Dressing the Part

You can't ignore the importance of your appearance and personal presentation if you want to succeed. Dressing appropriately for your shape, colouring, and the part you're playing, demonstrates that you care about how you present yourself. You feel confident when you know that you're well turned out. You look credible. People are drawn to the positive energy you exude when the clothes fit and the colours flatter.

Your choice of accessories and how you put them together reveal how you perceive yourself and how you want to be perceived. If you can afford to invest in high-quality items, do. They don't have to be the most expensive products on the shelf, although cost and quality often go hand and hand. What they do have to be is appropriate for the environment and reflective of you at your best.

Women's accessories

Forget about fashion and follow the styles that work best for you. Although leggings and smocked tops can look great on women at play or working in creative industries, they're out of place in a corporate environment. The same goes for short skirts and low-cut tops. These items draw attention to the wearer, which is fine for a date but not the office. The sexual messages they send out are better left outside of the office where the focus is meant to be on the task.

Excessive jewellery is also out of place at work if you want to head up the ladder. Dangly earrings are distracting, as are a wrist full of bracelets and fingers covered in ethnic rings. Stick to a few classic pieces to be seen as professional. Unless you're a Vivienne Westwood fashionista, in which case pile it on!

One of my first clients was a woman in her mid-20s working as a designer for ICI. Being a creative type, she went to work wearing dangly earrings, long skirts, and Indian blouses. She was good at her work and couldn't understand why she wasn't getting the promotions she believed she deserved. Part of my job was to help her understand the impact her clothing choices were making on her career. Working in a male-dominated industrial environment, her clothes and accessories were out of place. Recognising how her flawed judgement was holding her back, she agreed to leave the clothes that she believed reflected who she was at home and wear more simple and tailored clothes to work. Although she fought this change in principle, she discovered that she had several different styles of dress that she felt comfortable wearing and that reflected her at her best.

Dressing the First Lady

Much has been made of Hilary Rodham Clinton's dressing habits. Seen speaking in Congress wearing a pink blazer over a black top that rode low on her chest with a subtle V-shape pointing downwards to her bosom, the punters took note. Not that Ms Clinton was pouring out of her top like a bar-room chanteuse – she was simply nodding her head to her femininity and sexuality. Not one known to acknowledge comfortably her style and image, it was a slight surprise to see her bear this part of her body. During her husband Bill's first term in office in the early 1990s, she was photographed wearing a black Donna Karan shoulder-revealing gown, named by Karan as the 'cold shoulder dress'. Karan noted that regardless of a woman's age, her shoulders remain sensuous and appealing. Throughout the Clinton years, the first lady wore clothes that were feminine and stately, never sexy. Her second inaugural gown was an Oscar de la Renta, originally designed with cap sleeves and a wide neckline. After Clinton's alterations, the dress had long sleeves and a high, Victorian-like collar. In December 1998, at the peak of the Monica Lewinsky scandal (where Bill was revealed to have had an affair with Monica), Hilary appeared on the cover of *Vogue* wearing another de la Renta gown, with long sleeves and a boat neck, looking bold, glamorous, and regal.

Samantha Cameron, wife of the British Prime Minister David Cameron, and US First Lady Michelle Obama have become style-setters, as they take their clothing statements seriously without turning into fashionistas.

Men's accessories

The environment that you work and play in determines what's appropriate to wear. Gold chains hanging around your neck are fine if you're a DJ, bartender, rock star, or a gangster. If, on the other hand, you're working in industry, or in the professional or corporate world, leave the jewellery at home.

Accessories need to be clean and in good repair. A frayed belt, scuffed shoes, and a banged up briefcase look unkempt, as if you can't be bothered to look after them. You're sending out the message that you don't care about them enough to maintain them well. This may be interpreted as you being someone who's lazy and can't be bothered!

A tie with specks shows that you've been sloppy. Too much pattern on a tie confuses the eye and may draw negative responses. Keep ties clean, silk, and simple.

Graeme struggles to understand the impact that his clothes have on people's perceptions and why some people find his choices unacceptable. He has a preference for ties designed by a modern Italian artist whose designs would be better framed on a wall than displayed on a man's body. Their visual impact is so overwhelming that I was asked to advise Graeme about his clothes choices and the message they were sending. Because Graeme sought to distinguish himself from the corporate crowd, he purposely chose clothing items that made him stand out. We explored his values, needs, and belief systems and how he demonstrates them in his behaviour. Eventually, Graeme came to understand his need to be seen as different and how that was negatively manifested in the way he presented himself.

If you want to advance in your career, dress appropriately for your body shape and colouring. Making an effort with your personal appearance, and dressing appropriately for your environment, is a vital career skill. Whether you're working in advertising, the music industry or investment banking, if you want to move up the corporate ladder, look at the people who have the jobs above you and note how they dress. An image consultant can help you find the shapes and colours that suit you best.

Part IV

Putting the Body into Social and Business Context

The 5th Wave   By Rich Tennant

"When we met, we seemed to be on the same track, so we hitched up. Then, just when I thought the relationship was gaining steam, something derailed it. I don't know. Maybe I was sending the wrong signals."

In this part . . .

*H*ere, I take you on a trip from the office, to the bar, then overseas to experience different countries and cultures. In the boardroom, you find out where to place and position yourself for greatest effect. In the dating arena, you discover how to read and reveal signs of interest and dismissal and how to engage with a possible romantic partner. In sampling different cultures, I warn you of body language pitfalls to avoid, and tips to utilise for improving your relationships with people around the world.

Chapter 12

Being Aware of Territorial Rights and Regulations

In This Chapter

▶ Fitting into your space

▶ Staking your claim

▶ Positioning yourself to your best advantage

*I*f you've ever bumped into a stranger on the high street, if you've ever been squashed on a rush hour tube, or if you've ever been kissed by someone you'd rather hadn't kissed you, you've experienced space invasion. Unless invited, it feels a bit creepy when someone gets too close. And it feels, oh so good, when the distance's right.

In this chapter, you look at the different areas of space around you. You find out why what feels comfortable at ten paces feels differently at one. You also discover why cohorts sit side by side and adversaries sit face to face. Finally, you discover how the way that you position yourself, whether upright, supine or simply off kilter, impacts on your gestures, movements, and the impression you make.

Understanding the Effect of Space

The way you fill and move within space impacts on your attitude, your feelings and the way that others perceive you. People who know where to position themselves in relation to someone else control the interaction. They know when to get up close and personal, and when to back off. They know the different implications between standing so close to another person that you can feel that person's breath, and standing so far away that you have to squint to see one another. By knowing where and how to place yourself in relation to another person, you can consciously control that person's perception of you.

Territorial parameters aren't just a matter of manners. Foreign invaders, rival gangs, trespassers, burglars, pushy bullies and aggressive drivers all know that their invasion into another's territory can be met with varying degrees of resistance. Zoologist Desmond Morris sees humans as competitive as well as co-operative creatures. As humans strive for dominance, systems must be put in place to avoid chaos. Territorial perimeters, where everyone knows and respects one another's space, is one co-operative system.

A man is said to be king of his castle. As reigning sovereign, whether your castle is a flat in the heart of the city, a country farmhouse, or a caravan, you know that you've the right to be dominant in your own territory. And, everyone else has the right to be dominant in his. When someone enters your space without being invited, you may feel a little edgy. Whether someone is subject to fighter planes attacking from above, or a mother bursting into her teenage son's room, the likelihood is that the person whose space has been invaded is going to fight back.

Although you may feel perfectly confident, comfortable, and at home in one surrounding, when you enter another, your feelings change (see Figure 12-1). Say that you work in your own office. You feel comfortable and in control of your environment because you're in familiar surroundings. Then you're called into your boss's office. Suddenly, the comfort level changes. You're now entering someone else's territory and the control shifts from you to the person whose space you've penetrated. Your body language changes from dominant to submissive without you even realising it.

Figure 12-1:
Entering
someone
else's
territory
can feel
invasive.

Knowing Your Space

Humans have circles of space around them, which range from no space at all (touching) to far enough away that, even though you can be seen, you're not close enough to touch. As with animals, humans protect their territory by following accepted codes of behaviour. Whereas birds sing to proclaim their dominance over a particular part of a hedgerow, and dogs lift their legs to stake claim to a lamppost, humans indicate through their body movements what they perceive to be their territory, and how near and how far a person may penetrate it.

The five zones

In his book, *The Hidden Dimension*, the American anthropologist Edward T Hall, defined *proxemics* as the study of the human use of space within the context of culture. Understanding that cultural influences impact upon how people move within their space, and the amount of space a person is comfortable with, Hall divided space into five distinct areas. The relationship you have with another person determines how near you allow that person to come to you. (You can find out more about culture and space in Chapter 15.)

Hall defined five concentric spatial zones that affect behaviour (also see Figure 12-2):

- **Close Intimate (0–15 centimetres/0–6 inches):** This space is saved for lovers, close friends and family members. Close Intimate is a position for the most intimate behaviours, including touching, embracing, and kissing.

- **Intimate (15–45 centimetres/6–18 inches):** This space is where the lover, friend, and relatives are welcome. The distance is comfortable and secure. You feel uncomfortable, and your body reacts protectively, if a stranger, someone you don't know well or someone you don't like enters this space.

- **Personal (45 centimetres–1.2 metres/18 inches–4 feet):** For most Westerners, this distance is the most comfortable for personal conversations. If you step too far into the space, the other person may feel threatened. If you stand outside of the space, the other person can feel rebuffed.

- **Social (1.2–3.6 metres/4–12 feet):** When you're in a business-based interaction with shop assistants and tradespeople, this area is where you feel most comfortable. If you stand within the inner parameter, you're perceived as being too familiar. If you stand outside the outer ring, you're perceived as rude and stand-offish.

✔ **Public (3.6 metres +/12 feet +):** If you're speaking to an audience in a formal setting, the distance between yourself and the first row is in the public space. Any closer and you feel intruded upon; your communication feels cramped. Any farther away and you feel distanced from your listeners, making it harder to connect with them.

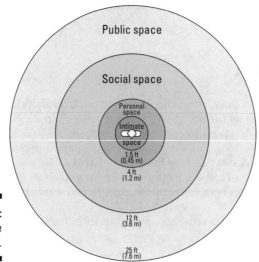

Figure 12-2:
Hall's space
bubbles.

The distance people keep between themselves reveals their relationship and how they feel about the other person.

Other territorial positions

In addition to your space bubble's five concentric circles, you have another set of territorial positions, private and personal to you. You have:

✔ **Inner space:** Your internal thoughts and feelings.

✔ **Immediate outer space:** Friends, family, close colleagues.

✔ **Your public arena:** The larger world in which you interact with an assortment of people.

People who enjoy their own company and prefer to keep to themselves have few requirements. They live quieter, simpler lives than those who surround themselves with people and fill their lives with social activities.

People who live lives that involve lavish entertaining need space to accommodate all the individuals and the accompanying accessories that go with a socially active life. Their personalities require a broad expanse of space.

A person who has many people taking up much of his time occasionally draws into his inner space for quiet contemplation. Executives, politicians, busy parents, and professionals – as well as the ubiquitous celebrity – need time alone to recharge their batteries.

Big personalities fill their space with their movements. For example, they hold their arms farther from their bodies than people with quieter personalities. Their gestures are definite and they move with purpose. People whose personalities are more internally directed use fewer and smaller gestures. (See Figure 12-3.)

Figure 12-3:
Big personalities take up more space than do internally driven people.

Space also works in proportion to status. Presidents, senior partners, and chief executives require a copious amount of resources, including space, in a practical sense and to fill status expectations, both their own and others.

Pauline is a Human Resources (HR) specialist, working in the telecoms industry. When she was promoted to the role of HR director, she moved from her open-plan office to a private office of her own. Although the room wasn't large, it had windows with blinds and a door to close herself off. Knowing that she needed thinking time as well as time for interacting with her team, Pauline appreciated the way that she was able to manage her public and private space according to her requirements.

Growing up in Palm Beach, Florida, a town of great opulence and wealth, I often saw 12-bedroom mansions for a family of four. The size of people's homes reflected their status – large homes indicated large incomes and large personalities. Small homes indicated lower income and lower status. My mother's home in Palm Beach had two bedrooms that cosily accommodated my mother, my sister and myself. Mom was a single mother, struggling to raise her two daughters. She didn't entertain much and had little use for a lot of space. Half a mile away was the winter home of the late President John F Kennedy. His home was huge in comparison, with high walls surrounding the property and bodyguards walking the grounds. The President's position of power, status, and authority came with more needs than that of a young divorcee on a restricted budget.

You can tell a person's status by how much personal space he requires. The more space expected and offered, the higher the status.

Reality TV?

The media has brought strangers into our lives to such an extent that some people believe that they know, or have a personal relationship with, actors and performers. Actors frequently tell stories of being treated as if they were the character they portray rather than themselves. When playing the part of Nurse Carol Hathaway on the television programme *ER*, Juliana Margulies was frequently approached by fans asking her how she would deal with a particular medical condition they were experiencing. The fans were infiltrating her private space based on their perceptions of her from her public space.

Television comes directly into a person's private space and brings its characters with it. People believe that they have a relationship with an actor because they've spent time together in the home.

How you view and define your space determines how others respond. By being clear about how far a person may come into your territory, you make it easier for others to know your boundaries and behave accordingly.

Using Space

Whether you're protecting your property, demonstrating dominance, or showing submission, the way that you fill your space indicates your attitude. Touch an object and you're saying, 'This is mine'. Turn away from it and you're saying, 'No, thanks'.

Demonstrating ownership

When you use your hands to lead and guide another person, you're taking control. Your behaviour becomes dominant as you touch what you consider to be yours. When you lead another person by the hand, when you guide someone by placing your hand on his back, or when you stand close to your partner and put your hand on his upper arm, you're demonstrating that you own that piece of property.

Victoria Beckham and Catherine Zeta Jones are masters of the female proprietorial pose. When they stand close to their husbands and place a hand on their man's chest or upper arm, you can't misread the signal telling you that the man belongs to them. Private property. Keep off.

Placing your hands on an object suggests a proprietorial relationship with it. Even if you don't actually own the object, by touching it you're establishing a dominant relationship with that item. When you touch an object, you're indicating that psychologically, if not in actual practice, you own, or are in control of, the object.

James and his new bride, Beverly, went to a party of James's work colleagues. Beverly knew very few people at the party. Throughout the evening James frequently touched his wife, as a sign of reassurance and of ownership. He guided her through the room by placing his hand on her lower back, he put his arm around her shoulders while introducing her to his colleagues and he often held her hand while they were in conversation with other people.

Max's friend, JD, recently purchased his first car. He worked hard and saved long to earn the money, and he's extremely proud of the car, including its personalised licence plate and alloy wheels. One day when he was at our home, he asked whether I'd take a photograph of him with his prized possession standing in our drive. As JD stood next to his car, he placed his hand on the bonnet for the first shot, and leaned against the door for the second. Both positions indicate his strong connection with the car and a real sense of his ownership of it.

Touching a person or an object implies that you've a relationship with that item. You can use this awareness to intimidate or dominate someone else, or you may observe someone trying to likewise intimidate or dominate you. Especially intimidating, for example, is when someone touches something that belongs to you.

If someone you don't know comes to your home or office, you can show ownership and dominance by leaning against your door frame in a proprietorial way.

Showing submission

Entering a foreign environment frequently causes people to feel uncomfortable and act in a submissive way. They wait to be invited to sit, refrain from touching objects in the space, and contain their gestures. Once they feel at ease, their body language opens up.

Amy's boss suggested that she attend one of our Positive Impact workshops. A potential high flyer, Amy's body language was letting her down. Although she was under consideration for promotion, her boss had concerns that when the time came, Amy wouldn't project an image of confidence and credibility. Amy wasn't claiming her space. Her movements were hesitant, contained, and mostly close to her body. This behaviour, in combination with her slightly hunched shoulders, gave the impression of subservience. Working with recording equipment, Amy observed how her non-verbal behaviour was displaying her inner world of doubt and insecurity.

If you purposely want to show submission, close your body by pulling your arms in close to your body and keeping your hands to yourself.

Guarding your space

In addition to clarifying ownership of people and possessions, people jealously guard the space that immediately surrounds them. Humans create an invisible bubble around themselves in which they function. Placing objects between yourself and others, spreading your arms across your desk, and wrapping your arms around yourself are ways of guarding your personal space.

In normal circumstances, most people respect one another's personal territory. Sometimes, however, space invasion is unavoidable. When an invasion of your space occurs, you feel uncomfortable. Another person entering your space can penetrate your guard. Fine, if you've invited that person in. Not so good if you neither know the person, nor want him there. Even when their personal space is invaded, people still find ways to limit the invasion as much as possible. Consider these examples:

- ✔ Turning your head away
- ✔ Avoiding eye contact
- ✔ Pulling into yourself

Beth was walking her dog, Bertie, along a country lane when Phillipa, a woman Beth knew and didn't much care for, pulled up next to them in her new Range Rover. 'Hello! Haven't seen you for ages,' Phillipa called out, jumping down from the car and giving Beth a hug. Grudgingly, Beth turned her head to avoid having to touch the woman's cheek with her own lips, and left her arms by her side, her excuse being that she was unable to let go of Bertie's lead. It wasn't until Phillipa had driven off that the stiffness around Beth's shoulders and neck was released, and she felt comfortable again.

Wait to be invited into the Close Intimate Zone to avoid causing offence, discomfort, or embarrassment.

Revealing comfort or discomfort

How near, how far and at what angle you position yourself in relation to someone else, indicates how relaxed you feel with that person. Sitting comfortably among friends, you probably sit close to one another. Your body leans towards them, and your eyes are engaged. Among people you prefer you weren't with, your body angles away. You avoid eye contact and you pull back. You're making it clear that you don't want to connect.

Putting distance and objects between yourself and another person can make for an awkward conversation. Stand too far away and you may come across as stand-offish. Get too close and you may be perceived as intrusive. Some people like to put objects and distance between themselves and others. It makes them feel protected and gives them the opportunity to observe someone from behind a barrier, whether actual or perceived. Others like to get up close right away. They want to burrow in and get connected.

If you turn your shoulder on another person, you're showing him that you're not comfortable with him. Your shoulder acts as a barrier keeping the two of you at arms length. When someone turns his back on you, he's shutting you out.

Giving the cold shoulder

The origins of the expression 'cold shoulder' are disputed. Some people believe it originates from when welcome visitors to one's home were fed a hot meal, but if they were unwelcome visitors they were lucky to be given a cold shoulder of mutton. In Sir Walter Scott's *St Ronan's Well*, 1824, the writer remarks: 'I must tip him the cauld shouther [cold shoulder], or he will be pestering me eternally.'

One of the reasons that open-plan office workers put photographs, pot plants, and mascots on their computers is to put distance between themselves and others. When people are forced to sit close together, they put up barriers in whatever way they can.

Open space between people can lead to accessibility. You sometimes see a person come from behind his desk to greet another without the desk acting like a barrier. Trainers, coaches, and teachers often prefer working in an open environment in order to connect with their listeners.

I recently ran a workshop in Portsmouth. Although scheduled to meet in one of the conference rooms, because of the large numbers who had signed up to attend we had to relocate to the large, formal assembly theatre. As the delegates entered the room, I noticed they were heading toward the back, leaving rows of empty chairs between them and me. I already felt uncomfortable in this formal setting, and my vain attempts to close the gap fell on deaf ears. Several of the participants justified their position by saying that only senior managers and directors sit in the front rows. As the event was designed to be interactive, it was vital that I connected with the delegates. I stepped down from the stage and walked among the group to break the ice and build the trust. I encouraged them to pretend that they were senior managers and could sit up front. After about 30 minutes, the group began to move forward and spread themselves out around the room, and a few of them even sat in the front row.

When your personal space is unavoidably infiltrated, such as in a crowded bus, and touching can't be escaped, only shoulders and upper arms should make contact. If the contact is any more intimate, people make an effort to move apart, in spite of the crowded conditions.

Maintaining your personal space

When strangers crowd in, you have to adjust your concept of how much space you need to conserve around you. Country people may initially feel quite uncomfortable in a large city. Where they're used to living in open spaces, they now find themselves confined within buildings. Crowded conditions take over where once there was distance. They may feel more constrained. Their gestures become fewer, smaller, and tighter as they adjust to their reduced space.

The next time you go to the doctor or hairdressers, observe where people sit. Normally, you find a row of chairs for waiting clients. The first client usually sits at one end of the row. The next person to enter sits halfway down. Both are at a comfortable distance from one another – neither too close to cause discomfort nor too far away to appear standoffish. The next person sits at the other end, and the fourth person sits between the middle and end position, and so on until eventually someone is forced to sit next to another person.

When people queue in Britain, they envelop themselves in an invisible space bubble. People have their own bubble and on a good day they respect one another's space. Interestingly, crowded conditions, such as those found on the rush hour bus, tube, or train, lead people to ignore one another. According to psychologist Robert Sommer, in crowded conditions people imagine that someone invading their personal space is inanimate. Therefore, no need exists to relay any social signals. Individuals stand or sit still when they're ignoring their surroundings. The larger the crowd, the less the individual body movement. People's faces take on a blank and expressionless look indicating that communication is not being sought. They avoid eye contact by staring at the ceiling or the floor.

Seating Arrangements

Seating positions should never happen by chance. When planning a dinner party or a special event, the hosts spend a great deal of energy deciding where their guests should sit. The position in which you're placed reflects your status, and impacts upon people's perception of you. Where other people place themselves in relation to you, signals their attitude toward you, their view of themselves in relation to you, and the level of cooperation you can expect from them.

Because rectangular tables enable people to have their own edges, equal space, and clear eye contact, everyone at the table can take a stance on a particular subject, although those at the shorter sides (the head) of the table are in a dominant position. Square tables are ideal for short, direct conversations. Round tables give everyone seated an equal amount of power and prominence.

Before you seat yourself, or direct people where you want them to sit, think about the outcome you want to have as a result of the people interacting.

Speaking in a relaxed setting

Sitting with the corner of a rectangular table between you and another person encourages relaxed, friendly conversation (see Figure 12-4). You can clearly see one another and open room exists for gesturing. The corner of the desk serves as a subtle barrier in case something is needed. This position also denotes an even division of space with both people on an equal footing.

Cooperating

When you work on a task with another person, or if you find that you and someone else think along the same lines, you're more than likely to find your-selves sitting side by side (see Figure 12-5). Most people intuitively sit in this configuration when they're working on a joint project with someone else. This position enables you to look easily at your partner. You can also reflect the other person's behaviour from this close position. You want to ensure that the person you're sitting next to doesn't feel that his space is being invaded.

Figure 12-4:
Sitting in the corner posi-tion diffuses tension and promotes a positive attitude.

When you introduce a third person to the cooperating position, the position in which you place yourself in relation to the other two determines how everyone at the table is perceived. By sitting next to the first person in the cooperating position, or at his side with the corner of the table between you, you're showing the new person that you and the first person are aligned. From this position you can speak and ask questions of the third person on the first person's behalf. In sales, this position is called 'siding with the opposition'.

Figure 12-5:
Sitting side
on to one
another
engenders
feelings of
cooperation.

Whenever you're influencing people, you should always aim to see their point of view, to make them feel at ease in your company and to ensure that they feel good about working with you. You gain more cooperation by sitting in the corner, or co-operative position, than you do by placing yourself in the combative position, in which conversations are shorter and sharper. (You can find out more about strategic positioning and persuading in *Persuasion & Influence For Dummies* by Elizabeth Kuhnke (Wiley).)

Combating and defending

Placing yourself across a table from another person sets up a barrier and a hostile, or defensive, atmosphere. The barrier serves as a foundation upon which each side can take a firm stand and argue their point. Standing or sitting directly face to face with someone else indicates that a confrontation may be imminent. (When animals attack one another, they come in head to head.) A person under attack throws up a shield to defend himself. It can be as subtle as folding your hands at chest level, or as blatant as putting a Star Wars defence mechanism into action.

In a business scenario, sitting directly across the table from another person implies a competitive atmosphere. In a social situation, such as at a dinner party or in a restaurant, this position is viewed positively because it enables conversation.

If you want to reprimand someone in a work environment, or demonstrate that you're in charge, sit directly across your desk or table from the other person.

Research shows that managers who don't use their desks as a barrier are perceived as active listeners, fair-minded and unlikely to show favouritism.

Keeping to yourself

If two people don't want to interact with one another, they sit diagonally across the table, at the farthest ends of the table. This position is typical in a library, when two people share a reading table.

The expression 'diametrically opposed' comes from this seating position and implies lack of interest, indifference or hostility. If you want to keep the discussions open between you and others, avoid sitting in this position.

Creating equality

King Arthur's Round Table empowered his knights with equal authority and status. No one was in a lesser, weaker or more dominant position than anyone else. Each knight was able to claim the same amount of table territory as his compatriot, and everyone could be seen easily. The circle is considered a symbol of unity and strength, and sitting in a circle promotes this effect.

Although the model of King Arthur's round table promotes equality, who sits where in relation to the perceived leader denotes positions of status and power.

The position in which people sit affects the dynamics of a group's power. The people sitting on either side of the person of higher status (and holding the most power), hold the next level of power, the individual on the right of the high-status person being granted more power than the individual on the left. The farther away from the high-status individual, the more diminished the power. Whoever sits directly across from the person with the highest status is placed in the competitive position and is most likely to be the one who causes the most trouble.

In business, a rectangular desk is effectively used for business activities, short conversations, and reprimands. A round table creates an informal relaxed atmosphere. Square tables belong in the company cafeteria. High-status people sit facing the door, not with their backs to it.

If you're seated at a round table, having a discussion with two other people and you want to make sure that they're both involved, begin by ensuring that the three of you sit in a triangular position. When one person asks you a question, look at that person first as you begin to answer, and then turn your head towards the third person as you continue your answer. Carry on like this, turning your head back and forth between the two people as you complete your answer. As you make your final statement, complete your remarks by looking at the person who first posed the question. This technique makes both people feel included and is particularly useful in helping the second person to connect with you.

You can tell a family's distribution of power by the kind of dining table they have, as long as they were free to choose any shape table they wanted. Families that encourage their members to share their opinions and points of view prefer round tables. Families with an authoritarian at the helm opt for rectangular tables.

Lefties and righties

The expressions 'left wing' and 'right wing' date back to pre-revolutionary France. In 1789, the French National Assembly was assembled to give power to the citizens and reduce the King's influence. Inside the chamber where the Assembly met, members of the Third Estate sat on the left and members of the First Estate sat on the right. The Third Estate was made up of revolutionaries and the First Estate consisted of nobles. Thus, the left wing of the Assembly was liberal and the right wing was conservative. The terms left and right wing have another meaning, as well. Whereas 'right' implies 'correct', the Latin term for 'left' (*sinestra*) implies 'sinister' behaviour.

Recently divorced, Anne was feeling shy, introverted, and somewhat unsure of herself. In spite of her lack of confidence, she accepted an invitation to a friend's dinner party. The hostess, knowing how Anne was feeling, seated her at the head of the table, facing into the room, with her back against the wall. Sitting in the most powerful position at the table, Anne found herself speaking throughout the evening with authority and confidence, and engaged comfortably with the people around her.

Orientating Yourself

Stand up, and you move and think one way. Lie down, and you think and move in another. Depending on whether you're standing to attention or slouching in your chair, you find yourself thinking and behaving differently. How you position yourself determines and sends out signals of how you view the world. The world, in turn, responds in its own way to the signals you send.

Horizontally

Someone who's lying out flat, or slumped over his desk, or is curled up in a ball, risks insulting his colleagues and companions. If the other people expect you to demonstrate polite attentiveness, you're going to have to change your posture and show that you're alert.

If you're extremely dominant, or among exceptionally good friends in an informal setting, you can get away with being horizontal. In the first case, you don't care what people think and say, and in the second case you know that you're safe with friends and trusted family members.

People in a supine position find that their thinking process is expansive – their thoughts free to meander and flow (see Figure 12-6). In an upright position, thoughts are sharper, clearer, and more coherent. You need both styles of thinking in order to explore all possibilities fully.

With the baby boomer and subsequent generations, people's posture has become more relaxed. Before World War II, people behaved more formally. Their clothes were structured and restrictive. After the war, fashions changed. With the advent of blue jeans as a wardrobe staple, our gestures and body placements reflect the new, relaxed atmosphere. People now move with more ease and less restriction because of the flexibility and freedom their clothes permit.

Figure 12-6:
Leaning
back in your
chair allows
you to think
freely.

You need a partner to do this with. Ask the other person to lie on the floor while you stand over him, accentuating the height difference. Give the person lying on the floor as loud and powerful a telling off as you can. Change positions, with you now lying on the floor looking up at your partner standing over you. Repeat the reprimand. You find that your voice lacks force and you've no authority.

Vertically

A person positioning himself lower than you is demonstrating a subordinate position. Someone standing above you is sending dominant signals. Whether you position yourself high or low, you're telling people where you stand in the pecking order. Kings and Queens are referred to as 'Your Highness'. Crooks, robbers, and other unsavoury characters are labelled 'low life'. People talk about the 'upper classes' and the 'lower classes'. The higher up you go, the more perceived status and authority you have. The lower down the scale, the less influence you wield.

Lowering yourself

In order to make himself appear small and deferential, a man removes his hat or tips his head when meeting someone in a position of higher authority.

Women curtsey, in a sign of deference and respect when meeting royalty. Men and women genuflect or bow their heads upon entering a church, and kneel for prayer. Beggars sit on the ground. When their eyes look downwards, they're at their lowest.

Short people suffer the indignity of being looked down upon. Because they're shorter than others, their credibility often gets overlooked. Short women are particularly susceptible to interruption and being talked over in meetings. In order to make up for their lack of height, short people must gesture and behave with strength, command authority, and demonstrate gravitas. Filling their space by standing up, holding their arms slightly away from their bodies, and gesturing with clarity and focus, creates an image of confidence, control, and commitment.

The more subordinate a person feels, the lower he positions his body. When a student or employee enters your office and you sit while he stands, you're demonstrating your power. The commanding officer doesn't rise when the junior lieutenant enters the Officers' Mess.

Sometimes, lowering yourself can raise your status. When you flop into a chair in someone else's home in front of the owner who's standing, you're demonstrating your comfort in that person's territory. By touching his belongings and behaving in unrestricted ways, you're indicating that although someone else may have a claim on the environment, you're more than comfortable taking over. This behaviour can be perceived as dominant or even aggressive.

Japanese businesses instruct staff members to bow at different angles, depending on the status of the customer. A customer who's 'browsing' receives a 15-degree bow whereas the customer who wants to buy is awarded up to a 45-degree bow. (See more about cultural influences on body language in Chapter 15.)

Elevating yourself

An Olympic gold medallist stands on a podium above the other medal winners and the judge sits above his court. To live in the penthouse is to live above, and look down upon, the crowd. People in 'high places' are looked up to and seen as superior. It would be most unusual to find the senior partner's or chief executive's office in the basement.

Look at the person sitting at the head of the table and you're likely to be looking at the boss.

Clients frequently ask me how they can project an elevated image when they're not tall. One female client who is just barely above 5 feet in her stocking feet tells me that she pretends that she's tall. Instead of straining and struggling to gain attention, she puts her efforts into visualising herself as a tall, slim woman, who fills her space and commands attention. By acting the part, she radiates the appearance.

Think tall

Whether people like to admit it or not, studies consistently conclude that taller people have more success, better health, and longer lives than short people. You look up to a tall person and subconsciously place him in a protective role.

According to research published in the *Journal of Applied Psychology*, a person who is six feet tall earns, on average, $789 (£400) more per year than their shorter counterparts.

In addition to their previous studies on the relationship between height and career success, University of Florida Professor Timothy A Judge and Professor Daniel M Cable of the University of North Carolina analysed data from four independent projects from the United States and the UK, following approximately 8,500 participants from their teens through adulthood.

The research findings show that tall people have greater self-esteem and social confidence than shorter people. The tall person is perceived to be more authoritative and in command.

The physical action of looking up towards someone elicits feelings of respect. The person in the limelight responds with feelings of confidence. Looking down on another person instils a sense of superiority on the viewer's part and submission on the person being looked at. The behaviour creates the feeling.

Not surprisingly, the study showed that the biggest correlation between height and salary was in sales and management, areas in which social interaction is vital for success. If the customer perceives the salesperson as tall and commanding, he follows the salesperson's lead.

At work, shorter women experience less height bias than men, a phenomenon that may be a result of evolution – a view offered by Professor Judge. He suggests that height was an indication of power in the early days of humanity and that, even though physical stature and prowess aren't as relevant today, those evolutionary appraisals remain. Professor Judge concludes that, subconsciously, people tend to apply the power appraisals more to men than to women.

The findings provide evidence that, in the same way as attractiveness, height, as well as weight and body image, impacts upon interactions and salaries.

Many of my clients work in the public arena and frequently appear on television. One of my shorter clients consistently received feedback that, although he was knowledgeable, on camera he lacked credibility and gravitas. Reviewing his tapes together, I devised a strategy for future public appearances to assure increased authority and presence: His lectern was to be customised in order that his chest was visible, and cameras were to be angled upwards, to give him the appearance of greater height. I coached him in speaking directly to the camera so that his viewing public felt that he was speaking to them individually. I put him in dark, single-breasted suits that elongated his body. His television performances improved dramatically. One observer reported that he had a new sense of gravitas and positive impact.

To project authority, breathe deeply from your diaphragm, release muscle tension, stand tall, and look people directly in the eye. Stand in a meeting to gain attention and control.

Asymmetrically

If you're sitting at your desk and one hand is resting on your desk and your other hand is placed on your hip, you're sitting in an *asymmetrical pose* (see Figure 12-7). Unlike a symmetrical pose in which corresponding body parts mirror one another, the asymmetrical position is two different poses. One side of your body is in one position while the other side is in another.

Straight posture commands respect and authority. Asymmetrical positions hold intrigue. They reveal more about the person. A man standing stiffly upright, with his mouth closed and his eyes staring straight ahead is giving little away. Someone whose body has fluidity and movement is more expressive. When your torso and limbs are in contrasting positions, they create impact and interest.

Figure 12-7: Asymmetrical positions are informal and intriguing.

Balancing the asymmetrical body

Studies of neuromuscular therapy and yoga provide insights into how humans stand, sit, and move. The ultimate goal is to have the outer body and the inner body working together to create an enhanced feeling of harmony and deportment. Yoga practitioners call this 'the dawning of the light of the spirit'.

People use their bodies asymmetrically, with the result that some sets of muscles work more than others. This leads to pain and discomfort as parts of the body have to work overtime to compensate for those muscles that are going slack. Diagonal gravity, misalignment, and poor balance lead to the body falling off kilter. Although the pelvis serves as a fulcrum, people often distribute their weight unevenly, causing their bodies to become unbalanced.

The Mexican poet and Nobel Laureate Octavio Paz writes in his poem 'Boy and Top', 'Each time he spins it / It lands, precisely / At the centre of the world.' These lines serve as a metaphor for our bodies.

The body, like the top, has a centre of gravity that it continuously seeks. The body's muscles work to keep you aligned. Because no one is perfectly symmetrical, the muscles pull in one direction or the other, away from, or towards, our centre. This happens from side to side and front to back. Any misalignment in the body causes one part of the body to overstretch while another part understretches. Muscles in one part of the body contract more than muscles in another part, causing a counter-contraction on the opposite side of the body. This counter-contraction occurs in the part of the body diagonally positioned to the first contraction. The width and length of these muscles is approximately the same. As the muscles pull and contract, they create an illusion of symmetry in an effort to create balance. Their efforts are misguided. Muscles move in complex patterns, some of which are obvious and many of which are not.

The back is an area where many people experience pain and discomfort. When the upper right thoracic muscles contract because of a slight curvature of the spine, the lower left lumbar muscles also contract because they're pulled in a counter direction. People with this condition who stretch to relieve the discomfort, at first feel rigid and stiff. As they become more aware of their bodies, and exercise carefully, they discover which muscles pull in which direction.

In both neuromuscular therapy and yoga, practitioners say, 'First you lengthen, then you strengthen'. By making the muscles more supple, flexible, and permeable, the pelvis stabilises and the body aligns itself.

Chapter 13

Rating, Dating, and Mating: Using the Body in Courting Behaviour

. . . .

In This Chapter

▶ Catching a person's eye

▶ Indicating your interest

▶ Following the romantic process

. . . .

*T*ry flirting without using body language. Go on, give it a go. Surprise, surprise! It can't be done. You simply can't convey romantic interest without the body getting into the act. To play a really successful game of flirtation, your body has to speak what your mouth mustn't say.

When you're feeling good about yourself you focus your eyes, position your mouth and manoeuvre your shoulders, hips and hands in ways that send out signals saying, 'Check me out! I think you're hot!' After you get a person's attention, you shift gears to hold onto your target's interest and move the attraction to another level. Having captured and conquered the unsuspecting or equally interested party, your body moves into a new mode of behaving that demonstrates comfort, ease, and familiarity. Observe how long-term lovers anticipate one another's actions by the way they move in sync with their partners.

How you use your body exposes how ready you are for a bit of romance, how attractive you feel and how interested you are in another's advances: some courtship signals are deliberate, others are unconscious. In this chapter I explore the wide, wild world of courtship behaviour and see how it can put a big smile on your face.

Attracting Someone's Attention

Watching people when they're in the company of someone they find attractive is fascinating. The stomach gets pulled in, whether it needs to be or not, slumping is exchanged for an upright stance, displays of health and vitality are conveyed through a lively walk, muscle tone becomes heightened and a youthful appearance replaces the ravages of time or too many late nights.

Men stand taller, thrust up their chins and expand their chests, making them look like the king of the jungle. Women tilt their heads, flick their hair and expose their wrists and necks, demonstrating vulnerability and submissiveness (check out Figure 13-1).

When you find another person attractive, your eyes dilate and you can do nothing to stop it (check out the later section 'Recognising dilated pupils: A universal sign of attraction' for details). If things go to plan, the recipient of your gaze unconsciously responds in a similar way and the excitement begins.

Figure 13-1:
You can spot the interest and sexual tension between these two people.

The allure of being sexually appealing

Research consistently shows that men are attracted to healthy looking women who demonstrate sexual availability. Both men and women want someone with an athletic body. Men see such a body as a sign of good health and an ability to provide him with progeny. Women see it as a sign of power, signalling the ability to provide for her.

Men are drawn to women with childlike faces, including doe eyes, petite noses, bee-stung lips, and full cheeks. These facial characteristics elicit fatherly, protective emotions in most men. Women prefer men with mature faces that show they have the ability to protect and defend. Strong jaws, large brows, and a prominent nose appeal to women.

The good news for women is that although good looks may initially give a woman a slight edge over her competitors, women don't have to be natural beauties to attract a man. Primarily, they need to display the signals of possible availability. Although you may need surgery to create a tilted nose or a rose bud mouth, and you can't always count on the results being what you hoped for, all a woman has to do to signal her availability is find out and practise the signals.

Granted, some women may be disturbed, if not appalled, to know that modern men are initially more attracted to a woman based on her looks and her sensuality than on her ability to discuss world affairs, balance a cheque book, play the piano, or stuff a turkey. But modern research concurs with what painters, poets, and writers have alluded to for thousands of years – a woman's ability to fill a man with the feeling of excitement and mystery appeals more to him than any family trust fund or intellectual capabilities she may possess.

Vickie is a particularly attractive woman. A former model, she has kept her figure trim and fit, wears just enough make-up to highlight her perfectly formed features and moves with purpose and energy. One day, Vickie and I went out to brunch. As she walked through the restaurant, I noticed a man tracking her while continuing his conversation with his partner. Although he didn't move his head, the muscles around his mouth raised, he slightly adjusted his seating position while expanding his chest, his eyes widened and he watched her out of the corner of his eye until she passed. After she was out of his line of vision, his body reverted to its original position and he continued his conversation as if nothing had happened.

David went for a walk one day after work. Worried about business and feeling overwhelmed with responsibilities, he walked slowly, looking at the ground in front of him with his arms across his chest, hunched shoulders, and a bent head. At one point he looked up and noticed an attractive middle-aged woman coming towards him with a smile on her face and a bounce in her step, looking right at him. Without thinking, he adjusted his posture to reflect hers by lifting his chest, squaring his shoulders and establishing eye contact. His energy heightened and he began feeling lighter and more positive as he noticed the woman continuing to smile at him. Before he knew it, he was smiling back. Although tempted to stop and engage her in conversation, he thought of his wife and young family at home and walked on by with a hint of a grin as he reflected on his and the mystery woman's brief flirtation. Putting a spring in your step, a twinkle in your eye and a smile on your face in this way makes you look attractive, feel appealing, and come across as hot.

When you're rating someone's attractiveness and in turn are being rated, messages that convey interest, keenness, and compatibility are relayed through posture, gestures, and facial expressions. Regardless of age, fitness, and capabilities, no one's immune to checking other people out.

Here are some things to keep in mind as you go courting:

- ✔ **Women usually make the first move.** Research shows that 90 per cent of the time women initiate the first move in the mating game. I can hear my mother now: 'Nice girls don't show that they're interested. They wait for the man to make the first move.' Well, apparently not. Women go for it. Men simply respond. Through a series of subtle expressions and movements (including covert smiles, eye contact and gestures that accentuate their femininity), women send out signals of interest. If she's a good flirt, the person in her sights thinks that he's taking the lead although in fact he's just dancing to her tune.

  If a woman is to succeed in the ritual, she has to count on the man to decode the signals she's sending out. When the man deduces that she's interested and shows he's interested too, the woman usually gives him the green light to move to the next stage. For a man to succeed in this game, he has to be able to recognise and interpret the signals correctly. The rating, dating, mating ritual is a complicated process, rather like ballroom dancing in which you follow a series of steps, moving in time with your partner.

- ✔ **Men aren't good at reading the signals properly.** Men tend to misinterpret friendly behaviour for sexual interest because men have 10 to 20 times more testosterone than women. *Testosterone* encourages dominant behaviour, increases sexual interest, and rises in the face of a challenge. Heightened levels of testosterone can make a man hunger for an evening full of lust, when all the woman had in mind was dinner.

- ✔ **Availability counts more than beauty.** Men pursue a woman who may not be the most sexually attractive as long as she gives off availability signals. A beautiful woman with all the right physical attributes is left on the shelf if she doesn't appear to be interested. In a contest between looks and signals, signals win hands down.

Going courting: The five stages

When you see someone you want to get to know better, often you go through a predictable pattern of courtship. The first order of business is to get that person's attention:

1. **Eye contact.**

   The woman looks across a crowded room. She spots someone she finds attractive. She waits for that person to notice her. She looks the person directly in the eye for 3–5 seconds and then looks away. The object of her interest watches to see what she does next. She establishes eye contact again, and then at least one more time. When a man sees a woman who catches his eye, he glances at her body first. After he makes eye contact with her, he slightly narrows his eyes and holds the gaze somewhat longer than he normally would, indicating his interest.

2. **Smile.**

   The woman flashes a fleeting smile or two – a hint of a smile with a promise of things to come rather than a toothy grin. The man needs to respond to this signal or the woman thinks that he's not interested and moves her sights. If interested, the man establishes eye contact with the woman and lifts his chin slightly as he smiles, inviting her to engage with him.

3. **Preen.**

   The muscles of both men and women become slightly tensed. Her posture straightens, accentuating her physical attributes. If seated, she crosses her legs to show them off. If she's standing, she shifts her hips and tilts her head to expose her neck. She plays with her hair, runs her tongue over her lips, and adjusts her clothes and jewellery. A man may straighten his stance, pull in his stomach, push out his chest, adjust his clothes, and touch his hair. Both point their bodies towards one another.

4. **Talk.**

   The man walks over to the woman, making it look as though he's the initiator, and gives her a few chat-up lines. Having given him permission to approach by the signals she's sent through her body language, a woman then waits for the man to begin the conversation.

   For a man, initiating a conversation with someone you find attractive can be a minefield. Here are a couple of tips to help you navigate it safely:

   - If you misread the signal and sense that you're about to be ignored or rebuffed, pretend that you just want to ask the other person about unrelated subjects, such as the time, what she's drinking or who won the evening's football match. You may sound a bit of an idiot but at least you aren't given a brusque brush off in response to a clumsy pass.

- If after a few minutes of speaking, the woman yawns, frowns, or sneers, you can count on the fact that she's not interested. If she crosses her arms, puts her hands in her pockets, and avoids your gaze, you may as well walk away.

5. Touch.

If a woman's interested in a man, she may create an opportunity for him to touch her arm lightly. When both people are happy with the touching process, they increase the amount. When people aren't interested in taking things further, they avoid touching. If you're going to touch someone, begin by touching her on the arm, which is less intimate than touching someone on the hand. If she doesn't pull away when you touch her on the arm, you can progress to her hand. If she continues to allow you to touch her, you may place your hand on her back or around her waist. A woman who doesn't want to be touched pulls away.

You may not have thought that so much choreography exists in the initial stages of courtship and the steps may seem incidental. They're not. Without going through these five stages, which may only take a few moments at most, the courting ritual stops before it begins. (Check out the *Body Language For Dummies* app to see these stages in action.)

Highlighting gender differences

People who want to attract the attention of the opposite sex emphasise their gender to make themselves sexually attractive and appealing. Women pout, arch their backs, and lean forward, bringing their arms close to their bodies to push their breasts together to create a deep and appealing cleavage (see Figure 13-2). Men stand tall and expand their chests (check out the later section 'Showing That You're Available' for more on male and female courting gestures).

Unless you want to be perceived as a hot totty or aggressively on the make, keep your gestures muted in the early stages of the courtship process. Otherwise you may find your signs of possible interest being interpreted as signals of immediate availability.

Figure 13-2:
By arching her back, pouting and accentuating her breasts, the woman's showing she wants his attention and he indicates that's he's prepared to oblige.

Walking, wiggling, and swaggering

The way you walk reveals your interest. Both men and women take on youthful characteristics when seeking the other's attention. They create the impression that they've an unlimited source of energy by the way they vigorously bounce along. Unlimited energy can be sexy because it indicates the promise of being a tireless mate.

When a woman wants to indicate her interest, she rolls her hips and swings her arms further back, exposing her soft and supple flesh. Because women have wider hips than men, as well as a wider crotch gap between their legs, they're able to walk with a rolling motion that draws attention to the pelvic area. Men, being built differently, can't emulate this walk and find the difference sexually appealing. If you've ever seen the film *Some Like It Hot* you're sure to remember the scene where Marilyn Monroe walks down the railway platform, while Jack Lemmon and Tony Curtis stare at her undulating bottom in awe. As Jack Lemmon says, this remarkable movement was 'like Jell-o on springs'.

Women in advertisements and commercials – especially those advertising fashion and beauty merchandise – are often directed to roll their hips and lead with their pelvis to draw attention to the products they're promoting. Watching women want to emulate the model and men want to engage with the model. Whatever the reaction, the movements create increased product awareness leading to increased sales, which is the bottom line for the ad agency and the client.

Some men swagger, thinking that it makes them look strong and domineering. They swing their arms across their bodies, elbows bent, hands at waist height, turning their arms inward showing just how manly they are. However, men who swagger tend to come across as boastful and arrogant, while men who stride with purpose, with a firm and relaxed gait, appear confident and assertive.

While sitting in an airport departure lounge, I noticed two men enter the room. Their chests were puffed out, their legs splayed wider than hip width, thus lowering their centre of gravity and drawing attention to their groins. Both men walked with a display of animal passion filled with power and purpose.

Filling the space

Men adopt dominant positions by sitting with their legs apart and their arms opened to show they need lots of space for their frames to fit into (see the example in Figure 13-3). They shift their bodies, change their positions, and use their hands frequently to emphasise what they're saying. When some men feel insecure, they become more expansive in their gestures, whereas others pull inside themselves.

Women accentuate their femininity by moving slowly and pulling their gestures towards themselves. They give the appearance of needing less space than men, making them appear little and subservient. Submissive gestures such as tilting their heads, entwining their ankles, and crossing their legs as well as touching their hair and face indicate not only that they're ready, willing, and able, but also that they're seeking protection and comfort.

Is she hobbling or flirting?

Besides wearing high heels to make themselves look taller and more powerful, women wear them to make themselves appear more feminine. The higher the heel, the stronger and more vulnerable the look. Men are in awe of women who can stride out in 15-centimetre (6-inch) Jimmy Choos without missing a beat, as well as captivated by the wily ways of a femme fatale in Louboutin platforms. Whether aware of what they're doing or not, in order to balance themselves women in high heels arch their backs and push out their bottoms, creating a wiggle to their walk that men inevitably notice. Marilyn Monroe is purported to have chopped 2 centimetres (three-quarters of an inch) off the heel of her left shoe to create her famous wiggle.

Figure 13-3:
The spread eagle position helps a man to fill the space, as well as drawing attention to the crotch where his manhood resides.

The next time you're watching a televised awards ceremony, notice how the women on the red carpet move. They revel in showing their sensuous shoulders, reflecting as they do, their breasts. Women cross their legs, one in front of the other, to give them a slimmer look than if they were to stand with their legs hip width apart. This position also squeezes the upper thighs, making the woman (and anyone paying attention) more aware of her vaginal area.

Discovering other 'is he, isn't he' clues

The clothes you wear and the way you wear them advertise your sexual availability. How much of your body you show and which parts are on display, as well as your facial expressions, also send signals as to your attraction and willingness to move forward in a relationship:

- ✔ **Clothing:** In addition to protecting you from the elements, your choice of clothing signals what you want to reveal about yourself. In response, people make assumptions about you based on what you wear. Clothes that draw attention to your sexuality indicate that you're prepared to be noticed. Low-slung or tight jeans draw the eye to the wearer's genitalia whereas tight-fitting tops enhance the chest.

✔ **Facial expressions:** Women use lively and animated facial expressions demonstrating interest, vitality, and energy, whereas in contrast men tend to be more controlled, reflecting a desire to convey dominance, restraint, and power.

Laura's a woman who knows the power of her body. She showed up at a recent concert wearing a skin-tight pink dress and black strappy high heels that would make Madonna envious. Laura's sexy, curvaceous figure encased in passionate pink, her full red lips, white skin, tousled hair, and painted nails, ensured that every man and most women looked at her with awe and appreciation.

Showing That You're Available

Having established that you're interested in the other person (as I describe in the earlier section 'Attracting Someone's Attention'), you need to show that you're available. Some of your gestures are studied and deliberate; others are completely unconscious. They all have the effect of showing that you're in place and ready to go, whether you know it or not.

Although men and women use the same basic preening gestures – such as touching their hair, smoothing their clothes, pointing their bodies in the other's direction, and increasing eye contact – a few subtle differences are worth noting.

Unlike most of the mammal population where the males are in charge of sexual advertising, in the world of humans women usually take the lead. They use clothes, hairstyles, make-up and fragrance to advertise their femininity. Whether a conscious choice or not, an interested and available woman sends out signals designed to lure a partner into her fold.

Looking at the many courting gestures of women

The list of female sexual behaviours is long and moves right down her body from her head to the tips of her toes.

Tossing her head and flicking her hair

When a woman sees someone she finds attractive, she tosses her head or runs her fingers through her hair, often not conscious of what she's doing. Whether her hair is long or short, the gesture is a subtle way of showing that she cares about her appearance and is making an effort to look appealing. An added benefit of this movement is that it exposes her soft underarm, a highly sensual part of a woman's body that most men find irresistible.

Canting her head

A head tilted to the side gives an appealing and helpless look. By exposing the neck, a vulnerable part of the body, the head-cant is an ideal courtship signal because it implies that the woman trusts the man so much that she's prepared to display a defenceless part of her body to him.

The origins of the head-cant can be traced to infancy. A baby rests its head on the parents' shoulders when being comforted. The head-cant is a stylised version of the infant's gesture and unconsciously sends out an appeal for protection. Without knowing why, men feel a sudden surge of compassion, probably because the woman looks so vulnerable and helpless that the pose appeals to men's masculinity.

Showing her neck

A woman uses two ways to expose her neck to make herself look appealing (see Figure 13-4). In one she raises her chin slightly; in the other she turns her head so the man can get a clear view of her neck. By showing her soft skin on a vulnerable part of her body, she makes herself look helpless and sexy, which is a lethal combination that no hot-blooded male can resist.

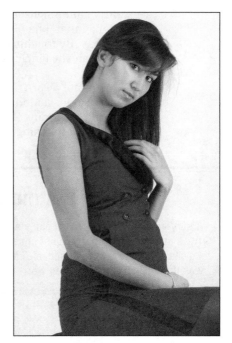

Figure 13-4: In both positions, the woman looks vulnerable and appealing.

Dipping her head

One way a woman can make her eyes seem bigger, and herself seem smaller, is to lower her head when she's looking up at her lover. The result is that she looks vulnerable and in need of protection. Women also lower their heads when they're flirting with a man because lowering the head is a sign of submission. The late Princess of Wales made this pose popular and it continues to be copied by women across the globe as they recognise the (paradoxical) power of submission.

Pouting and wetting her lips

Full lips are seen as a female characteristic and are considered full of sexual promise. When a woman pouts, the size of the lips increase, as does the man's interest.

The facial bone structure of men and women is vastly different. During the teen years, as testosterone increases in men, their features become stronger, larger, and more pronounced. Women's facial features change only slightly. Owing to more subcutaneous fat, their faces seem full and childlike, particularly their lips.

Touching herself

Women have a much larger number of nerve sensors than men, making them more sensitive to touching sensations. A woman may leisurely stroke her neck, throat and thighs, drawing attention to that part of her body and signalling to a man that if he plays his cards right she just may let him caress her in a similar way. By touching herself, a woman can fantasise about how it would feel if the man she fancies were the one doing the touching.

Often you're not aware that you're touching or stroking yourself. The gesture is an unconscious action in response to your interest in the other person. Women who *are* aware of the effect this behaviour elicits become adept at performing self-touching actions to call attention to themselves.

Putting on a Clara Bow

A fiery-haired legendary silent film star of the 1920s and 1930s with a free-spirit encapsulating charm, charisma and sex appeal, Clara Bow was the original 'It' girl, having starred in the 1927 film *It*. One of the most duplicated features of all time is the actress's cupid bow-style lips, always enhanced with a splash of bright red lipstick.

Lips, labia, and lipstick

A woman's labia are in proportion to the thickness of her facial lips. According to zoologist Desmond Morris, women 'self-mimic' their outer genital lips by making their facial lips wet by licking them or using lip gloss, thus creating a sexual invitation.

When a women is sexually aroused her lips, breasts, and genitals enlarge and become redder as blood flows into them. The use of lipstick dates back 4,000 years to the time of the Egyptians. Women painted their lips to mimic their sexually aroused and reddened genitalia. Modern research shows that when men look at photographs of women wearing different lipstick colours, they're consistently drawn to the bright reds which they describe as the most attractive and sensual.

Susan had been dating Dennis for several weeks when she invited him to her house for dinner. This occasion was the first time Dennis had visited her house, and from the moment Susan opened the door to him she began to feel a tingling sensation throughout her body. She found him powerful, sexy, and exciting and anticipated that by the time dessert was served, he would be stroking her body. During the meal, Susan caught her reflection in the dining room mirror, noticing that as she leaned in towards Dennis she was stroking her bare shoulder with her middle finger and the hollow at the base of her neck with her thumb in anticipation of what she wanted to happen.

Exposing her wrists

The underside of the wrist is considered to be one of the most erotic places on a woman's body, probably because the skin highly delicate. A woman showing interest and availability reveals this smooth, soft skin, increasing the rate of frequency as her interest grows (see Figure 13-5).

Fondling cylindrical objects

If you find yourself fondling any object that remotely resembles a phallus, you're acting out what's going on inside your head. The same is true for someone else if you notice them stroking a firm, upright object. The scene in *Ghost,* in which Demi Moore and Patrick Swayze work a mound of wet clay on a potter's wheel is an erotic, emotive, and classically graphic example of the sexual arousal that can be ignited by fondling a phallic object. Don't be surprised if a person you're speaking with fondles a personal item of yours while you fiddle with your earring, pen or the stem of your glass. The stimulus is too much to resist and he has to respond in a similar way to show that he's paying attention and wants to possess you.

Figure 13-5:
Exposed
wrists are
a sign of
availability.

Sliding a ring on and off your finger can show a desire to have sex with the person you're speaking to.

Glancing sideways over a raised shoulder

A woman who raises her shoulder is performing an act of self-mimicry by using her shoulder to emulate her rounded breasts. By turning her shoulder towards a man, holding his gaze with slightly lowered eyelids just long enough to get his attention and then quickly looking away, a woman can drive a man to distraction (see Figure 13-6). If he's interested, that is. This gesture tantalises the man and suggests a peep show, which most men find hard to resist.

Putting her handbag in close proximity

A woman's handbag is her personal domain. Even most married men live in terror of entering this most forbidden territory. Because a woman treats her handbag as if it were a personal extension of her body, it becomes a strong signal of sexual intimacy when she places her bag close to a man.

If a woman finds a man attractive, she may deliberately stroke and caress her bag in an inviting manner, tantalising and teasing her male admirer.

Figure 13-6:
A raised shoulder highlights a woman's roundness and curves.

A woman who places her handbag close enough to a man for him to see or touch it is sending out signals that she's attracted to him. If she keeps her bag away from him, she's creating an emotional distance.

Pointing her knee in his direction

Watch the direction a woman's knee points when she sits with one leg tucked under the other. If a man is at the end of the sight line, you can bet that she finds him interesting. From this relaxed position, she's able to flash a bit of thigh and gain her target's attention.

Dangling a shoe

If a woman is sitting with a man and dangles a shoe off the end of her foot she's sending out the message that she's relaxed and comfortable in his company. In addition, the foot acts like a phallus as it thrusts itself in and out of her shoe. Many men become unsettled by this gesture and they don't know why.

If you want to test a woman's comfort level as she swings her dangling shoe off her pedicured toes, say or do something that unsettles her or makes her anxious and observe how quickly that shoe goes back on her foot.

Entwining her legs

Men consistently rank the leg twine as the most appealing sitting position a woman can take. Women consciously use this gesture to draw attention to their legs. When one leg is pressed up against the other it gives the appearance of highly toned muscles, which is the position the body takes just before engaging in sex.

Women who want to entice a man and demonstrate their own interest slowly cross and uncross their legs and gently stroke their thighs as an indication of their desire to be caressed. Think of Sharon Stone's provocative leg cross in the film *Basic Instinct.*

Examining the few courting gestures of men

Compared with the vast amount of courtship signals women possess, men have a sad and paltry few. In their effort to attract a woman, men often rely on their power, money, and status as a means of flexing their muscles. Men's idea of a sexual invitation is to rev their engines, flaunt their wealth, and challenge other men.

This is not to say that men don't preen when a potential partner comes into view. In addition to pulling in his stomach, expanding his chest, and lifting his head like a conquering hero, a man smoothes his hair, straightens his tie, adjusts his clothes, and flicks real or imaginary dust from his lapel.

If you're a man and you want to see whether a woman finds you attractive, tidy up your appearance by wearing a smart suit or a jacket and tie. A loosely knotted and slightly off-centre tie elicits a nurturing response in a woman. She instinctively reaches out to make the necessary adjustments, brushing your shoulder or lapel just in case a bit of fluff needs removing. If she's drawn to you, she wants to make you look like the well-put-together man she wants you to be.

The most sexually aggressive posture a man can display is to hook his thumbs over his waistband, into his belt or into the top of his trouser pockets. With his arms in the ready position and fingers pointing subtly to his genital area, men take this stance to stake their claim or show other men they're not to be messed about. If a man uses this gesture in front of a woman, he's indicating that he's both dominant and virile (check out Figure 13-7).

Penile enhancements

In the 15th century, the male codpiece was introduced. (Refer to Chapter 10 for more on the codpiece.) The purpose of this not-so-subtle item of clothing was to display the purported size of the man's penis, which determined his social status. New Guinea male natives still display their penises, while western men do so more subtly by wearing tight-fitting jeans, pocketsize swimsuits, or dangling a bunch of keys in their nether regions.

Figure 13-7:
A man whose fingers point towards his crotch is drawing attention to his source of power.

If a woman sees a man with his thumbs in his pockets and his fingers pointing toward his crotch combined with dilated pupils, a longer-than-usual gaze and one foot pointed toward her, she's on a winner if she guesses he's displaying interest in her.

Studying pupils

University of Chicago bio-psychologist Eckhard Hess developed *pupillometrics* to assess the size of the eye's pupil as a means of gauging emotion or interest. Hess discovered that the pupil enlarges when people look at something that stimulates them. When someone looks at unpleasant or uninteresting things, the pupils contract. In one of Hess's studies, heterosexual men were shown retouched photographs of women. In half the photographs the women's pupils were made to look larger, in the other half the pupils were made to look smaller. With few exceptions, the men perceived the women with the larger pupils as being more attractive and friendlier than the same women whose pupils appeared smaller. When asked why they found one set of women more attractive than the other, the men were unable to give an answer. None of the men remarked on the difference in the size of the pupils.

Although controversy is rife in the advertising industry over the practice of air-brushing photos and the negative effects it has on people's perceptions of themselves in relation to the enhanced versions of their idols, retouching photographs of male and female models for print advertisements is common practice. The pupils are enlarged to make the models more attractive and alluring. Sales of manufactured goods measurably increase where close-ups of the face are used to promote merchandise, especially in the worlds of fashion, cosmetics, and hair products.

Recognising dilated pupils: A universal sign of attraction

Anyone who has ever gazed longingly into another person's eyes knows how powerfully the eyes convey the message that says, 'I find you incredibly attractive.' What you may not realise is that your pupils dilate when something arouses and stimulates you. As you can do nothing to control this reaction, give up playing hard to get because anyone paying close attention sees your pupils enlarging and knows that they're in with a chance.

If you want to kick-start a romance, arrange to meet your person of choice in a dimly lit place. Both your and your partner's pupils dilate because of the lack of light, creating the impression that you're interested in one another. The rest is up to you.

For more information on what messages you can send with a gaze alone, go to Chapter 5.

Progressing Through the Romance

As I describe in the earlier section 'Going courting: The five stages', the court-ship procedure is made up of a series of stages. Depending on how each person reacts to the other's signals, the courtship progresses or comes to a screeching halt. If you find yourself laughing, tickling, and generally engag-ing in playful behaviour when you're with Cute Guy or Gorgeous Gal, you know that you're at least 'in like' if not yet 'in love' with one another. Goofing around and acting like puppies in a basket is harmless, unthreatening behav-iour that allows you to show one another your nurturing and loving sides.

Matching each other's behaviours

The closer two people are emotionally, the more similar their postures become. Certain postures and emotions are linked – especially those pertain-ing to sexual interest and anger – so when two people adopt the same physi-cal position they may well be experiencing similar feelings. Observe a couple who are in tune with one another and you can see that their movements are coordinated and their postures match.

Take a look at photos or videos of the Duke and Duchess of Cambridge together and you may notice how their bodies move in sync with one another. An easy energy exists between them, and their bodies fit comfortably together. They walk in time with each other, with William often guiding his wife by placing a gentle hand on the small of her back. This intimate gesture reflects the sensual-ity they experience together.

Displaying that you belong together

People who establish a physical closeness give the impression that they're emotionally close as well. A man may put his arm around a woman's waist or shoulders, sending out the message that she's his woman. A woman may remove a piece of fluff from her man's jacket or straighten his tie, giving the message to anyone who's watching that he belongs to her.

Other signs of togetherness are linking arms or holding hands while you're walking with your partner. People don't usually hold onto one another in these ways to keep from falling over, but to show that they're connected.

Angelina Jolie and Victoria Beckham are often photographed touching their partners, Brad Pitt and David Beckham. Whether they're stroking their partner's upper arm or resting a hand on his chest, both women are sending out clear signals that while others may look at and fancy her man from afar, only she may touch him (see Figure 13-8).

Figure 13-8:
Touching your partner demonstrates that he belongs to you.

When people hold hands, each person's hand may be in front or behind, and the position of the hands can indicate who's in charge. Usually, the man's hand is in front with his palm facing towards the back (perhaps because men are taller or because they like to lead from the front). If a woman has her hand in the front position, usually she's taller than her partner and finds that putting her hand in the back position is uncomfortable. If she's shorter than her man and still puts her hand in front, however, she likes to be in charge, regardless of the physical discomfort it causes her and her partner. (For more about what certain hand movements and positions mean, go to Chapter 9.)

After the inauguration of George W Bush in 2001, Hillary and Bill Clinton left the ceremony walking hand in hand. Bill looked composed and in control and Hillary looked supportive. Photos and film coverage show that Hillary was holding Bill's hand with her hand in the front position. The difference in their heights and the male-female relationship would normally dictate the opposite position. What the position clearly demonstrated was that Hillary, not Bill, was in charge.

Chapter 14

Interviewing, Influencing, and Playing Politics

In This Chapter

▶ Creating the right initial impression

▶ Conveying positivity and confidence

▶ Weighing up your best position

▶ Discovering effective negotiating behaviour

*H*ow you perceive and project yourself determines how people perceive and receive you. If you want to be seen as positive, powerful, and influential at work, you have to act the part. Your gestures, actions, and expressions need to celebrate and reflect your strengths and abilities. Based on what you reveal in the way you appear and move, people want to know more – or close the door on you.

From the moment you enter the work environment to your last day on the job, you're being watched. Make sure that the way you're moving, gesturing and behaving projects the image you want. The higher up the hierarchy you go, the more focused your actions and the more contained your gestures need to be, in order to project the expected authority. You never see chief executives running down the hall or senior partners flapping their hands. You never see prime ministers and presidents sitting with their backs to the door.

Self-awareness is paramount if you're to work your way successfully through the office maze.

In this chapter, I look at how you can make a positive impact from the first impression through to the final exit. You discover that how you position your body impacts upon how people perceive you, and you gain skills to display confidence, commitment, and credibility.

Making a Great First Impression: The Interview

I know, I know, you've heard it a hundred times or more, but here it is again: you never have a second chance to make a first impression. Make a good one and you're on a winner. Make a poor one and you're going to struggle long and hard to be invited back.

Going for an interview involves being on show. People begin making evaluations from the moment they first see you. From top to toe, how you groom, dress and accessorise yourself sends out signals about who you are and the message you want to convey. Add to those ingredients your body language, your manners, and your demeanour, and in less than seven seconds the impression you make is set. Although you may appeal to some, others may be less than impressed. This section describes how to push the odds in your favour.

Perfecting your interview behaviour

Getting yourself ready for a successful interview requires preparation and practice. In order to go in feeling good about yourself, and in control, follow the suggestions below:

- **Warming up:** Remind yourself of the purpose of the interview, what you want to achieve and how you want to be perceived. Think hard about the strengths and special qualities that make you unique and add value to all that you do. Before setting off for your interview, visualise yourself at your best. Only enter the interview room when you're looking, sounding, and feeling like you do when you know you're in top notch form.

  Concentrate on breathing from your abdomen, allowing the air to flow into your body with ease and strength. Visualise unzipping your torso and freeing the nervous butterflies in your stomach. See them fly out of you in a forward-facing, straight formation – light and free – guiding you to where you want to be. Notice how relaxed and energised you feel. Practise vocal warm-ups – humming and quietly repeating the phrases, 'The tip of the tongue, the lips and the teeth' and 'Red leather, yellow leather, red leather, black leather' or any of your favourite tongue twisters. Shake out your arms and legs, and again, breathe deeply. You may want to do these exercises in the privacy of a rest room if you're concerned about appearing a bit odd as you walk down the street and into the building. These exercises help to release any tension you may be harbouring in your body, connect with your voice, and clarify your speech.

REMEMBER

Physical exercises including raising and lowering your shoulders, letting your head roll from side to side, and shaking your hands and fingers out before undergoing any tension-filled task, prepare you mentally, vocally, and physically, enabling you to face your fears and get on with the task at hand.

✔ **Claiming your space:** Wherever you are, make the surrounding space yours and own it. (Check out the later section 'Claiming your space' for loads more tips.) Remind yourself that you wouldn't be there if you didn't have the right to be. You want to send out the message that you're ready and raring to go. Follow these tips:

- Relieve yourself of unnecessary clutter. Carry only what you need. Too much mess sends out messages of a muddled mind (see Figure 14-1).

- Enter the reception area with a strong stride and greet the receptionist with a smile and a polite word. Give your name and say whom you've come to see. Remove your coat and ask the receptionist to store it, if possible.

Figure 14-1:
People carrying the least amount of items look more in control than their colleagues.

Move away from the receptionist's area and in spite of the invitation to 'take a seat', remain standing, unless the chairs are upright and easy to get in and out of. Some seating arrangements include soft, low chairs and couches that make you look small and can be awkward to navigate. Most reception areas have literature about the company, as well as newspapers and periodicals. If you haven't already read up on the company – and you really should have – flick through their annual report. If you prefer to stand, allow your hands to rest, one in the other in front of you at waist height, while taking in your surroundings. This position, known as the Power Position, makes you appear strong and in control and calms your nervous energy.

✔ **Making your entrance:** How you move signals how you perceive yourself and expect to be treated. When you're invited to enter the interview room, do so with focus and energy. If you want to be perceived as someone with an upfront, upbeat, and positive attitude, move confidently, smoothly and purposefully. And smile. Put down whatever you're carrying, shake the interviewer's hand if offered and only take a seat if you're invited to do so. You're demonstrating that you're comfortable with yourself entering another person's territory.

Move purposefully, avoiding any slight hesitation that may cause a small shuffle that makes you appear unsure of yourself. In order to project a commanding image, walk at a brisk pace, taking medium-length strides.

✔ **Showing that you're approachable:** Smiling at someone you're meeting for the first time makes you appear approachable, prompting the other person to open up and to relate with you. When you smile, you're indicating that you're willing to share yourself and connect at an emotional level. Smiling also lightens and relaxes a potentially tense atmosphere; it costs you nothing and yet enriches the lives of people who are at the receiving end. Although it may not last long, the memory of a genuine smile can last forever.

When you smile, make sure that you mean what you're doing. A fake smile is easy to spot and leaves the impression that you're not genuine.

✔ **Shaking hands:** Instead of shaking hands across the desk, which puts a barrier between you and the other person, move to the left of the desk to avoid receiving a palm down handshake and being put in a subservient position. Hold your palm straight and return the same amount of pressure that the other person gives. Let the interviewer decide when the handshake should end.

When you match the force of the interviewer's handshake, you're showing that you're sensitive and flexible and able to reflect that person's approach. If you crush the other person's fingers or offer a wet fish handshake in return for a firm one, you're showing that the two of you are mismatched and out of sync.

Include the person's name in your remarks twice within the first 30 seconds of having introduced yourself, including when you first meet. Speak for no longer than 20–30 seconds at one time.

✔ **Positioning yourself:** When you're invited to sit, make sure that your body is at a 45 degree angle from the other person. Move the chair to this angle, if you can. If you can't, shift your body. (The later section 'Creating a relaxed attitude with the 45 degree angle' contains lots more info on the importance of the 45 degree angle.) Facing your interviewer directly, especially if you're seated across the desk from one another and your chair is lower than his, makes you look like a child about to be reprimanded. If you're invited to sit away from the desk in a more informal area, silently rejoice. Few rejections are made from this position.

If the seat you're offered is soft and low, sit on the edge, leaning slightly forward to avoid sinking into the seat and lowering your status. If you don't, you're going to look like a mini head perched on two sticks.

Respecting the other person's personal space is bound to win you points. In determining what the appropriate space is, keep these guidelines in mind:

- The greater the familiarity between you and the other person, the closer you sit; the less familiar, the farther away.

- Men tend to move closer to a woman they're speaking to, whereas women generally back away.

- If you're being interviewed by a person of a similar age, you sit closer than if you were being interviewed by someone significantly older – or younger.

As the meeting progresses, and all being well, the parameters of this area close inwards, inviting you to come closer. If you move in too soon, the other person feels invaded and moves back and away from you.

✔ **Making your exit:** When the time comes to leave, move calmly and focus on what you're doing. Smile, shake hands with your interviewer, turn and head towards the door. No matter how fit you are, and even if your bottom puts Pippa Middleton's to shame, the final impression you want to leave your interviewer with is your face, not your buttocks. Of course, backing out of the room appears odd, and so to ensure that your face is the last thing your interviewer sees, when you reach the door, slowly turn, look your interviewer in the eye and smile again (see Figure 14-2). Finally, when you exit the room, leave the door in the same position as it was when you entered.

Figure 14-2:
When leaving a room, turn to ensure that the last image the interviewer has is your friendly face.

People who show that they're similar to the people they want to work with, sharing values, goals, and beliefs, and demonstrating that they can benefit the business, are more likely to gain further interviews and land a job than the person who shows little interest or a lack of initiative.

Using minimal gestures for maximum effect

You see fewer and more precise gestures displayed higher up the business hierarchy. Innocent, inexperienced and insecure people flap their hands, toss their heads, and jiggle their feet, whereas people at the top keep their movements cool and contained; their gestures look precise, concise, and devoid of extraneous activity.

During an interview, keep your gestures clear, simple, and deliberate. When appropriate, mirror the other person's gestures and expressions. (I discuss mirroring in the later section 'Establishing rapport'.) Keep your hands away from your face and mouth and avoid any nervous-looking behaviour such as straightening your tie or fiddling with your hair. Leave alone any items you may nervously toy with, such as a pen or a piece of jewellery. (Check out the later section 'Avoiding nervous gestures' for more details.)

TECHNICAL STUFF

Speak more, move less

Research shows that a direct link exists between people's vocabulary and their status, power and position. The higher up the corporate ladder someone rises, the greater that person's facility with words and phrases. Further research shows a connection between people's control of the spoken language and the number of gestures they use when communicating. People at the top don't need a lot of gestures to get their point across because they have their words. Lower down the pecking order, people rely more on gestures to convey their meaning, perhaps because they haven't acquired the skills or had the training or opportunities to develop their vocabulary.

Creating a Positive Environment

If you want to get ahead at work, you need to treat people with respect. Not everyone you work with is going to be the same as you – thankfully – or even like you (which you may find hard to believe, being the likeable person that you are). But each person brings a unique quality that can contribute to the success of an organisation when steered with sensitivity and compassion.

As well as treating people with respect, aim to establish rapport. When two or more people are reading from the same page and playing with the same goal in mind, miracles can happen. Or at least, deadlines can be met.

Demonstrating respect

Over and over again as I was researching material for this chapter, people told me that what they really wanted at work was to be treated with dignity and respect. When I broke down what they said, the following messages came through:

✔ Treat people with courtesy, kindness, and politeness. Keep your body in an open position – where your weight is evenly distributed and your muscles are relaxed (see Figure 14-3) – to allow a free flow of information, inviting people to feel comfortable in your presence.

Encourage colleagues and staff to express their ideas and opinions. Look them in the eye as they speak, and appear interested. Pay attention to people's facial expressions – are they frowning or smiling, are their lips taut or trembling? Refrain from multi-tasking when someone's speaking: fiddling with your phone and playing with paper, pens, or pencils is rude and potentially distracting. If you don't agree with what you hear, keep your facial expressions and gestures neutral.

✔ Listen to what others have to say before expressing your opinions. Never interrupt or butt in while someone else is speaking. If you struggle not to interrupt, make a conscious effort to keep your mouth closed while others speak. Refrain from clenching your teeth, however, as this causes tension in your mouth, mind, and body. Allow your lips to lie lightly together and your tongue to float gently in your mouth. Make sure that your eyes are open and not burrowed in a frown.

✔ Encourage someone who offers an idea that may improve conditions to implement their idea. Lean forward, smile, look them in the eye, and smile as you speak if you want to let them and others know that you think someone's making sense.

✔ Never insult, bully, or disparage someone or their ideas. Raising your nostrils as if you're smelling something past its prime, pulling up your upper lip, laughing with derision, or physically pushing or punching another person is rude, unproductive, and about as far away from demonstrating respect as a person can get.

✔ Praise more often than you criticise. Encourage a culture of praise and recognition among employees as well as from management. When you praise people, look at them face to face and smile. Doing so may feel uncomfortable at first because many people shy away from giving and receiving praise, but persevere to see the benefits.

✔ Practise giving and receiving praise. When you offer praise, be sure that you believe what you're saying or the person you're praising won't believe you. Like animals, people can pick up on physical vibrations including facial expressions and bodily tension. Nod as you speak in confirmation of what you're saying. Look the other person in the eye. Smile with pleasure as you give and receive the praise.

Treat others as they want to be treated. Maintain an open mind and reflect your attitude in your open body language. Nobody wants to be spoken to in tense tones with tight gestures.

For more about body language in the office, refer to *Persuasion & Influence For Dummies* by Elizabeth Kuhnke (Wiley).

Establishing rapport

When you're in rapport, you feel a harmonious connection between yourself and others. All's right in the world and communication flows. You can find yourself smiling and nodding in agreement as you converse.

The word *rapport* derives from the French word *rapporter,* which translates as 'to return or bring back'. English dictionaries define rapport as 'a sympathetic relationship or understanding'. The result is that people in rapport can create outstanding results.

Figure 14-3:
An open body invites others to enter the space.

When you've rapport with someone, taking on that person's style of behaviour – also called *mirroring and matching* – helps you become highly tuned to the way the other person thinks and experiences the world. Your whole body becomes involved in the observation process. *Mirroring* is a direct replication of the other person's movements while *matching* is more about moving in sync with them. Be attuned to the difference between moving in rhythm with someone and mimicking their actions, though, because people know when you're making fun of them or being insincere.

Mirroring

People who are in rapport tend to reflect one another's physical patterns. They move in time with each other and mirror behaviour that they observe.

Research on rapport indicates that, from an evolutionary perspective, mirroring body language facilitates interaction between people. When you mirror people – whether in the way they speak or move – you're unconsciously reproducing their state of mind within yourself (check out Figure 14-4). The more effectively you can do so, the more able you are to understand the other person's perspective.

Figure 14-4:
Mirroring
body
language
helps build
rapport.

When you're reflecting other people's behaviour back to them, be sure to avoid mimicry. If you recreate muscle movement for muscle movement and replicate exact gestures and expressions with precision, the other person feels mocked and disinclined to engage in a meaningful conversation with you.

Matching

Matching someone's behaviour indicates that you're in sync with one another, experiencing similar feelings and emotions. When you're matching someone's behaviour, you create a similar state to the other person that helps you understand their point of view.

When you match someone, look to match their:

- ✔ Body postures and gestures
- ✔ Breathing rates
- ✔ Rhythm of movement and energy levels
- ✔ Voice tonality including pitch, pace, and volume

Mirroring and matching effectively

People attempting to create rapport through mirroring and matching without attempting to understand and convey the state of the people around them come off like the worst of used-car salesmen. Those best at creating rapport match the *state* of the other person, feeling it within themselves much as the other person does. The goal in matching and mirroring behaviour isn't to replicate the behaviour, but that ability comes naturally when you adopt and replicate the state of the other person you're interacting with. Mirroring and matching the behaviour enhances communication only when the adopted physiology assists in replicating emotional state. For more about creating rapport through mirroring and matching, see *Neuro-Linguistic Programming For Dummies* by Romilla Ready and Kate Burton (Wiley).

Standing tall and holding your ground

Having a superior position carries with it an implied authority. The same goes for tall people: they can command respect because of their height. Others have to look up to them and because of their physiological make-up, they look down on others.

Some people don't feel comfortable being taller than others, so they stoop or slouch (see Figure 14-5). They diminish themselves in size and statue, giving away their authority. Shorter people have to create an image of height and stature. They do so by standing with their centre of gravity deep in their loins while lifting their upper torsos upwards and outwards. Rather than placing their energy in their upper chests – making themselves top heavy – they place their energy in their pelvic area, giving them a sense of firmness and control. Nicholas Sarkozy, Tom Cruise, and Al Pacino, for example, are no taller than 1.7 metres (5 feet 7 inches), and yet with Cruise's bright smile, Sarkozy's purposeful stride, and Pacino's brooding passion, all exude the aura of powerful men.

To experience what being in control feels and looks like, try this short exercise, practising from both the seated and standing positions:

✔ Visualise another person who's challenging you, at an interview, in a meeting or at an assessment.

✔ Place your feet firmly underneath you, hip width apart.

✔ Maintain flexibility in your knees and ankles to avoid becoming stiff.

✔ Keep your head upright and maintain eye contact with the other person.

✔ Let your arms and hands be visible.

✔ Keep your chest open, feeling as if your shoulder blades were gently melting down your back (see the earlier Figure 14-5).

✔ Keep your mouth closed while you're listening.

✔ Inhale from your abdomen. Breathing deeply from your core grounds you and provides a firm foundation from which you can move, gesture and position yourself.

✔ Reflect on what you're going to say before speaking.

✔ Remind yourself of your strengths and how you want to be perceived.

✔ Respond.

Stooped shoulders, caved-in chest and hands in the fig-leaf position (covering your private bits) are protective signals and indicate that you're subconsciously feeling defensive.

Figure 14-5:
The
sloucher
fails to
project
authority.

Cecile stands at just over 1.82 metres (6 feet) tall. As an athlete, she was used to being with people of equal height, and felt comfortable with them. When her sports career ended, she obtained her law degree and joined a city firm. After several months, Cecile noticed that she was hunching her shoulders and sinking into her hips. Her chest caved inward, her head sunk into her neck, and she was looking at people from under her eyes.

As we explored the reasons for this new behaviour, we discovered several issues. Cecile was experiencing a lack of confidence and low self-esteem because she was still finding out about the job. Highly competitive, she was uncomfortable, fearing that she was being perceived as lacking in her work. In addition, the male partner she reported to was shorter than Cecile. She discovered that she was purposely making herself smaller to make him look bigger. With practice, Cecile regained her stature. We explored her mental attitude and made the necessary self-perception adjustments. Her new way of thinking and perceiving herself was reflected in the way she stood and gestured. Now, when Cecile sits and stands using her full stature she feels confident, looks credible, and commands respect.

Moving with purpose

Whether you stride into a room with focus and direction, or wander in as though you've forgotten why you're there, you're going to create an impression. Unless you're purposely playing the role of someone from La-La Land, I suggest that if you want to be noticed in a positive light, put your muscles into your movement and propel yourself into the fray with focus, direction, and positive energy. Other people then perceive you as vibrant, interesting, and engaging.

Before projecting yourself into other people's territory, test the waters. Moderate your movements to mirror those of the people you're with (I discuss mirroring in the earlier section 'Establishing rapport'). If you come bounding into a room full of silent, contemplative folk, you may be perceived as a bit of a buffoon, if not an outright annoyance. Reflect back the energy you observe in the room and adapt your behaviour to match what you notice, still moving with focus and direction.

Positive energy draws people, whereas negative energy repels them. You don't have to bounce like Tigger or Tony the Tiger to demonstrate focus and energy. Slow actions performed with integrity project authority and command attention.

An intentionally deliberate movement draws attention to the action and highlights the meaning behind the gesture.

Matching mood and movements for results

I recently attended two training events led by two different trainers and the contrast was highly informative. At the first one, the trainer bounded into the room like a basket of puppies. Feeling overwhelmed by her exuberance – it was 6 p.m. and I was tired from a long day's work – I struggled to engage with her and left the session feeling disappointed, like I hadn't gained anything.

The second training session took place early in the morning, and again I was tired – this time from a long journey to the venue. Here, the trainer established rapport (check out the earlier section 'Establishing rapport') by matching my mood and movements. Instead of imposing her energy onto me, she allowed me to set the tone until I was ready to become more engaged and energised. By noticing my movements and purposely matching them to enhance our communication and build our relationship, I left the training singing the trainer's praises, having gained a valuable experience while enjoying the process.

Pointing Your Body in the Right Direction

How you position your body in relation to other people impacts upon their perception of you, which is particularly relevant in the work environment. If you stand directly in front of them, face to face, hands on hips, and jaw jutted forward, you become a threatening force. Turn your shoulder to people, cross your arms, and look down your nose at them, and you indicate that you think they aren't up to scratch. Turn your back completely on people and you better pray that they don't stick anything in it as a response to your dismissive attitude!

To create a more positive interaction, stand facing another person at a comfortable distance – with your arms open, your hands visible, and a welcoming expression on your face – and see how constructive the mood becomes. Sit or stand side by side at a distance that feels right for your relationship, and sense the connection. Both consciously and subconsciously you're adjusting your body position in response to what's happening in your environment.

People who sit side by side tend to work in a collaborative way. People sitting across the table from one another are often at odds, relying on the furniture to act as a defensive barrier.

To make a positive impression, hold your head up, keeping your chin parallel to the ground. Let your eyes engage and sparkle. Allow yourself to smile. Free your shoulders and permit your chest to open as if it were a plane about to take off (but don't puff it out, which overeggs the pudding and reveals vulnerability, not strength). Breathe from your abdomen. Ground yourself by connecting with your environment. Imagine roots coming out from the soles of your feet, providing you with a firm foundation. Pretend that you've a deep tap root driving deep from the centre of your sole making you solid and strong. In addition, make believe that you've shallow roots coming out from the soles of your feet, providing you with flexibility.

If someone you're engaging with seems distracted, uninterested, or even annoyed, aim to match that person's movements and energy as a means of creating rapport. When the person feels that you're more connected, you can more easily lead the conversation to where you want it go by making subtle changes to your movements and gestures that are in line with your feelings and attitudes.

Creating a relaxed attitude with the 45- degree angle

The angle at which you position yourself in relation to another person affects the outcome of your communication. If you want your interaction to be comfortable, co-operative, and congenial, place yourself at a 45-degree angle to the other person.

The benefit of sitting at a 45-degree angle to another person is that the position encourages openness and trust. By positioning yourself at this angle, you form a third point where you avoid being perceived as aggressive or flirtatious. Whereas face to face is confrontational, and side by side is intimate, placing yourself halfway between the two creates an atmosphere of confidence and equality. Neither confrontational nor intimate, the 45 degree angle allows people to see one another, gesture freely and maintain a comfortable space between themselves.

The 45-degree angle is a co-operative space that encourages discussion and the flow of ideas: this angle is perceived as a neutral territory. The third angle allows another person to join you in the space, creating an equilateral triangle. If a fourth person enters the group the group can form a square, and if one or two more people join, they can form a circle or divide themselves into two triangles.

Positioning yourself for cooperation

Say that you're the newly appointed head of a well-established and successful team. One by one, you invite your new colleagues into your office for a 'getting acquainted' session. They may feel a little wary of you and watch to see how you manage the meeting. By placing yourself in the neutral 45-degree zone, you encourage openness and honest discussion. No threatening aspect is associated with this position. Turn 10 degrees in either direction and the dynamics change. If you turn inwards, you indicate that intimacy is in the air. If you angle your body away, you shut out the other person.

Sitting with subordinates

When you want to create a relaxed, informal atmosphere when speaking to a subordinate in your office, open the session with both of you sitting in the 45- degree angle position, directing your bodies to a third point forming a triangle, suggesting agreement. From this position you can reflect the other person's gestures, creating a sense of ease and rapport.

If you want a direct answer to a question and you feel that you're not getting it in the 45-degree pose, shift your position to face directly towards the other person. This action says that you want a direct answer to your direct question.

Taking the pressure off

Positioning your body at a 45-degree angle relieves the potential stress of the meeting. When a sensitive issue needs addressing, go for this position. It takes the pressure off and encourages more open answers to your open questions.

Facing directly for serious answers

If someone asks you a direct question, look at the person directly – that is, if you want to be taken seriously. If you drop your head, avert your eyes, and peer over your shoulder, you're conveying that you're unsure, doubtful and perhaps even scared; you've lost your power.

Serious questions require a serious attitude and so you need to reflect that attitude in your pose. When you're asked a direct question, follow these steps (which you can do seated or standing):

1. **Close your mouth.**

2. **Breathe deeply from your lower abdomen.**

3. **Hold your head vertically as if your chin is resting on a calm lake.**

4. **Square your hips and shoulders with your knees.**

5. **Place your knees directly over your ankles, with your feet planted firmly on the ground.**

6. **Open your chest as if a treasured book that you open with tender respect.**

7. **Look the questioner in the eye.**

8. **Pause.**

9. **Answer.**

Emma worked in the HR department of a city law firm. She was ambitious and wanted to progress in her career. She received feedback telling her that her superiors weren't taking her seriously. She was told that, although she was a pleasant person to have around and worked well organising events behind the scenes, as regards working directly with clients, she seemed unorganised, flighty, and unsure of herself.

When Emma came to me, she had an abundance of nervous energy that was creating the image the clients described. She shifted her weight from leg to leg and slouched into her hips. Her shoulders stooped and her hands fidgeted. She tossed her head and frequently giggled. She had difficulty establishing and maintaining eye contact. Her words said that she wanted to progress in her work, but her body language conveyed that she wasn't up to the job. Working with a video camera – positioned so that she was able to see herself – Emma discovered how her gestures and behaviour were impacting upon people's perceptions of her. By adjusting her stance, she stood taller. By controlling her breathing, her actions calmed down. By opening her chest, she filled her space. Her fidgeting lessened and she began to project the image she wanted. Emma's new presence looks, and sounds, confident and credible, and she's now working in the position she sought.

Picking the power seats

As regards seating at work, and without beating around the bush, the message is simple: stay away from seats that make you look small, awkward and insignificant (see Figure 14-6). These seats are the kind where you're forced to look upward, lifting your chin and exposing your neck, which happens to be one of the most vulnerable parts of your body. The person on the other chair is sitting upright and in control. Even if he's leaning back in his chair, he's still in a higher position than you. He can look down on you along the length of his nose. He can lower his glasses, looking over the top at you, all cramped, awkward, and feeling uncomfortable.

The height of the back of the chair

The higher the back of the chair, the higher the status of the person it belongs to. The person with the support behind his back, the protective shield and frame that surrounds him, holds a more powerful position than the person sitting on a stool at his feet. Kings and queens, popes and prime ministers, chief executives and oligarchs sit in chairs that reflect their power and position. The higher the back of the chair and the more luxurious the fabric, the higher the status of the person.

On the reality television show *The Apprentice,* Sir Alan Sugar sits in a black leather chair with a high back. The back of the chair frames his face and gives him authority. The would-be apprentices sit in front of him. The backs of their chairs are lower. Before a word is spoken, the positioning makes clear who holds the authority in the room.

High-status people prefer to sit on high-backed chairs.

Rolling on casters

Chairs on casters have a power and mobility that fixed chairs lack. The person sitting in a chair that swivels has more freedom of movement and can cover more space in a shorter time than someone sitting in a fixed chair. When a person is under pressure, being able to move quickly expels energy and expedites the process.

The person who's sitting in the chair on wheels, with the arm rests and the high, reclining back, tends to be the person in charge.

Gaining height advantage

Height is associated with status and power: the higher you are, the more authority you hold. Savvy business types know that by adjusting the seat height of their chairs they gain a competitive advantage.

If someone invites you to sit in a chair that puts you at eye level with the other person's desk, decline, saying that you prefer to stand.

Placing the chair

When you seat yourself directly across the desk or table from another person, face to face, the atmosphere is immediately confrontational. But place the chair at a 45-degree angle in front of the desk and you create a welcoming environment (flip to the earlier section 'Creating a relaxed attitude with the 45-degree angle' for the advantages of the 45-degree angle). If you want to reduce a visitor's status, arrange for the person to be seated as far away from your desk as possible, into the public zone at least 2.5 metres (8 feet) away from where you're sitting.

Negotiating Styles

When crunch time arrives and you're at the final stage of a work or business negotiation, you want to win, right? The best negotiations result in everyone feeling like a winner. And to feel that you're a winner you have to look, sound and behave like one (in other words, act the part). If you want to know more about how to position yourself when negotiating, persuading and influencing, take a look at *Persuasion & Influence For Dummies* by Elizabeth Kuhnke (Wiley).

Acting the part

The Russian director, Constantine Stanislavski, popularised a style of acting that became known as *method acting,* which requires actors to base their characterisations on the emotional memory process. The actors immerse themselves in their characters' lives, to experience that life as the characters would. Actors draw upon memories and incidents from their own lives and incorporate them into their roles, enriching and enhancing the portrayal. Devotees of method acting include Dustin Hoffman, Jane Fonda, and Robert DeNiro.

In a similar manner, by recalling how you felt and behaved when you negotiated a favourable outcome in your past, and by emulating the behaviours of negotiators you admire, you too can act yourself into the part.

Before you go into any meeting where you want to be seen performing well (interview, negotiation or assessment), find yourself a quiet spot in which you can gather your thoughts in peace. Five minutes is ample. Reflect on how you want to be perceived and visualise yourself behaving in that manner. See and hear yourself performing at your best and experience the feeling. By creating your desired image, you're able to act the part and convince others that you really are like that. Who knows, you may actually be that person.

Claiming your space

When you enter a negotiation, you need to claim your space right from the beginning. If you don't, the competition is going to have you for breakfast. *Claiming your space* means that you're taking responsibility for yourself and your actions, and that you act as though you've got the right to be where you are, doing what you're doing. When you walk into a space and make it your own, you're telling others that this territory's yours and woe betide anyone who tries to take it away from you. Dogs spend much of their time marking out their territory in order to let the rest of the pack know that they've been there and the same applies with people (although I suggest that you mark your territory differently!). Your intention is to let people know that you own this space and you're to be taken seriously.

When you claim your space successfully, you can act as if you belong there. Your gestures appear fluid, your posture's upright and you engage in eye contact with ease. You send out positive signals indicating that you're comfortable and in control.

Getting acquainted with the environment

One way of demonstrating that the space you're in belongs to you is to make contact with an item in the area. Say, for example, that you've been invited to speak at an event attended by many influential people, some of whom you know, others you don't. You want to appear confident and in charge of yourself and your material. To do that, follow these suggestions for getting comfortable in the space and making it your own:

- ✔ Walk into the room where the negotiation is taking place as if you own the space. Move with purpose and authority.

- ✔ Pull your chair out and sit down without waiting to be invited. (Be advised, though, that if you do take this action at a first interview, you may be perceived as forward or rude.)

- ✔ Place your notes and pen in front of you with confidence and authority.

- ✔ Establish eye contact and open the discussion clearly and concisely.

Tracy is a highly qualified and respected lawyer. Practising for her partnership interview, Tracy felt nervous and awkward, as though she didn't belong. She fidgeted with her clothes, avoided eye contact, and played with her jewellery. Her behaviour began shifting as she practised entering the room and taking her seat at the table in front of the imaginary panel. Before Tracy sat, she let her hands rest on the top of the chair's back as if staking her claim to that seat. By making contact with this object, she established a sense of ownership with the room. Her nerves steadied, and she gained an appearance of confidence and credibility.

Choosing a good seat

Arrive at the meeting early enough so that you can pick your spot. Sitting facing the door gives you the upper hand. Research shows that people seated with their backs to the door experience stress, increased blood pressure and shallow, rapid breathing as the body prepares itself for a possible attack from behind. Save this weak and defensive position for your competition.

Filling your space

People who fill their space look more commanding and in control, which can be a challenge for small or slim people, who may appear to be devoured by space. The following tips can help people of smaller stature appear more in command of their territory:

- ✔ Hold your elbows slightly out from your sides when standing or sitting. (People who hold their arms close to their bodies look subservient, timid and fearful.)

- ✔ Lean forward when seated behind a table, letting your hands, elbows, or lower arms rest on the table's surface.

- ✔ Never pull your arms in close by your sides at a meeting; you're reducing your stature and diminishing your influence.

Large people also need to consider the amount of space they fill, because lolling and ambling along, spreading across their space, can be perceived as invasive. You don't need to draw your shoulders and arms in towards yourself. Just be aware that you take up more space than smaller people and that you may need to adjust your position to allow others in.

To avoid overwhelming others with your large presence, contain your gestures, making them concise and precise.

TRY THIS

Try This

Building confidence

To be perceived as confident, you have to demonstrate confident behaviour, which requires that you know what confident behaviour looks, sounds and feels like. To clarify your concept, try the following exercise:

- Ask yourself: 'What's important to me about behaving confidently?'

- Describe some of the gestures, movements, and facial expressions that you believe demonstrate confident behaviour.

- Reflect back on a time when you felt confident. Describe the feeling. What gestures and expressions did you incorporate into your behaviour?

- Think of someone who you believe demonstrates confident behaviour.

- Describe how that person acts, including specific gestures, fluidity of movement, eye contact, and facial expressions.

- Ask what do you currently do that's similar to that person 's behaviour.

- Define how your behaviours differ.

- Identify what you have to do to adjust your behaviour to more closely resemble someone who displays confidence.

- List the benefits of behaving with confidence.

- Practise the gestures, postures and expressions that denote confidence for you and avoid those that don't. In this picture, the woman appears relaxed and at ease, looking quietly confident, whereas the man's his puffed-out chest makes him look defensive rather than quietly confident.

Displaying confidence

The way you stand and sit, your gestures and expressions, the actions you choose and the way you perform them, all reveal who you are and what you're about. Captains of industry, masters of the universe, and doyennes of the theatre instinctively know, and are well trained, in projecting a confident countenance. With eyes clear and focused, posture erect, and facial muscles engaged, they reveal a look of positive expectancy.

Avoiding nervous gestures

People who fidget and fiddle, pick at their fingernails, and scratch their head, face, neck, and/or chest during a negotiation, are displaying nervous gestures and giving the game away. You don't need a microscope to see that such people are in a real state and creating a nervous environment around themselves. Spend too much time with someone who's demonstrating nervous behaviour and you start feeling uncomfortable as well.

You can't avoid gesturing nervously unless you're aware that you do it. Watch yourself on video, ask a trusted colleague for feedback and pay attention to yourself as if you're an outside observer. When you recognise the behaviour, you can do something about it.

Replace a nervous gesture with another action. If you're fiddling with a pen, put it down whenever you're not writing. Let your hands rest on the desk or table in front of you. If you don't have a surface that your hands can lie on, rest them in your lap. If you find yourself picking at your fingernails, swap that action for another, such as taking a quick note then folding your hands in your lap. You can also shift position in your sitting or standing position. When you reposition your body from where you were feeling uncomfortable to a different pose, you can shift your thoughts, feelings, and emotions as well. After you shift your position, settle in. If you're bouncing from pillar to post, you're showing your nervousness.

Changing behaviours takes time, commitment, and practice. In fact, research shows that habits can take anything from 18 to 254 days to form. For example, a relatively simple habit like drinking a cup of hot water and lemon every morning, or going for a 10-minute walk every lunchtime, can take up to 66 days. Changing your habitual behaviours in stressful conditions may take longer.

In today's highly competitive business world, you need simple strategies to provide the extra *oomph* to get you where you want to be. Being good at what you do is no longer enough; you have to be *seen* to be good. Take stock and evaluate what you do well and where you see room for improvement. Consider your behaviour and the impact it makes. When you're aware of these things, you can make the necessary adaptations.

Standing up for meetings

Research shows that when people participate in meetings standing up they speak for a shorter length of time. It encourages quick decision making, and cuts down on time spent socialising. The studies also demonstrate that the perception of people who conduct their meetings while standing is that they've a higher status than the seated people.

Kate attended a marketing meeting at a company in Denmark. In the middle of the room was a tall stone table and the room had no chairs.

The table was at a comfortable height for people to stand at and lean on it, and the room had enough space for them to walk around the table easily. The participants in the meeting were encouraged to mill around the room speaking with one another, and come to the table when a point was being made and a decision required. Kate found the experience liberating, because the thinking in the room was more creative and energising than in meetings where people remained seated.

Opening or closing your fingers

Short, sharp gestures hold more authority than open hands waving in the air (see Figure 14-7). By keeping your fingers closed and your hands below chin level when gesturing, you look confident, in control, and so command attention.

Figure 14-7:
Hands
waving
above your
head makes
you look
flustered.

If you want to appear caring, approachable or subservient, also keep your hands below chin level but gesture with open fingers.

Carrying only what's necessary

Keep your accessories slim and compact. Bulging briefcases indicate that you're the worker bee and not the one making the strategic decisions. They give the impression that, although you may be buzzing away hard, you're not in control of your time.

Accessories are meant to enhance your image. Decide what image you want to project and choose your accessories accordingly. Also, to make a positive impression, invest in good quality accessories.

Watching your buttons

Tightly closed jackets indicate a tightly closed point of view. People who button up their jackets while making decisions indicate that they're closed to the idea put forward. When they fold their arms across their chests with their jackets buttoned, they're displaying real negativity. If you notice one or two people unbuttoning their jackets during a meeting, you can safely assume that they're changing their opinions and opening up to what's going on (see Figure 14-8).

Figure 14-8:
When you unbutton your jacket, you appear open and receptive.

Chapter 15

Crossing the Cultural Divide

- -

In This Chapter

▶ Understanding different cultures

▶ Abiding by status-based conventions

▶ Examining problematic gestures

▶ Playing by the rules to avoid offence

- -

*W*ith businesses spanning the globe, students travelling the world and the media bringing foreign lands into people's homes on a daily basis, no group can any longer believe in the infallibility of its own customs and culture. As the singer/songwriter Paul Simon says, 'One man's ceiling is another man's floor'.

In spite of the 'shrinking' world, or perhaps because of it, cultures are holding onto their customs and traditions with pride and determination. Behaviours as simple as counting on your fingers, walking along the street and shaking hands vary widely across the globe.

But when you know the rules that govern behaviour in cultures other than your own, you can avoid making major mistakes that, in addition to insulting your host, may lead to a diplomatic crisis – or at least an uncomfortable embarrassment.

A huge number of countries, cultures and customs exist in the world and as I have relatively few pages in which to write about them, this chapter can simply give you a taster: a few examples, tips, and techniques to get you started on a safe path while you trek the globe.

I assume that you don't want to make a fool of yourself, insult your host or cause an international calamity simply because you don't know the differences between acceptable and unacceptable behaviour. So when in doubt, ask. Natives are usually more than happy to guide you in the ways of their country and are flattered that you want to behave in a respectful manner. One gesture that you're always safe to use, no matter where you go, is the smile. This gesture is the one truly universal behaviour that's understood by the most sophisticated city person as well as by desert nomads.

Recognising the Different Strokes for Different Folks

As more cultures interact than ever before, knowing the acceptable non-verbal behaviours – and those that are verboten – can help you to make a friend and seal a deal. Although you may not need to become au fait with all the cultural intricacies around the world, discovering the basics – for example, meetings and greetings, handling business cards, managing personal space as well as establishing and maintaining eye contact – sets you up for the next promotion or puts you in the driver's seat as regards building positive relationships with people from races, religions, and creeds different from your own.

Some cultures – such as the Italians – are known for their upfront exuberance while others – including the Japanese – are acknowledged as the keepers of the keys when it comes to revealing emotions. Some encourage openness (such as the Spanish), whereas the English, Scots, and Scandinavians prefer to protect their privacy. Even within the same country, behaviours differ. For example, northern Germans tend to be contained in their expressions and movements whereas their southern cousins tend to demonstrate more freedom in their gestures and mannerisms.

By accepting differences and adapting your behaviour to meet what's expected in cultures dissimilar to yours, you can build respectful relationships and sail smoothly through challenging cross-cultural communication.

Pay attention to how the natives are behaving. Unless people's behaviour goes against your values, emulate their movements and expressions. Treat people's beliefs and customs with respect in order to communicate with honesty and openness as you engage with them.

Positioning yourself and setting boundaries

One problematic convention that differs from country to country and culture to culture is the issue of accepted personal space boundaries. In Latin America, the common and expected behaviour is for people to stand close to each other, whereas in Anglo-Saxon countries people give each other a wider berth. For example, the Spanish and Italians stand close to one another when they're speaking and a casual touch on the arm or shoulder during conversation is the norm. Good friends typically greet one another with a hug or a kiss and seeing people of the same sex walking down the street arm in arm is normal. If you back away when an Italian or Argentine speaks to you, they may think that you're shy and move closer to fill the gap. In complete contrast, Australians require a lot of personal space – if you get closer than an arm's length an Aussie feels hemmed in.

People in Nordic countries are all quite restrained in the way they use their bodies. As opposed to their southern European cousins, who embrace public physicality, northerners shy away from effusive gestures and consider hugging to be taboo.

If you want to avoid embarrassing your Nordic friend or acquaintance, particularly in public, refrain from behaving in an intimate manner. Save your hugs for home.

If you were a fly on the wall in an American manufacturing company, you'd see the plant manager walking around, chatting informally with the staff and factory workers. The manager may be dressed in a suit for a business meeting, or more casually if not. In France, by contrast, the plant manager always wears a suit and begins the day by greeting everyone in the office and in the factory with a handshake. This difference shows the hierarchic style of the French company, whereas the American plant has a flatter management structure.

In many Western cultures, when friends greet each other, you may see them perform the 'air kiss', in which a kiss to the right and left cheeks is directed towards the sky rather than landing on the face.

Like southern Europeans and unlike their Japanese neighbours, the Chinese demonstrate their regard for members of their own sex by publicly holding hands or making other forms of physical contact. Opposite sexes, however, don't engage in public displays of affection.

Getting up close and personal

Whether you kiss, bow, or shake hands when you greet someone and say goodbye, how you do so indicates your culture's attitude toward bodily contact. In some countries – including France, Italy, and Greece – the standard practice is to touch, whereas other cultures – such as New Zealand, Australia, Great Britain, and the United States – view touching as intrusive, if not outright rude.

Islamic countries forbid public touching between the sexes and to break that taboo can lead you to a stern talking to from the authorities, if not a public hiding. On the other hand, same sex couples walking down the street hand in hand or with their arms intertwined or draped over one another's shoulders is normal in Arab countries and implies nothing more than friendship or camaraderie. (Two men walking arm in arm in downtown Dallas may cause a few raised eyebrows whereas in Dubai no one would notice.)

If you've ever travelled to Latin lands, from South America to the Mediterranean, you know that the locals are comfortable with getting up close and personal. Embracing one another with big hugs and pats on the backs while planting kisses on your friends' and family's cheeks is natural and expected behaviour. Even the workplace is filled with bear hugs and mutual kissing in place of a handshake.

In 2009, when Michelle and Barak Obama attended a G20 dinner, Silvio Berlusconi – Italy's rambunctious president – was desperate to embrace the bare-shouldered, elegant woman with toned arms and body. Tapes of the three show Berlusconi pursing his lips, raising his shoulders, and rubbing his fingers while extending his arms in a 'come-to-padre' pose. President Obama keeps a close and steely eye on Berlusconi with taut lips and not a hint of a smile. His right arm, next to Berlusconi, is tense and tight. The First Lady smiles only with her lips while her eyes remain fixed on the Italian president. Her right arm juts forward like a steel rod and her fingers are tight, offering a handshake with no welcoming touch. The message from the Obamas was, 'Don't even think about it!'

No kissing please, we're German

The Knigge Society in Germany, an organisation that advises on etiquette and social behaviour, has called for a ban on kissing in the workplace. The society's chairman, Hans-Michael Klein, is purported to have received emails from workers expressing their concern about this overly familiar practice. His response is to stick to the traditional handshake. Although he admits that banning kissing outright may be impossible, he believes that society should protect people who don't want to be kissed. He suggests that if staff and employees don't mind being kissed at work, they announce their feelings by placing a paper message on their desks. Mr Klein is reported as saying that kissing isn't typical German behaviour and that the habit is imported from countries such as Italy, France, and South America. He indicates that kissing belongs in a specific cultural context and says that he's been told that Germans don't like to kiss while at work.

A survey shows that most German workers feel that kissing contains an erotic aspect and that the gesture is a way for men to get close to a woman. Other issues that the Knigge Society has responded to include the appropriate way to end a relationship via text message and how to deal with a runny nose in public. Interestingly, the Russian custom of men exchanging kisses hasn't got in the way of Germany conducting commercial relations with Russia.

Gearing up your greetings

Greetings can be loaded with landmines: to kiss or not to kiss; to shake hands or to refrain? The following are a few examples of the types of greetings you can expect in different areas around the world:

- **Brazil:** Upon greeting and departure, the custom is to shake hands with everyone present. After you establish a friendship with someone, expect to embrace.

  Brazilian women exchange kisses on alternating cheeks: twice if they're married, three times if they're single. The third kiss is to ensure 'good luck' in finding a spouse.

- **China:** The Chinese are more comfortable greeting another person with a handshake than in many other Far Eastern countries. A slight nod or bow is also a proper form for greetings and departures. Wait for them to initiate the gesture and follow their lead.

  The Chinese don't like being touched by people they don't know. This convention is especially true of older people and individuals in important positions. If in doubt, leave out the double-handed handshake.

- **France:** If you make friends with French people, expect them to kiss your cheeks three times when you say hello and goodbye.

- **The Middle East and the Gulf States:** Males touching upon greeting in the Middle Eastern and the Gulf States is common. Wait for your counterpart to initiate the exchange because several styles of greeting are used.

  When shaking hands, some people don't seem to want to let go, whereas a mere flutter of fingertips is more than adequate for others. The standard Asian handshake between men is more of a handclasp: it lasts between 10–12 seconds and is rather limp. (This long hold contrasts with the North American handshake that lasts approximately 3–4 seconds and is firm.)

  Personal distance between male speakers is close in the Middle East, and so backing away can be interpreted as an insult. Be prepared for more touching and physical contact in conversations. In fact, for Arab men, holding hands is quite common (check out the earlier section 'Getting up close and personal').

  In Saudi Arabia, be prepared to go through an elaborate greeting ritual with another person. Although a westernised Saudi man shakes hands with another man, the customary Saudi greeting between men is a more complicated affair. After saying the traditional 'salaam alaykum', you shake hands and say 'kaif halak'. Then you and your Saudi counterpart put your left hands on the other's right shoulders and kiss one another on each cheek. Finally, your new-found friend takes your hand in his. Unless, of course, you're a woman, in which case no bodily contact is involved at all. (So if you're a woman, don't be offended if a Saudi man doesn't shake your hand.)

> Traditionally, if a veiled Saudi woman is in the company of a Saudi man you don't introduce her. Although westerners may wonder why women hide behind black veils, the ladies in burkas can watch how others behave while revealing little about themselves.

Nadia's father is from Saudi Arabia and her mother is British. Nadia was raised in England, has travelled across the globe and respects the cultural differences between countries. When she's in Paris, London, and Rome, she wears her miniskirts and fashionable shoes with gay abandon. When she's in Delhi, Cairo, and Riyadh, she covers herself. She leaves Heathrow dressed in tight jeans and heels and disembarks in Saudi dressed from top to bottom in a black shroud. Nadia quite enjoys being covered because she can observe how other people are behaving and make decisions about their personal qualities without revealing any of her own.

Acknowledging the no-touching rule

Although in many Far Eastern countries, people greet one another by shaking hands, the Japanese in particular have an aversion to informal bodily contact. Japanese doing business in the West force themselves to shake hands although they may feel uncomfortable doing so. In their own country, the usual form of greeting is a long, low bow from the waist and a formal exchange of business cards.

Although young people are defying the norms of their parents, be aware that throughout the Middle and Far East male-female touching in public meets with disapproval.

Even if you feel awkward bowing to Far Eastern colleagues or customers, seeing it as a sign of subservience, do so anyway if you want to make a favourable impression. What you're saying is that you value their experience and wisdom and respect their culture and customs.

In the Far East, never put your hand or hands in your pockets when you're bowing, greeting someone or saying farewell, or while you're giving a speech. Doing so is considered rude, despite being accepted behaviour in the US and UK.

Cities in Japan are crowded places and sometime you need to push through the throng, as the locals do. To do so, hold your hand in front of your face, with a bent elbow (rather like a child pretending to be a shark or as if preparing a karate chop), while bowing and saying 'excuse me'.

When presenting your business card in the Far East, hold it with both your hands with your details facing towards the other person. When people from the Far East present you with their card, receive it with both hands and study it with respect before looking back smiling at the person who presented it to you and accepting the card with a slight bow.

Whether you're working in the Indian subcontinent, Central Asia or any country throughout the East, avoid slapping your colleagues on the back, playfully punching them on the arm or hugging the breath out of your new best friend. You'll be perceived as rude, disrespectful, and invasive.

Waving farewell

The simple act of waving someone goodbye isn't so simple after all. What you may believe is a straightforward signal saying '*ciao bella*', '*à bientôt*', '*sayonara*', or 'see you later', can be interpreted as an offensive gesture or a sign to return. For example, if you ever make a business presentation in a Latin American country such as Argentina, and you wave goodbye to your audience, be prepared to present again. Your gesture of 'farewell' in fact signals to your audience that you want them to stay.

Most Europeans face their palms front and wag their fingers up and down with their arm stretched forward and held stationary. Americans hold their palms forward with their arms outstretched and wave their hand back and forth from side to side.

Throughout most of Europe, the American wave would be interpreted as 'no', except in Greece where the gesture is highly insulting and you can easily find yourself pleading innocence to the local authorities.

Observing the Conventions of Higher- and Lower-Status Behaviour

The concept of status refers to how important an individual is in society. People with *high social status* are perceived as valuable and dominant and often fulfil leadership roles. *Low social status* people come across as being dispensable in spite of their often playing important supporting roles in society. Across cultures and continents, people of lower status demonstrate deference to the person holding the higher status. Their body language is closed and they take up as little space as possible so to appear non-threatening. People with high status fill the space they occupy. They're confident that they can handle whatever comes their way and aren't afraid of looking threatening. Their body language is relaxed, even in times of tension and panic (see Figure 15-1).

Figure 15-1:
People of
high status
appear
relaxed.

Crouching in defence

The fear-crouch reflex is a universal position with the intention of protecting yourself from harm. Whether you're African, Asian, or Alaskan, when someone shouts at or hits you, you may find yourself wincing in fear or discomfort. Your shoulders rise to protect your ears and your face scrunches up as if to block out the sensation. Your head drops forward to protect your vulnerable throat while your chest and knees fold into your waist to protect your inner organs, turning you into ball of flesh and bones.

How you feel about yourself internally and externally determines how you behave in society. Internal status and the associated behaviour is driven by your sense of self and is affected by your personal sense of worth and confidence; it's independent of external factors. In contrast, external factors including your job, money, and qualifications affect how valuable others perceive you and the status they place upon you.

The most reliable way of determining people's internal status is to observe their non-verbal behaviour while they're interacting with others, particularly when under stress or pressure. Instinctive responses kick in at these times, revealing a person's true self-perception. Someone who remains calm under pressure most likely has a positive internal status. On the other hand, someone who shouts, screams, and runs in panic at the first sign of stress is probably (internally) crying out for protection.

People in low-status positions often demonstrate deference and can also appear defensive and anxious. Around the world, people are taught to show respect to those who are older, wiser, and in positions of authority. Usually, to show respect you put yourself in a lower physical position to the other person, bowing your head and making yourself appear smaller. At other times, you snap to attention and stand upright to show respect.

When the commanding military officer enters a barracks, enlisted soldiers stand up with shoulders back, stomachs in, eyes straight forward, and not even a thought of smiling. When the soldiers are told to stand at ease, they widen their stance and clasp their hands behind their backs. At no time do they engage at a familiar level with their superior. Similarly, school students are taught to rise when an adult enters the classroom and staff members straighten up when the boss strides through the office. In Asian countries, subordinates don't look their superiors in the eye, whereas in western cultures eye contact is the norm. (Check out the later section 'Playing by the local rules: Eye contact' for more on where to look around the world.)

If you want to see clear examples of internal and external status behaviour, watch Downton Abbey, the costume drama television series that portrays the lives of the Crawley family and their servants.

Bowing, kneeling, and curtseying

Bowing, kneeling, curtseying, and lowering the head are low status behaviours. Within royal households, staff bow or curtsey when the monarch passes. By curling up the body and lowering it, you make yourself look small in relation to another person. This behaviour can be traced to the animal kingdom, where creatures under attack cringe and crouch to protect themselves.

Bowing is of particular importance in Japan, where you can tell someone's status in relation to another's by how long and low the person bows. Someone holding a lower status bows lower and longer. If equals are bowing to one another, they match one another's bows. If one of the two people wants to show more respect, she adds an extra bow. The Japanese also add another bow for someone who's much older, as well as for a customer whose business they're hoping to obtain.

When you're bowing to someone who holds a higher rank than you, make sure that you out-bow the person and keep your eyes respectfully lowered. If you're unsure of who holds the higher status, bow slightly less low than the other person. Slide your hands down the front of your legs towards your knees, or down the sides of your legs. Maintain stiffness in your back and neck and avert your eyes.

Standing to attention

Standing with a straight back, legs close together with your weight distributed evenly between them, arms by your sides, and your hands remaining still, is a sign of deference the world over. If you've ever been called into the head teacher's office, stood up in court or served in the military, you know the position. You look straight ahead and don't move a muscle until you're spoken to.

My sister Paula and I were taught from an early age to stand up when an adult entered the room. We were also taught to look the person in the eye, shake hands firmly and say a polite 'hello'. This rule also applied when we were dining out and an adult stopped by the table to say hello. When we became adults, we were permitted to remain seated, although our husbands, sons, and any other men at the table are expected to stand (see Figure 15-2).

Figure 15-2:
Men who stand up when a woman comes to the table are perceived as polite.

Getting Specific: Common Gestures, Multiple Interpretations

Just when you thought you knew the meaning of laughter, the 'thumbs up' sign and giving the 'okay' signal, you find yourself creating the most embarrassing faux pas. All you can plead is ignorance, which is hardly a viable excuse. This section fills you in to keep you out of trouble.

Giving the thumbs up . . . cautiously

The thumbs up sign means different things in different cultures. In North America and Great Britain, the sign means 'good'. The same gesture in the Arab world, Nigeria and parts of South America, however, conveys negative connotations, and in Germany holding up your thumb indicates the numeral one.

If you're travelling in Japan and want to indicate that everything's just great, stick your thumb up in the air with a clenched fist.

Ensuring that the okay sign really is okay

Traveller, beware. North Americans make a circle with their index finger and thumb – with the other fingers slightly raised – to indicate approval, but you're regarded as being vulgar if you make this sign in Brazil. To complicate the issue, when the Japanese make this sign they're signalling money, whereas, for the French, the gesture stands for zero.

Ask your host, or read ahead of time, what the okay sign means in a particular country. In Arab countries, it's a rude sexual gesture. You can't assume that it means the same thing universally. Giving the okay sign can be a blessing or a curse. It may be safest to avoid using the sign at all!

Never give the okay sign in Japan while shaking your fist – it's considered to be an extremely rude gesture.

Laughing your way into (and out of) trouble

When people laugh in the western world, you're safe in assuming that they're happy. If you hear the same laughter – with a slightly different accent – in Asia , don't think that everything's fine. Individuals in the Asian world laugh as a means of controlling their displeasure and also to conceal embarrassment, confusion, and shock. A young Japanese, Vietnamese or Korean woman may reveal her embarrassment by giggling behind her hands, which are held in an upright position, slightly away from her mouth, with the palm towards her face.

Cultures have personalities, like people. Some are open, outgoing, and extrovert. Others are less expressive, and their gestures are fewer, closer to the body, and generally more restrained. Sit in a restaurant in Rome and watch the people laughing, interrupting one another, and touching a lot. Take yourself to Stockholm and experience the difference. People are quiet, more contained in their gestures, and demonstrate less emotion. Both groups are equally friendly and caring; they simply express their feelings and goodwill quite differently.

Laughter is associated with humour. Have you ever watched the same film in two different countries with different national audiences? I remember watching *Four Weddings and a Funeral* in Britain and then in the US. The two audiences laughed at different places. What the British think is funny seems odd to Americans and American humour is often lost on the British. That being said, American sitcoms such as *Friends* and *Two and a Half Men* have a big following in the UK and *Monty Python* and *Fawlty Towers* go down a treat with cosmopolitan Americans. As in these examples, humour can translate across borders, although time can be needed to grasp the subtleties. If you're in a culture different from your own and you're in doubt about what's funny and what's not, observe how the natives respond and follow their lead. You can also ask other people to tell you their experiences of humour in different cultures, too.

Avoiding Problems and not Causing Offence

This section focuses in on an issue that in some ways runs through this whole chapter, which is to help you avoid embarrassments and steer clear of upsetting people in different countries and from different cultures.

A potpourri of local customs

Many conventions and common gestures can prove problematic when travelling. Here are a few to watch out for:

✔ When visiting Asian and Middle Eastern societies, use only your right hand for greeting and eating. The left hand is considered the 'unclean hand' and using it in any greeting is highly insulting and eating with the left hand is considered vulgar.

✔ Muslims consider pointing at anyone or anything rude.

✔ Asians and Arabs consider the feet to be unclean. When visiting Arab and Asian countries, be sure to sit with your feet flat on the floor; showing the soles of your shoes is highly insulting. Never prop your feet up on a piece of furniture such as a desk or a chair, or cross them over your knee.

✔ In Thailand, never step on a doorsill when entering someone's home. Thais believe that friendly spirits live below.

✔ Some Asian cultures, including Thailand and India, consider the head to be a sacred area where the soul resides. To touch the head of a Thai or an Indian, even a child or close friend, risks terminating the relationship.

Smoothing over difficult situations

Different cultures have different ways of dealing with difficult or embarrassing situations. Brazilians, for example, avoid giving bad news and saying no. They may change the subject, stretch the truth or put such a positive spin on the information that you don't notice the negative aspects. They're not trying to deceive or avoid losing face: they simply want to keep things positive and not disappoint.

On a cold winter's day, Caroline, an American living in Tokyo, was travelling in the packed underground during rush hour. No seats were available and in spite of her being pregnant, no one offered her theirs. She was forced to stand, pressed up against the safety glass of the door that divides the trains. Her train companions leant against one another for support rather that holding onto the straps.

With one lurch of the train, the passengers all swayed towards Caroline and pressed against her. Her back went through the safety glass leaving her covered in broken glass. In spite of her condition, people ignored her. When the train came to its station, the passengers piled out of the train as the next group piled in. A few minutes later, a young man who was in the carriage with Caroline when the accident occurred, knocked out the rest of the glass to minimise the danger. Another person moved away to offer her a seat. All these actions took place with no eye contact. Caroline had discovered that she'd inadvertently created a scene and the Japanese, by not overtly paying attention to her, were 'saving her face'. Their lack of emotional reaction was their way of smoothing over an embarrassing situation for Caroline, in spite of the incident being an accident. This behaviour was their way of keeping the situation harmonious without offending her.

If you find yourself in a similar situation to Caroline, follow your personal values and customs. If that means that you'd offer a pregnant woman your seat, do so without making a meal of the gesture. Establish eye contact with the person, smile, stand, and indicate with your hand that your seat is for them. Make no contact with other people in the carriage, as that would cause them to feel uncomfortable and lose face.

Playing by the local rules: Eye contact

In North America and throughout much of Europe, eye contact is a necessary ingredient for demonstrating respect and signalling that you're a powerful business professional. The opposite is true, however, throughout much of Asia, Africa, and Latin America, where eye contact is viewed as being rude, personally challenging or displaying a lack of respect. For example, in Africa, China, and Japan you show respect to your superiors by avoiding eye contact.

As with so many of the issues I discuss in this chapter, though, things can be even more complicated. For instance, in the Middle East eye contact is considered a sign of trust or truthfulness, but Muslims consider eye contact between the sexes as inappropriate (eye contact within your own gender is acceptable).

Wherever you are in the world, as a general rule avoid staring or fixing your gaze on someone, because doing so can often be interpreted as confrontational.

When conversing with someone from the Far East, avoid making eye contact, except for an occasional glance to make sure that they're still present. Then, quickly avert your eyes again.

Certain cultures place a lot of importance on what the eyes convey and so, although often very difficult, always watch for the smallest of eye gestures because they can highlight or undercut the spoken words.

Maria, for example, was working in Japan with a Japanese colleague, preparing a client presentation. She asked him whether he was pleased with the work they'd done together. He told her that, yes, he was. A couple of days later, Maria heard through the grapevine that her colleague wasn't happy with the result and wanted to rework the presentation. When she asked him why he'd told her that it was all right when it wasn't, he replied: 'But I told you with sad eyes, Maria.' Maria left her colleague wondering how she could have spotted his sad eyes when she struggled to see his eyes at all.

In Nordic countries, Germany and Great Britain, eye contact is important for demonstrating sincerity and trust. If you're ever invited to a Scandinavian's home for dinner, be prepared for serious eye contact (see the sidebar 'Toasting the host and each other').

Toasting the host and each other

Inge and Jesper, friends from Denmark, invited us to their home for a long weekend. On Saturday night they hosted a formal dinner party for the four of us and ten other friends. Throughout the meal, toasts were frequently made. Every time our generous and gracious host raised his glass, he looked each guest directly in the eye as we raised our glasses in response. No one failed to engage direct eye-to-eye contact with Inge and Jesper, as well as with the other guests at the table. Fortunately, we only toasted once during the serving of the hot food!

Although the toast details vary throughout the Nordic lands, direct and prolonged eye contact throughout the ritual is required.

I hold round-table discussions in the office for trainees in an international accountancy firm who represent a variety of cultures. Many Asian participants say that looking at a superior or colleague in the eye is difficult because that suggests arrogance and disrespect on the part of the younger person. Because they're working with British and American colleagues, they need to practise establishing and maintain eye contact if they're to be seen as adept in a global business environment. Conversely, when westerners visit a culture where eye contact is restricted, they need to experience how it feels to create a relationship by averting their eyes, usually downward, with clients, superiors, and colleagues.

When you meet and deal with people from other cultures, pay attention and take every opportunity to discover more about how they behave in different situations. Doing so is bound to pay off as your personal relationships blossom and your career develops.

Adapting your style for clear communication

If someone asks me, 'Why do I have to adapt, why can't they?', I hear Aretha Franklin singing 'R-E-S-P-E-C-T, oh, what it means to me!' Many people can't understand why they should adapt their behaviour to communicate successfully with people whose traditions and cultures are different. Take a moment to consider what that thinking leads to. Although business may be competitive, being deliberately disrespectful gets you nowhere; sooner or later you come unstuck. And on the way down, you have to face all the people you offended on the way up! For example, if you refuse to shake hands with a western business woman when she extends hers in greeting, don't be surprised if she doesn't answer your phone calls or respond to your emails.

Remember that what seems strange to you is perfectly normal for someone else. For example, in North America and Europe men and women socialise individually and in groups; friendship between men and women isn't strange or unorthodox. This custom doesn't apply in Muslim countries, however. Men greet other male friends with a handshake, an embrace and by touching one cheek to the other, and when they're among their friends Muslim women's behaviour is warm and affectionate: but never the male and female twain shall meet. The men stick with the men and the women hang out with the women.

You may be effusive in your style, wanting to put your arm around your friend with a big hug when you meet. This behaviour is great in Latin countries, and acceptable in China, too. However, unless you want to embarrass your Nordic buddy, a polite hello suffices. You're not being unfriendly, simply respecting the norms of the culture and making your friend feel good. And isn't that what acting in a friendly manner is all about?

Being friendly means that you respect and conform to the traditions of the other person's culture, and are considerate of how your behaviour may be perceived in a land very different from yours. For more about communicating across cultures, pick up a copy of *Cross-Cultural Selling For Dummies* by Michael Soon Lee and Ralph R Roberts (Wiley).

Chapter 16

Reading the Signs

In This Chapter

▶ Showing that you're interested

▶ Paying attention to all the signals

▶ Recognising different types of gestures

*1*n order to interpret body language accurately, you have to notice it first. If you think this sounds pretty obvious, you're right. And yet some people just don't pay enough attention to how someone else is behaving. Then they're surprised when the person tells them he's unhappy, he's angry, or he's packing up and leaving home. 'But you never told me', is the response. 'If you'd paid attention, you'd have realised', comes the reply.

Noticing how people behave is the first step towards understanding. After that, you can begin to interpret what their behaviour means. Be careful at this point. The experienced observer knows that it takes more than one gesture to convey a message.

Think of body language in the same way as you do the spoken word. If you want to communicate a concept you have to speak several words, or even a few sentences, to express what you mean. Body language works the same way. One gesture doesn't tell the whole story. It takes several actions, working together, to signal a person's feelings, thoughts, and attitudes.

In this chapter, you explore and interpret gesture clusters and see where there may be contradictions between what someone says and how he says it.

Taking an Interest in Other People

When people are wrapped up in themselves, they often don't notice how someone else is behaving. Big mistake. By failing to spot the signs, you edit out valuable information. The way a person behaves can complement, supplement and even supersede what he's saying.

By observing people's body language, you're on the inside track to knowing what's going on between them. Whether you're observing participants in a business meeting, a family negotiation, or watching a couple in a restaurant, by being aware of how the people position and move their bodies, you may end up understanding more about their relationship than they do.

Here's a list of the telltale, mainly facial, expressions for different emotions:

- **Happiness:** Lower eyelids are slightly raised, crinkling around the outer edges of the eyes, eyes sometimes narrow; the corners of the lips move up and out and lips may part to expose upper teeth; cheeks are raised with an apple-like bulge; C-like wrinkles pull up from corners of raised lips to the sides of the nose. The body is open and forward moving.

- **Surprise:** The eyebrows zoom upwards in a curve, wrinkles spread across the forehead; eyes open wide showing their whites; jaw drops; mouth slackens. The head hunches into raised shoulders.

- **Sadness:** Inner ends of the eyebrows rise; eyes appear moist; mouth drops at the corners and the face appears limp; lips may quiver. The shoulders hunch forward; the body is slack.

- **Fear:** Similar to surprise with subtle differences. Raised eyebrows are pulled together (not as much curve in the brow as in surprise). Forehead furrows in centre (when surprised, furrow carries across the brow). Whites of the eyes show; lips are pulled back; mouth is slightly opened. Shoulders are hunched, with a backward movement to the body.

- **Anger:** Eyebrows pulled down and inward; vertical crease between the brows; eyes narrow and take on a hard, staring look. Lips close tightly, and turn down at the corners; nostrils may flare. Hands are clenched, body is forward moving.

Be subtle when watching other people. If they feel they're being scrutinised, they may become antagonistic toward you.

James, a highly respected and acclaimed prize-winning scientist, is quite a bit older than his current wife. At a private dinner party held in his honour, he was invited to speak informally while coffee was being served. Earlier in the day, he had been the guest speaker at a luncheon meeting of colleagues and supporters. At that time, he spoke with reasonable authority and clarity. In public view, his wife looked at him adoringly, laughed at his jokes, and led the applause. By the end of the evening, James was tired. His stories rambled, his words were mumbled, and his jokes fell flat. As he spoke, his wife whispered and giggled with her young, handsome dinner partner, occasionally casting a glance towards her husband and pointing to her watch as if to tell him that it was time for him to wrap it up. When he finally sat down, his wife scowled at him across the table before turning again to the man on her right and resuming their intimate discussion. By the way James's wife behaved throughout the day and evening, it was clear that their relationship was both complex and complicated.

Drawing Conclusions from What You Observe

To read body language signals accurately, you have to consider the combination of gestures, whether they match what the person's saying and the context in which you're seeing them. For example, when someone scratches his nose, that's not necessarily an immediate indication of guilt. He just may have an itchy nose. If, however, his eyes dart about, he's chewing his lip, his legs are crossed, and one arm is tightly folded over his body, you're safe in betting that he's in a negative state.

The following sections explain how to go about drawing thoughtful conclusions.

Looking at the sum total of the gestures

When observing body language, watch for all the behaviours. Making a judgement based on one gesture may lead you down the wrong path. If the sides of a person's lips are lifted up, don't assume he's happy. Look to see what his eyes are doing. If he's got a vertical line running between his brows and is leaning forward, he's showing you that he's interested, not angry.

A smile is not just a smile and a kiss is not just a kiss, no matter what the song says. The sides of the mouth going up while the sides of the eyes pull down gives two meanings. The mouth says happy and the eyes say sad. When in doubt, trust the eyes. (You can find out more about how eyes send messages in Chapter 5.)

If you want to be believed, make sure that your body language accurately reflects what you're saying. People always believe what they see more than what they hear.

Drumming fingers can indicate boredom, but can also indicate anxiety, nervousness and other types of stress. Staring into space with dull eyes says he's bored. Staring into space with engaged eyes tells you that he's listening. Crossed arms across his chest may indicate that he's feeling cold, or that he's adverse to what you're saying. Observe the gestures in context. When in doubt of a person's attitude, look to see how his body's positioned.

If you want to tell a person's mood, look to the following for clues.

Signalling stress

One way of telling when someone is feeling stressed is to observe his face and hands. If he's rubbing his eyes or the bridge of his nose, holding his head, or stroking his neck, you can bet he's feeling under pressure. When you respond in a way that relieves that pressure, he's forever grateful.

Holding and rubbing the head is self-comforting and by shutting the eyes the person is blocking out both internal and external distractions (see Figure 16-1). Even if he tells you that he's just got a headache, he's still dealing with the pressure that comes from the pain.

Signalling boredom

If someone's eyes are dull and drooping and his head is resting in the palm of his hand, you can bet he's suffering a severe case of boredom. To keep himself awake, he may doodle or occasionally shift in his seat.

Figure 16-1:
Self-
comforting
gestures
relieve inner
turmoil.

Morten decided to go to a business conference where a client was making a presentation. After a few minutes of listening to the man's ramblings and mumblings, Morten realised that the client was neither as smart nor as interesting as he'd thought. Sitting towards the front of the hall in the middle of the row, Morten was unable to easily get up and leave. Observing his fellow delegates, he noticed that the majority of them weren't looking at his client and many were leaning backwards, resting their heads in their hands. A few were doodling in their notebooks, not looking up. The speaker's lacklustre presentation was reflected in a feeling of boredom throughout the room.

Showing happiness

Signs of joy can be seen in someone whose torso leans forward, whose arms are outstretched with the palms of his hands exposed, and who sports a wide grin in which his eyes crinkle and his teeth are showing. This is a typical position of a greeting when loved ones return after a long absence.

After leaving school, Nicky's daughter Kiera went on a six-month tour around the world. This was the first time that Kiera had been away from home for such a long time and Nicky could hardly wait to see her return home safely. As Nicky stood in the airport's arrival hall, she noticed parents of other young travellers rushing forward to embrace their children as they came through customs. The longer Nicky waited, the more anxious she became. Finally, Kiera came through the double doors. Nicky couldn't restrain herself and ran forward, arms outstretched, and embraced her daughter, rocking back and forth while holding her tightly, as if she'd never let go. She stroked Kiera's head and kissed her repeatedly as she laughed and cried with relief and happiness.

Dealing with a mismatch between spoken and non-verbal messages

Words convey factual information and gestures convey feelings and attitude. People believe what they see more than what they hear. Say, for example, that you and your partner have had a disagreement. As you both agree that it was a foolish argument and it's time to make up and move on, you notice that your partner is sitting with his arms crossed over his chest, his fists clenched, his legs tightly crossed, his head bent, his mouth turned down at the corners, and a big frown covering his forehead (see Figure 16-2). When you suggest that he may still be harbouring some resentment, anger, or other negative feelings, he scoffs at the suggestion and assures you that you're putting too much emphasis on what you see. Trust your instincts. Here is a case of actions speaking louder than words.

Figure 16-2:
Everything in this person's body language indicates negativity.

Stephen went into his boss's office for his quarterly review. Although Kate, his line manager, said that he was doing a fine job she avoided his gaze during the meeting, focusing instead on the report in front of her and only occasionally lifting her head. At no time did she smile. When she did lift her eyes from her desk, she looked over Stephen's shoulder or at the floor. When her hands weren't folded, her arms crossed over her body and her fingers played around her mouth. Her facial expression was serious. From the way she was presenting herself, Stephen knew that Kate was holding back negative comments. Although her words were supportive, her body language said that she wasn't happy with the job Stephen was doing. He left her office feeling confused and worried.

Think back to a conversation you may have had when you knew that something wasn't quite right. Something about the way the words and the gestures didn't match had indicated to you that the person didn't mean what he was saying. What gestures was the person using? What words was he saying? How were you able to tell that the gestures weren't supporting the spoken message?

Over lunch with her friends, Jacqui was talking about her relationship with her husband, Michael. Although her mouth was formed in a smile and her words were positive, her eyes looked sad. She seemed distracted and kept twisting her wedding ring on and off her finger as she spoke. Several months later, Jacqui told her friends that she was leaving Michael. Remembering how she had behaved at lunch that day, none of them was surprised.

Considering the context

Just because someone sits bent forward with his head tucked into his shoulders, his arms crossed tightly over his chest, and his hands balled up in fists and tucked under his arms, doesn't mean that he's angry. Look at the bigger picture. It may be cold where he's sitting and he just may be trying to keep warm. Or perhaps he ate something that he now wishes he hadn't.

If you want to read body language correctly, you have to take in all the signs.

Dr O'Connor is a tall, handsome, and physically fit man. He gives the appearance of being strong and active. When I first saw him, I was pleased that my mother was in his care. However, when we shook hands I had my doubts. His hand felt limp in mine and I was aware that I was exerting more pressure than he was. Based on that handshake, I began to doubt how committed a man he was. After thinking about it later that day, however, I recalled how gentle his touch was when taking my mother's blood pressure and listening to her heart, and how he lightly rested his hand on my mother's shoulder as he encouraged her to take her medications. Because his hands are vital for his work, he must protect them and use them gently.

Practice Makes Perfect: Improving Your Reading

Wanting to read body language accurately is the first step. Paying attention to the signs is the second. Finally, in order to improve, as in any other endeavour, you have to practise. Give yourself 15 minutes a day to observe other people's gestures and see whether you can make sense of what their bodies are saying. Choose a good place to practise, where lots of people are busy with their own lives. Train stations, airports, and restaurants afford the opportunity to observe people without being obvious.

The New Zealand haka

The Maori haka, an action chant with hand gestures and foot stamping, is traditionally performed by the New Zealand rugby team, the All Blacks, before an international test match. Originally acted out by warriors before battle, the haka proclaimed the soldiers' strength and prowess and served as a verbal challenge to the opposition. The most famous haka 'Ka Mate' tells of the wily ruse that a Maori chief used to outwit his enemies and is interpreted as a celebration of the triumph of life over death.

On August 28, 2005 before a match against South Africa, the All Blacks unexpectedly introduced a new haka, 'Kapa o Pango'. The climax of this new haka is particularly aggressive as each player, staring at the opposing team, performs a throat-slitting action. Answering allegations that the gesture was offensive, the New Zealanders explained that in Maori culture and haka traditions the throat-slitting gesture signifies the drawing of vital energy into the heart and lungs. The All Blacks went on to win the match 31 to 27.

Watch television with the sound turned off. See whether you can figure out what's going on by observing how the people on the screen are interacting. After a few minutes, turn the sound on and check how closely you came to interpreting their attitudes correctly.

Part V
The Part of Tens

"I wouldn't read much into Mona's body language. She actually enjoys meeting new people."

In this part . . .

Every *For Dummies* book has a delicious and dainty group of chapters at the end of the book for you to consume with relish. Here you find ten subtle give-aways to identify whether someone's lying to you, and ten ways of showing that you're interested in someone. I share my overall top 20 body language pointers – 10 tips for reading other people, and 10 tactics for improving your own silent communication skills. *Bon appetit!*

Chapter 17

Ten Ways to Spot Deception

In This Chapter

▶ Watching facial expressions

▶ Looking for body signals

▶ Listening for voice patterns

'Oh, what a tangled web we weave when first we practise to deceive!' The problem with trusting body language as the sole source of information is that human beings are complex creatures. One gesture cannot and does not reveal an entire story any more than a book's message can be contained in one word. Context is key and even forensic professionals can be stumped when it comes to spotting the giveaways. That being said, by carefully watching for those uncontrolled gestures that appear when least expected, you may just be able to detect the deceiver.

Spotting deception is awfully difficult to do. If you know the person, the task can be easier, but not foolproof, because you can compare behaviours between how she acts when telling the truth and when you think she may be pulling the wool over your eyes. So, focus on a wide range of clues. If you think that just one single gesture is going to give the game away, you're just deceiving yourself.

Catching Fleeting Expressions Crossing the Face

If you've ever fibbed, fudged, or fabricated – your secret's safe with me – you may remember how important it is not to reveal yourself. You adjust your behaviour to be the opposite of what you think people are looking for.

What you can't control are those tiny, barely perceptible micro expressions that flit across your face in a nanosecond and die the moment after they've appeared. However, the well-trained observer and the highly intuitive bystander can spot this involuntary process that, like a traitor, betrays what you're thinking and feeling. The minor muscular twitches, the dilation and contraction of the pupils, flushed cheeks, and the slight sweating that occurs when you're under pressure can give away your game.

Watch someone's face carefully if you think she may be deceiving you. While the face may look calm and composed, at some point there comes a moment when the mask falls to reveal the true feelings.

Imagine that you've recently taken up skiing. Someone asks you how you're getting on. You tell her you love it, that after your first week you tackled a black run and even though you wiped out and spent most of the run careering down the mountain flipping between your front and back sides, you're mad about the sport and can't wait to give it another go. While your words say 'Yes!' and you're smiling and laughing as you're telling the story, for the briefest of moments a look of fear crosses your face, immediately replaced by your previous enthusiastic and excited expression. If spotted, that momentary look exposes your terror. It shows that, although you want to convey the impression of loving what you'd been doing, during that fall you feared for your life.

See Chapter 4 for more about facial expressions.

Suppressing Facial Expressions

A composed face, lacking expression, is the one that may be masking emotion. This face is what's known as a 'poker face' and is the easiest and most successful way of concealing what you'd rather not show. Narrowed eyes, a tense forehead, and tightened jaw muscles are other small, subtle signs that an emotion is being suppressed.

Say you're at the funeral of a dear friend. While what you may really want to do is cry uncontrollably, you feel it is inappropriate to expose your emotions so openly. You voluntarily compose your facial expression, replacing your instinct to cry with a tight-lipped pose or even a slight smile as people pay their condolences. The giveaway signs here are that your eyes are filled with sorrow, your forehead is holding tension, and your smile is crooked or the sides of your mouth are turning downwards. Your lips may well tremble as you fight to contain your emotion and deceive others into thinking that you are bearing up well.

You can find out more about masking emotions in Chapter 4.

Eyeing Someone Up

Some deceivers look you straight in the eye while telling a barefaced lie. Others look away. What you, as a lie detector, have to do is look for the intensity of the action and compare the behaviour to what you've noticed in the past. Possible signs of deception include:

✔ **Eye rubbing:** Deceivers often rub their eyes as they're speaking, as if their brain is erasing or blocking out the deception. Men rub their eyes vigorously whereas women use a small, gentle touching action just below the eye.

✔ **Inability to look you in the eye:** Both men and women may also look away, avoiding your gaze. You know this as the familiar shifty-eyed character, where the deceiver can't look you in the eye. You notice that the eyes dart back and forth or fail to connect with yours at all.

If you think someone is telling you a tall story, interject a few simple, uncontroversial questions that you know will elicit honest answers. Check where she's looking. Follow this up with a trickier question. See where the eyes go then. If she has to make up an answer, her eyes go in search of it. If she's telling you the truth, her eyes follow the pattern established when answering the first set of questions.

Look for unusual patterns and over-compensation. If, for example, the deceiver doesn't usually look you in the eye when speaking to you and now can't connect with you enough, you can safely assume that something suspicious is going on.

Turn to Chapter 5 for more about the eyes.

Covering the Source of Deception

Hand-to-face actions provide a basis for spotting deception. People who are holding back their feelings and emotions and who want you to believe something that isn't true, often touch their faces, particularly their mouths. This action stems from their younger days when, as children, they covered their mouths when telling a lie. (Not that you ever did, of course.) With age, that gesture modifies and becomes less obvious.

Adults use the mouth-covering gesture in more subtle ways. If you're having a difficult conversation with someone and notice her resting her chin on her hand with her index finger surreptitiously touching the corner of the mouth while she's speaking, she's possibly giving you a sign that she's holding something back. Several fingers playing across the mouth are another sign of containing information.

People who are trying to deceive you receive subconscious instructions from their brain telling them that the best way to suppress their deceitful words is to cover their mouth. Up go the fingers or closed fist. A single finger over the mouth is like the shh-ing gesture. They're telling themselves to be quiet. They may even put their fingers in their mouths in an unconscious attempt to revert to the childhood security of being at their mother's breast when they're feeling under pressure. Finger in mouth is an outward sign of an inner need for reassurance.

Finally, when someone is holding back information, she quite often suppresses her words with a fake cough or a clearing of the throat.

In Chapter 6, you can discover more about mouth movements.

Touching the Nose

If the mouth cover is the easiest gesture to spot when you think someone may be deceiving you, the second easiest is the nose touch. As the hand comes towards the mouth it is deflected to avoid being obvious. The nose, conveniently close by, serves as a suitable landing point.

When someone lies, it releases chemicals known as catecholamines, triggering the nasal tissues to swell. This is known as the Pinocchio Response because, although the reaction may not be visible to the untrained observer, the nose becomes slightly enlarged with the increased blood pressure. A tingling sensation in the nose develops, resulting in an itch that screams to be scratched. The hand, already in position, vigorously squeezes, rubs, or pulls at the nose, to soothe the sensation.

During his Grand Jury testimony over the Monica Lewinsky affair, President Clinton touched his nose 26 times when answering probing, uncomfortable questions. When asked questions that were easy for him to answer, his hands were nowhere near his face.

The nose touch is an overworked deceit action, so if you're ever in the position of having to be duplicitous, find yourself another gesture.

Faking a Smile

The smile is the easiest facial gesture to produce and is therefore the one most often used when someone is being deceptive. A smile is disarming. It makes other people feel positive and less suspicious.

But there's something about a fake smile that causes warning signals to flash. Whereas a genuine smile involves many facial muscles, including the ones that crinkle the eyes as well as those that pull up the corners of the mouth, counterfeit smiles are different. Firstly, they are confined to the lower half of the face. The teeth may show but the eyes remain unresponsive.

Secondly, the timing of a fake grin is an indicator. Someone assuming a phoney smile puts it on hastily and holds it longer than its genuine counterpart. While the artificial smile swiftly disappears, the genuine smile evolves slowly and fades gradually.

Finally, a real smile is usually symmetrical with both sides of the mouth raising. A deceptive smile is asymmetrical, appearing more pronounced on one side of the face than the other and giving a lopsided effect. Look for a smile where the mouth corners turn down. People find it hard to make the corners rise if they're feeling sad or depressed.

Refer to Chapter 6 for more details about spotting smiles.

Minimising Hand Gestures

A valuable means of spotting deception is the way people use their hands, because most people are unaware of how they use them. When you're excited, you may wave and flap your hands about without being aware of exactly what you're doing. Unconsciously, when you're being deceptive – surely not – you sense that your hands can give you away so you suppress them. You may tuck them into your armpits, shove them in your pockets (where they can nervously jingle and jangle your keys and coins), or even sit on them. When all that fails, one hand may hold the other in a tight clasp. Whatever you choose to do with your hands, your observer is on alert. You may also see the hand shrug, in which the palms of the hands face upwards, signifying helplessness. The hands disclaim any responsibility for what the mouth is saying.

A man who is being deceptive tends to keep his hands still. He keeps to a minimum, if not completely contains, actions that would normally be used to emphasise a statement, drive home a point, or underscore an idea.

Conversely, when a woman is being deceptive she tends to use her hands more than usual. She keeps them busy, as if deflecting attention from what's really happening.

You can find out more about hand gestures in Chapter 9.

Maximising Body Touches

In their unease, deceivers stroke their bodies in an effort to provide comfort and reassurance. They also touch certain parts of their bodies as if to block out information or prevent it from escaping. Excessive chin stroking, lip licking and pressing, eyebrow scratching, and hair grooming when taken in context are potential giveaway signs that something is amiss:

- ✔ **The ear fiddle:** This person tugs at her earlobe, rubs the back of her ear, and may even shove her index finger deep within the ear canal as she seeks the comfort of bodily contact.

- ✔ **The collar tug or neck scratch:** When someone's holding back information, she often tugs at her collar or scratches her neck. This action is in response to the tingling sensation in the delicate neck tissues that is caused by increased blood pressure. When a person's being deceptive and senses that you know it, her blood pressure increases causing a slight sweat to form on the neck. An irresistible urge to relieve the sensation causes the person to pull at her collar or stroke her neck. The neck scratch, in which the index finger may rub the neck up to five times, signals distrust and reservation.

- ✔ **The nose rub:** Several quick rubs below the nose or one quick almost imperceptible nose touch can also signal that someone's being deceitful. Like all possible signs of deception, however, you must be careful when interpreting the nose touch. The person may just need to give it a quick wipe for hygienic reasons.

- ✔ **Crossed arms and legs:** These are further signs of holding back an attitude or emotion. As always with body language, in order to obtain as clear a reading as possible, read the signs in context to avoid misinterpreting the message.

You can find out more how your feet and legs give the game away in Chapter 10, and Chapter 8 looks in detail at arm movements.

Shifting Positions and Fidgeting Feet

Feet shuffle, toes twitch, and legs cross and uncross when someone's being deceptive. That person avoids bodily contact with another person, preferring to keep her distance. While she may wriggle and squiggle, her actions appear stilted rather than animated.

Signs of deception are most prevalent in the lower part of the body. Legs and feet are farthest away from the brain so they're under the least amount of mental control. Therefore, they reveal vital signs that the deceiver may not even know that she's sending.

When a person is being deceitful, you may notice an increased number and more frequent slight changes in body posture, as if the body is saying, 'Get me out of here!' These non-verbal leakages show that an inner/outer conflict is going on that's making the deceiver uncomfortable.

A flapping foot, a jabbing toe, and repetitive foot jiggling alone or in combination with squeezed or shifting legs, reveal the conflict between what's being said and what's being felt.

See Chapter 11 for more about how inner turmoil reveals itself in body language.

Changing Speech Patterns

People don't think of speech itself as body language, but the *way* you speak *is*. How you say something can tell the observer more about your feelings and attitude than the words you utter. Someone observing you watches for the pattern of the speech and how that fits with the words you choose to say.

People who are purposely misleading you tend to say less, speak more slowly, and make more speech errors. They may be likely to take longer pauses before replying to a question, and hesitate more during their replies. They're inclined to quickly fill in any potentially awkward gaps in conversation.

Another giveaway area is the tone of a deceiver's voice, which is likely to be higher than usual in register, with a lift at the ends of sentences. (To learn more about how the voice reveals what's going on inside have a look at *Persuasion & Influence For Dummies* by Elizabeth Kuhnke (Wiley).)

Chapter 18

Ten Ways to Reveal Your Attractiveness

. . . .

In This Chapter

▶ Showing that you care

▶ Demonstrating openness

▶ Being yourself at your best

. . . .

*B*eauty is in the eye of the beholder and attractiveness takes many forms. Some people like fair hair, others prefer brown. Although you may favour a well-defined body, your best friend may fancy one that's soft and cuddly. Whatever your preference, the truth is that you don't have to be a Hollywood starlet or the next George Clooney to be attractive. What most people find appealing is openness and someone who takes an interest in them.

'But why should I bother?' you may ask yourself. Because people who are perceived as attractive are also considered to have other positive attributes. Numerous studies show that people think of attractive individuals as likely to be talented, warm and responsive, kind, sensitive, interesting, poised, sociable, and outgoing. And if that's not enough reason, attractive people are also perceived as more intelligent and happier. Whether this is true or not doesn't matter. If that's how you're perceived, why would you want to argue the point?

Although physique and appearance are contributing factors in determining your attractiveness, a person overlooks a less-than-perfect face or physique if the body language is appealing.

Using Eye Contact

Think about the time someone gave you his full attention when you were speaking. Chances are that he looked you in the eye, kept his body still, and offered you encouragement to express your thoughts and feelings. His attention was focused on you. Establishing and maintaining eye contact with other people shows that you're interested in them. And if you show interest in other people, they're going to be attracted to you.

When you look at someone, make sure that your eyes reflect your curiosity for who that person is. Refrain from frowning, squinting, or avoiding eye contact all together, unless you want to make him feel as if he's being judged or simply ignored. And scrunching up your face gives you lines and wrinkles long before they're due.

By paying attention and demonstrating care, you make the other person feel important. Anyone who makes another person feel significant and worthwhile is automatically perceived as attractive.

Refer to Chapter 5 for more info about the eyes.

Showing Liveliness in Your Face

Smile and the world smiles with you, cry and you cry alone. At least, that's what my grandfather told me. A natural, genuine smile, where both the eyes and the mouth are engaged, is appealing. People want to be with someone who makes them feel good. Frowning, pouting, and a generally miserable face are definite turn-offs.

A face that shows liveliness, interest, and enjoyment is like a magnet. It draws people to you and makes them want to be in your company. By smiling, you can directly influence how other people feel about you. You can control their reaction to you by the look on your face. By making judicious use of your facial expressions, you can guide people into responding positively to you and to perceiving you as an attractive person. This is not to say that you should walk around with an artificial grin plastered to your face; that's a definite turn off.

You can find out more about facial expressions and mouth movements in Chapter 6.

Offering Encouragement

By nodding, tilting, and cocking your head in another person's direction, you show that you're listening and are interested in what he's saying. And anyone who shows interest is consistently perceived as attractive.

Nodding encourages the person to continue speaking and shows that you care. Tilting your head to one side also shows that you're involved and paying attention. Appealing minor head gestures, showing concern, fascination, or involvement in someone's story, make you seem connected and empathetic. And who doesn't find those characteristics attractive and appealing?

You can read more about head positions in Chapter 3.

Using Open Gestures

Open gestures welcome people and invite them to come into your territory. By showing that you are attentive, comfortable, and at ease with people, you make yourself appear warm and approachable. And warm and approachable equals attractive.

If your tendency is to cross your arms over your chest or to shove your hands into your pockets, resist the temptation and open your arms, showing the palms of your hands instead. Barrier signals keep people away and make you look cold, distant, and uninviting. Open gestures encourage others to enter your environment and demonstrate that you accept and appreciate who they are.

Turn to Chapters 8 and 9 for more about open gestures.

Showing Interest Through Your Posture

Upright, erect posture is infinitely more appealing than a slumped, unresponsive physique. That's not to say that you have to be rigid and stiff. On the contrary, you want your body to be flexible and alert to draw people to you and make them comfortable in your presence.

When you're seated in an informal situation, lean backwards and adopt an asymmetrical position. Have a go at resting one arm over the back of the chair. Try other positions. Open, relaxed postures are more inviting and attractive than having both arms squeezed tightly by your sides. They take less effort, too.

If you want to show interest, lean slightly forward using a symmetrical posture. This balanced position shows that you're focused on the other person and paying attention to him. If you act as if you're curious about that person and care about him, he's automatically going to be drawn to you.

In Chapter 7, you can discover more about the power of posture.

Positioning Yourself

Attractive people respect others. They take into account another person's point of view and show consideration for the other person's feelings. They seem to have an innate understanding of what makes someone feel good and what causes offence. They know when to be close and personal, and when to back off.

Respecting someone's personal space is an attractive quality. In a work or social context, when you choose to position yourself next to another person you're telling him that you value him and are interested in what he has to say. Attractive people don't purposely embarrass someone else and never intentionally invade someone's territory. They position themselves close enough without being so close as to cause embarrassment.

If you want to reveal your attractiveness, respect the other person's space. If you sit or stand near the person you're engaging with and look at him directly, he feels confident and comfortable in your company.

You can find out more about positioning yourself in various spaces in Chapter 12.

Touching to Connect

Attractive people aren't afraid to make physical contact. They know the powerful effect an appropriate touch can have. Touching can be used to encourage, to express affection or compassion and to show support.

An attractive person demonstrates respect when touching someone else. Your attractiveness quota rises if you intentionally touch another person in these situations:

- ✔ When you're listening to someone's problems or concerns, touching the other person indicates that you care and are offering support.
- ✔ When you're persuading someone to your point of view, your touch serves as a bridge connecting the other person to your position.
- ✔ When you're giving information or advice, your touch conveys encouragement and co-operation.

Only touch another person if you have a relationship that permits deliberate physical contact. Touching implies that a bond exists between the people involved. Observe the kind of contact people feel comfortable with before initiating contact. If in doubt about how your touch is going to be received, best not do it.

Lookin' good

Attractive people take pride in their appearance. They know what clothes look good on them and which ones they should give to the charity shops. You don't have to spend copious amounts of money to make yourself attractive. Start by being clean and well groomed. See that your hair is washed and styled to suit you. Are your fingernails clean and trimmed? Do you visit the dentist regularly? Are your clothes and shoes in good repair? How you present yourself reflects how you feel about yourself. If you don't take the time and effort to present yourself at your best, don't expect to be seen as an attractive individual.

If in doubt about what colours and shapes suit you best, treat yourself to a session with a personal stylist who can guide you when your friends, family, and your own personal taste take you down the wrong path.

If you're physically out of shape, do something about it now. Life's short. Not only are you going to look better, you're going to feel better as well. You don't have to join an expensive gym or health club, although if that works for you, do it. You don't have to invest in lots of fancy kit to do stomach crunches, though a good pair of running shoes is vital if you're heading off for a jog. What you do need to do is find what works for you, commit to a plan, and stick with it. Fat and flabby isn't healthy or attractive.

Being on Time

The most attractive people are those who demonstrate respect and care for others. Although you may not think that how you manage your time has anything to do with body language, time management is an integral aspect of non-verbal communication, which is why I've included it here.

If you've ever been kept waiting, whether for an appointment, a date, or even a response to an email, you know how annoying it is. Keeping to schedule and being punctual is more than a demonstration of good manners; doing so is a reflection of your core values. It demonstrates how you feel about and treat other people.

In some cultures, such as India and Saudi Arabia, being kept waiting would not be an issue. It is even expected. But in western culture, we're obsessed with time. (See Chapter 15 for more information about time in different cultures.)

If you're habitually late, consider the impact of your behaviour. Don't be surprised if people consider you to be a bit of a flake, if not rude and selfish. Although you may think that arriving at a dinner party 'fashionably late' is appealing, the host whose soufflé depends on precise timing won't be thrilled.

Synchronising Your Gestures

For successful communication to take place, your actions and gestures in face-to-face encounters with others need to be synchronised. Watch people as they speak and you see how their bodies move in a rhythmic pattern, whether their heads are nodding or their hands are gesturing. Then observe yourself. Notice how, even if you seem to be perfectly still, you're moving in time with the speaker's rhythm. Your eyeblinks or head nods synchronise with the words you're listening to. These subtle body movements, echoing those of the speaker, show that you're paying attention.

When you're speaking and you want to prevent someone from interrupting you, keep your hand slightly raised as you end your sentences. Then, when you're willing to let someone else speak you have several options of handing over the air space. When you've finished your sentence you can pause, look steadily at the other person, or conclude a hand movement that was accompanying your speech. By using these signals you're demonstrating the attractive quality of sharing conversation, rather than keeping it all for yourself.

Balancing Your Non-Verbal Aspects of Speech

Attractive people know how to adjust their voices to suit the environment. They control volume, pitch, and tone to the requirements of the situation. They choose language that is appropriate for the circumstances and speak clearly, confidently, and with commitment. In addition, the most attractive people give their full attention as others express themselves.

Because attractive people also like to share their opinions and tend to talk more, being able to balance listening and speaking is vital.

Behaving with confidence, moving with purpose, and demonstrating that you comfortably abide by the rules of whatever environment you find yourself in, are sure signs that you're an attractive person whose company others seek. (You can read more about non-verbal aspects of speech in *Persuasion & Influence For Dummies* by Elizabeth Kuhnke (Wiley).)

Chapter 19

Ten Ways to Find Out About Someone Without Asking

. . . .

In This Chapter

▶ Observing the signs

▶ Reflecting on the meaning

. . . .

So, you've seen someone who's caught your eye. Although she's interesting enough to investigate, you don't want to pump your friends for information at this stage. What do you do? Pay attention.

You have two eyes, two ears, and one mouth. Use them in that order and you may discover what qualities this person possesses that floats your boat or rings your bells, without you giving your game away.

Observing Eye Movements

Do they flash? Do they flicker? Are they dull and dreary? Turn to the eyes, the gateway to the soul, as your first point of reference.

No matter how much your mouth churns out information, your eyes reveal more. Eyes that turn downwards like Antonio Banderas's give the impression that the person is authoritative and caring. Women swoon at Banderas's combination of soulful eyes and strong physique. They also quiver at the new James Bond, Daniel Craig, he of the steely blue eyes and climbing-frame figure, and swoon at Hollywood heart throb, Ryan Gosling. What are those men's eyes saying?

Queen Elizabeth II seldom gives her emotions a public viewing, and quite rightly, too. Even though she shows a down-to-earth kindness in her eyes, they're covered by a gauze curtain to keep her feelings concealed from her public. Long live the Queen!

Princess Diana, on the other hand, drew her public in with her soulful eyes, averted looks, and vulnerable appearance. She was naturally skilled at creating empathy and captured the world's compassion by the tilt of her head and her upward gaze. Women today still copy this helpless and submissive pose that triggers nurturing reactions in most people if they're paying attention.

Both Samantha Cameron and Michelle Obama have direct eye gaze which makes them look confident, credible, and in control. Both women project an image of being comfortable with who they are, and are able to make other people feel comfortable in their company.

If the person in your sights returns your gaze with lowered eyelids, raised eyebrows, and slightly parted lips, she's showing you that she's interested in you and wants to take this further. How you choose to respond to that message is up to you.

For more on how to read eyes, head to Chapter 5.

Looking at Facial Expressions

By looking at the position of the mouth, the movement in the lips and what the nose is doing, you can quickly spot another person's happiness or pain, anger or despair, or just plain boredom. The most successful people in the public eye manipulate their facial expressions in order to elicit desired responses. They know what to show and when to show it.

The saying goes that behind every successful man is a strong woman. The best wives of accomplished men have a way of looking at their husband that raises his stature in the eyes of others. Their gaze is unwavering, full of attention, awe, and adoration. Former actress and second wife of President Ronald Regan, Nancy Reagan, was expert at influencing public opinion by the looks she showered upon her man. Like a love-struck teenager, she would gaze upon him with Bambi-like devotion. Her public displays of affection sent the message that Ronnie was a terrific guy.

At President Gerald Ford's funeral, his widow Betty, a highly respected and accomplished woman in her own right, showed the world how to behave with dignity and grace during times of loss, sadness, and public scrutiny. She didn't display a great outpouring of grief. At least, not openly. Television permitted you to see her lips quiver, her eyes moisten, and her occasional faltering step throughout the mourning period. You only had to look at her face to absorb both her pain and her fortitude.

Chapter 4 has details on the range of emotions that faces display.

Watching for Head Movements

Observe someone nodding in agreement, understanding or with the desire to add her point of view to the speaker's. The eyes look engaged, the head is held upright, and her face is mobile. Slow nods tell you that she's following the speaker, and fast nodding indicates a desire to jump into the conversation. A shake of the head tells you she's not buying the speaker's opinion.

Cocked, canted, and tilted heads tell you the other person's

✔ Thinking about what's going on

✔ Contemplating a retort

✔ Responding submissively

When you register head movements in combination with other gestures, such as lip and eye actions, you're better equipped to determine a person's attitude and its underlying message.

Head to Chapter 3 for more on head movements.

Noticing Hand and Arm Gestures

Look at a person's hands for revealing gestures. If the fingers are tapping and the nails bitten, you can be sure she's filled with nervous anxiety. Someone flapping her hands like Prissy in *Gone With the Wind* is, well, in a flap!

When someone's hand goes to her mouth, you're safe in betting that she's holding back some kind of feeling, emotion, or attitude. And when her lips are firmly sealed, she's keeping her thoughts to herself.

Anyone rubbing her hands and licking her lips at the same time is feeling happy and excited, as long as the speed's up tempo. If the hand and lip rub is slow and deliberate, be careful. This person may be dreaming up a scheme, calculating her chances, or devising a strategy that benefits herself – and not you.

Arms crossed against the chest, hands tucked into the armpits, or a lowered head and furrowed brow are not signs of a warm and welcoming person. Of course, she may just be reacting to a cold blast of air. Opened arms, a dropped-jaw smile, and an eyebrow flash conveys a sense of pleasure and excitement, whereas a pointed finger wagging in your face belongs to someone who's aggressive, controlling, and domineering. You may want to stay out of that person's way.

For more on hand and arm gestures, go to Chapters 8 and 9.

Observing Posture

An upright stance, with legs parallel and feet under knees, knees under hips, and hips under shoulders, marks out the strong and powerful individual. If her chest is thrust forward, with chin jutting out, and the jaw clenched, beware. She may have moved into aggressive territory.

Slumped shoulders, hands protecting the privates, and a downcast eye all indicate that the person's depressed or despondent. In a woman, crossed ankles and hands neatly folded in her lap suggest a prim and proper attitude, whereas men who sit with their legs splayed, their arms stretched across the back of their chair, and their chests pumped out, are showing how manly they are.

You can read more about posture in Chapter 7.

Considering Proximity and Orientation

Does a person get up close and personal when she's not been invited? Does she turn her back when you approach? You can tell a lot about a person's nature, attitude, and culture by the amount of space she places between the two of you, as well as how she positions her body in relation to yours.

If someone is feeling co-operative and helpful, she sits next to you. If she's feeling competitive, she sits across from you. If she really doesn't get on with you, she turns away.

Look at where a single person places herself in public places. Someone sitting with her back to the other people is clearly indicating that she wants no engagement with anyone, thank you very much. Although facing other people head on may indicate a fearless attitude, it can be a bit overwhelming for both the person assuming the position as well as other people. The person who sits at an angle is indicating that she is open to speaking with another person if the opportunity comes along.

Those with a sense of high status remain seated while others stand. People with a low sense of status hang back by the door when entering someone's office. Someone who believes she's of equal status with a colleague sits next to that person's desk.

Go to Chapter 10 for more information on the messages you send through positioning yourself in relation to others.

Paying Attention to Touching

Favourable judgement is most often given to the person who is able comfortably to touch someone else. Granted, Anglo-Saxons have more difficulty embracing the gesture, because their culture is one that refrains from touching. That small point aside, the people you see touching are the ones who are

- ✔ Offering information or advice
- ✔ Giving a command
- ✔ Making a request
- ✔ Persuading another person
- ✔ At a party
- ✔ Conveying enthusiasm
- ✔ Listening to another person's troubles
- ✔ In a dominant role

When another person touches you, that person is implying that a bond exists between the two of you. Unless, of course, that person's a politician, in which case you can figure that she just wants your vote.

Go to Chapter 9 for more on messages conveyed through touch.

Responding to Appearance

With some exceptions allowed for, the first impression you get of people comes through what you observe about their physical appearance. You may start by noticing their clothes. Clothes, as a reflection of the wearer, send out messages for others to interpret. They're a sign of what the person wearing them is like. If the person you're analysing wears clean, well-fitting clothes, has had a recent hair cut, and brushes twice a day, you're looking at someone who has a sense of personal pride.

And what about fitness? Whatever the investment in clothing and accessories, without a fit body reflecting an active mind, a person has trouble convincing an observer that no confidence issues exist that aren't being addressed. To find out more about how confidence is reflected in the way you present yourself, take a look at *Building Self-Confidence For Dummies* by Kate Burton and Brinley Platts (Wiley).

People who want to present themselves at the top of their game pay attention to their outward appearance. They know the impact the visual message has on people's opinion of them.

Go to Chapter 11 for more on how personal appearance can influence others' perceptions of you.

Checking Timing and Synchronisation

A skilful communicator knows the impact that time has on perceptions and relationships. Others may struggle with time and use it ineffectively, adversely affecting their ability to communicate.

In western culture, people place great importance on time. They value pace, punctuality, and a pre-determined schedule. The person who acts by this code is viewed positively. Europeans and North Americans find the concepts of tardiness, slowness, and unstructured time difficult to grasp, much less view in a positive light. If you want to keep your mother-in-law happy, show up on time.

In India, Saudi Arabia, and other far- and middle-eastern cultures, people have a more relaxed approach towards time. In these countries, keeping people waiting for appointments and allowing interruptions during meetings is common. Doing so is not intended to be rude. Time is considered to be flexible and schedules are simply loose guidelines to work around.

When you're interacting comfortably with another person and have established a good rapport, you may find that your body movements match one another's. Your gestures and actions harmonise while you both subconsciously copy or reflect the other person's actions. Your movements are co-ordinated, or synchronised. Like two dancers, you're both moving to the same rhythm. Imagine the ensuing chaos if your movements were waltz-like while the person you're interacting with moved in time to the jitterbug. Figuratively speaking, you'd be bumping into and tripping over one another and your communication would suffer.

If you pay attention to the other person and match your body movements, your communication is going to be more effective. So, if you want to keep your father-in-law happy, get your body in sync with his. By nodding at his jokes, smiling at his stories, and recognising by the cant of his head that cocktail hour has begun, your body reflects and responds to the signals he's sending out. And that is going to make him feel good.

After listening to a long-winded conversation, the person who wants to make a point moves quite conspicuously when she thinks the speaker is about to come to a conclusion. Her body rhythm differs from the speaker's, indicating that she now wants to speak.

Scrutinising Non-verbal Aspects of Speech

Because we take meaning from the way a message is delivered as well as from the words themselves, you do better to pay attention to the non-verbal aspects of speech. The volume, the pitch, the pace, and the tone of a person's voice can give you a pretty good idea of someone's mood and attitude. Add in accent, rate, and emphasis and the picture becomes clearer.

You can usually tell a person's mood by the way she uses her voice. If the voice is low in volume, sombre in tone, slow in speed, and lacking in emphasis, you can figure that she's feeling sad or depressed. If the pitch is high, the pace quick, and the words tumble out of her mouth, chances are that she's in a state of excitement.

If a person lifts the pitch at the ends of her sentences and is neither asking a question nor Australian, you may be right in thinking she's feeling a bit insecure or uncertain about what she's saying.

Nervousness and deception, characterised by stuttering, stammering, or adding 'ums', 'ers', and 'ahs', indicate that someone's not clear about what she wants to say. Polished performers eliminate those space fillers and count on the pause to provide authority and indicate confidence.

Anyone who can make you laugh has got to be okay, right? Laughter is infectious. It makes you feel good. Laughter lifts the spirits and as long as you laugh with, rather than at, another person, the results are positive and beneficial.

Finally, the person who wants to demonstrate that she has higher status than another, aims to have the last word on a subject.

Chapter 20

Ten Ways to Improve Your Silent Communication

. . . .

In This Chapter

▶ Deciding how you want to be perceived

▶ Being willing to adapt

. . . .

*I*f you've ever stood in awe of someone who's comfortable asking for what he wants, dresses in a way that you admire, and leaves people feeling good about themselves, now's your chance to discover the secrets. Actually, they're not such big secrets. It's more a matter of attitude. If you're aware of your current behaviour and are willing to do what you have to do to get the results you want, you're well on your way to achieving them.

Taking an Interest

The best communicators take an interest in other people. They can empathise with you, and just by looking at you, know how you're feeling. Think about those people whose company you thoroughly enjoy. I'm willing to bet – and I'm not a betting woman – that the ones whose company you seek out are the ones who make you feel good about yourself.

If you think that you're a good communicator but for some odd reason no one's seeking out your company, perhaps the problem is that you're so busy focusing on yourself and your interests that you're failing to notice other people, what they're saying, and how they're behaving.

 I once described another person as 'boring'. The friend I was speaking to admonished me by suggesting that if I think someone is 'boring' I should think about that person for five minutes, and if I still think he's boring I should think about him for another five minutes, and continue to do so until I find something about that person that I find interesting. He also suggested that

I may want to consider my own behaviour. Was I acting in a way that brought out the best in the other person? Was I demonstrating an interest in the person, or was I focusing only on myself and my own interests?

Knowing What You Want to Express

A clearly formulated thought, simply expressed and without apology, makes life so much easier for both the speaker and the listener. Instead of umming, erring, or ahhing, the expert communicator leaves those space fillers to the people who are afraid to state their beliefs and hesitant about saying what they feel.

Before speaking, whether stating an opinion or asking a question, have your thoughts clearly formulated in your mind. If you're speaking as you're thinking about what you want to say, you may have to make several attempts before you get your words out the way you want them to be heard. By then, your listeners and observers may have departed.

Modelling Excellence

Every so often you meet someone who has the knack for communicating in such a way that keeps you hanging onto his every word and makes you long to be in his company. That's the person whose behaviour you want to model.

Observing other people gives you the chance to see what works and what doesn't. If someone uses body language that's inclusive and encompassing, and open and welcoming, you're going to feel comfortable in his company. If someone presents himself in such a way that commands your attention and elicits your respect, you sit up and take notice.

Deciding what you consider to be excellent behaviour requires that you establish your standards. Review your current behaviour and acknowledge where you may have some blind spots. Concede that some of your behaviour may put people off. By recognising what you do well and where there's room for improvement, you give yourself a foundation to build on. By following the examples of people whose behaviour produces the kind of results you aspire to, you have, in effect, a template to follow.

Mirroring Others

By mirroring, or reflecting the behaviour of another person, you can create a natural rapport that leads to effective communication. Mirroring the behaviour of another person tells him that what he's doing is acceptable in the context of your interaction. Mirroring demonstrates that you're willing to echo what you're observing in order to create an environment where both you and the other person can communicate freely and comfortably.

Once you have matched the other person's behaviour, you can then take the lead yourself and get him to mirror yours. For tips and techniques for effective mirroring techniques, head to Chapter 1. I also recommend *Neuro-linguistic Programming For Dummies* by Romilla Ready and Kate Burton (Wiley).

Practising Gestures

Some people struggle when it comes to using appropriate gestures to express themselves effectively. Smiling, opening their arms, and standing upright just doesn't sit comfortably with them. One person I know, who's a thoroughly pleasant fellow, habitually frowns, making him look angry and out of sorts. He wasn't aware that he had this habit until someone pointed it out to him. His genuine interest in other people means that he really concentrates on what they do and say, causing his brow to furrow. He thought he was showing interest. Other people thought he was showing disapproval.

If you want to project a specific image or attitude, you may need to practise the appropriate gestures until they become a natural part of your behavioural repertoire. It may feel uncomfortable at first, as any new habit does, but the more you practise the more at ease you feel and the gestures become second nature. As Cary Grant once said, 'I pretended to be somebody until I became that person'.

Developing Timing and Synchronisation

How people relate to time is central to who they are. In western cultures people are obsessed with time and place a high value on punctuality and keeping to a pre-determined schedule. They consider keeping another person waiting to be rude and hostile.

If you want to impress others in a time-sensitive culture, fill your time with meetings, appointments, and activities. Moving and working at a fast pace earns you more respect than if you move at a slower tempo. Slowness is equated to laziness, although someone who takes a more measured approach towards time may actually accomplish more than those people who dash about, often accomplishing little or nothing. (See Chapter 15 for more about the impact of culture on time.)

One way that you can improve your use of time is to anticipate what's coming next. Before completing one task, think about what may follow and plan your approach. This anticipatory scanning technique is particularly useful for anyone working with the public, such as waiters and airline personnel. A skilled employee anticipates the customers' needs in advance by identifying cues and specific signals, and responds to them before being asked.

Sometimes you feel good and can communicate with ease and enthusiasm. At other times, all you want to do is turn out the lights and pull the covers over your head. The body's natural time rhythms influence these moods. When the rhythms become disrupted, as happens when you're suffering from jet lag or too many late nights, you may find yourself making mistakes and behaving irrationally. Go get yourself a good night's sleep and see how you do in the morning.

If you want to show that you're paying attention to a person who's speaking, synchronise your body movements with his. It has been argued that by having your gestures echo those of others, a rhythmic pattern is produced that enhances communication.

Dressing the Part

Glad rags, jeans, or a pinstriped suit? What's it to be? It depends on how you want to be perceived and the impression you want to make. The way you dress sends out messages about you. Observe how your friends, clients, and colleagues present themselves and adapt your style to meet theirs.

The key is knowing what's expected and what's acceptable. If you work for a traditional organisation where a suit and tie for men and jackets and skirts or trousers for women are the norm, you're tempting fate to show up in tracksuit trousers and a hoodie. To do so makes other people uncomfortable. They would also question your judgement.

Sure, you want to be comfortable and dress in a way that reflects who you are. You also want to be appropriate. You really do. Your clothes needn't be expensive. They do need to be clean, in good repair, and suited to your shape and style. They need to represent you at your best and make the people you're with feel comfortable.

Acting the Way You Want to Be Perceived

First, you decide how you want to be perceived. Then, you behave in a way that creates that impression.

You may never have thought about the way you act, thinking that how you behave is just fine. And it probably is, most of the time. Just remember, if you want to be perceived in a certain way you have to give some thought to your behaviour. If you want people to think that you're the life and soul of the party you smile, laugh, and make an effort to put other people at their ease. If you want to be taken seriously, your actions need to be more contained, and your facial expression more sober. The trick is to determine how you want people to perceive you, and after that, to take on the behaviour of that kind of person.

Demonstrating Awareness

Some people just don't get it. They seem to be blind to their own behaviour and the impact it has on others. If you pay attention to the reactions of other people, you develop an awareness of what works when and where.

You may say that what other people think about you doesn't matter. And in many ways you're right. Yet at particular times someone's opinion of you can matter very much. By knowing how certain people respond to specific behaviours, you can adapt your style to meet theirs thus creating an environment that's conducive to successful communication.

In addition to focusing on your own behaviour, observe how other people behave. By paying attention to how someone else is conducting himself, you can respond in a way that makes that person feel noticed and valued. And if you make someone feel that he matters, you're going to matter very much to him.

Asking for Feedback

It doesn't hurt, well, not too much, to ask how people perceive you. If their response matches your vision of yourself, all's well. If, however, they tell you one thing and you thought you were projecting something else, you may want to spend some time re-evaluating your perceptions.

When you ask for feedback, be specific. Otherwise you leave the door open for all kinds of information to come flooding through, some of which may not be pertinent or helpful. By getting honest reactions to your behaviour, you can continue what's working well and adjust what's not, in order to assure that you communicate accurately and that your actions support your message.

Make sure that you're open and receptive to the feedback you get and that you listen attentively. If you don't, the person responding may get exasperated and walk away, leaving you none the wiser. If you don't understand, ask for clarification. Respect and acknowledge the other person's point of view. This doesn't mean that you have to agree with what he's saying, just that you value and allow him his observations. Finally, thank him for his opinions. After all, you asked for them.

If you're giving feedback, make sure that you're clear about what the other person wants feedback on. Comment on observable facts and avoid making assumptions about personality or motives.

Index

• *Numerics* •

45-degree angle
  in business situations, 277–278
  in interviews, 267

• *A* •

absorbed actions, 44
accessories. *See also* smoking
  clothing, 213–215
  eye glasses, 204–207
  inner turmoil shown through interaction
    with, 202–203
  jewellery, 213
  makeup, 211–212
  men's, 214–215
  mental state reflected through, 201–204
  necessities, only carrying, 287
  pausing for thought, using accessories
    while, 203–204
  playing with, 202
  women's, 213–214
actors. *See also* celebrities
  creation of a character, 34
  non-verbal gestures, use of, 46
  relationship with, television causing
    people to think they have a, 224
adaptors, 42–43, 182
Adoboli, Kweku (rogue trader), 106
advertisements, 258
affective displays, 41
aggression, displaying, 51–52
agreement and encouragement
  eyebrow flashing, 100
  head gestures, 56–58
  with nodding, 56–58
  offering, 326–327
  understanding, showing, 57
air punch, 170

America
  management style, 291
  okay sign, 301
  thumbs up sign, 300
  waving farewell, 295
amplifier, 136
anger
  aggression, displaying, 51–52
  deep breathing to combat, 80
  facial expressions, 79–80
  reading, 308
animals
  attention, head tilt when paying, 82
  bonobos, studying gestures in, 39
  chimpanzees and body language, 38, 39
ankles, locking, 197
anticipation of movements, 32–33
anxiety, 105–106
appearance
  of attractive people, 329
  observing someone secretly, 335–336
The Apprentice (television show), 280
approachable, in interviews showing that
    you are, 266
Arab countries. *See* Middle East
Argentina
  personal space, 291
  waving farewell, 295
arm gestures. *See also* touching
  cold shoulder, 146
  crossed-arm position
    clenched fists and crossed arms, 142
    deception indicated by, 322
    gripped crossed arms, 142
    overview, 140–142
    thumbs up and crossed arms, 142–143
  defensive barriers, 139–146
  fig leaf, 144, 145
  friendliness and honesty, conveying, 146
  half-hugs, 144
  hugging/stroking yourself, 144

arm gestures *(continued)*
  observing secretly, 334
  public personalities, arm gestures used
      by, 147
  self-touching movements, 144
arrogance, demonstrating, 50–51
Asian cultures
  eye contact, 304
  laughing, 301
  local customs, 301
assertiveness, demonstrating, 51
asymmetrical positioning, 238–239
attention and interest
  communicating, 339–340
  courting behaviour, 242–250
  eye signals, showing, 85–88
  facial expressions demonstrating, 82
  head gestures, displaying, 58–61
attitude
  posture used to change, 130–131
  stance used to show, 185–186
attraction
  eye contact, showing attraction by, 94
  eye signals indicating, 87–88
  sideways glance, 95–96
attractive people
  appearance, taking pride in, 329
  encouragement, offering, 326–327
  eye contact, using, 325–326
  liveliness in face, showing, 326
  non-verbal aspects of speech, 330
  open gestures, using, 327
  overview, 325
  personal space of others, respecting, 328
  positioning of, 328
  posture, showing interest through your,
      327
  punctuality of, 329
  sexual appeal of, 243
  smiling, 326
  synchronising gestures, 330
  touching to connect, 328
Australians, 291
authority and power. *See also* dominance;
      status
  aggression, displaying, 51–52
  arrogance, demonstrating, 50–51
  beckoning with your head, 55
  business situations, 273–275

defiance, tossing your head in, 55
disapproval, showing, 52–53
eye glasses as prop for, 205–206
gripping hands, 173
head gestures, 49–55
horizontal positioning, 234–235
intimidation, catapult gesture used for, 54
rejection, conveying, 53
space invader handshake, 180
steeple gesture, 172
straddle stance, 187–189
superiority, signalling, 50
touching someone on the head, 55
vertical positioning, 235–238
vocabulary as indicator of status/power/
      position, 269
availability, showing, 250–258
avoiding eye contact, 90, 93–97

• *B* •

babies' eyes, 86, 100
bad mood, getting out of a, 123
Banderas, Antonio (actor), 331
Basic Instinct (film), 256
Beckham, David (footballer), 260
Beckham, Victoria (singer), 25, 225, 260
beckoning with your head, 55
behaviour. *See also* courting behaviour
  demonstrating awareness of, 343
  feedback on, asking for, 344
bent blade stance, 193
Berlusconi, Silvio (President of Italy), 292
Birdwhistell, Ray (anthropologist),
      33, 40, 127, 172
Blair, Tony (Prime Minister), 147
blind person, holding their hands in
      position of gesture you would make to
      communicate more effectively to, 16
blinking
  average number of times people blink per
      minute, 98
  less frequently than normal, 99
  longer than usual, 98
  more often than normal, 98–99
blushing, 29–30
body, in deception maximising touching,
      322

body language
first seven seconds of meeting someone, image projected during, 11–12
gesturing
to illustrate what you are saying, 15–16
to reinforce your message, 16–18
improving your, 339–344
overview, 10
physically supporting the spoken word, 16–18
revealing thoughts, attitudes and beliefs, 18–21
substituting behaviour for spoken word, 13–14
unconscious transmission of messages, 12–13
Bonaparte, Napoleon (French military and political leader), 23
bonding. *See* rapport
bone cruncher handshake, 176
bonobos, studying gestures in, 39
bore, controlling a, 92
boredom
head gestures showing, 63–64
reading, 310–311
Bow, Clara (actor), 252
bowing, 294–295, 297–298
Brazil
difficult situations, handling, 302
greetings and farewells, 293
okay sign, 301
breaking or avoiding eye contact, 90, 93–97
Brown, Gordon (Prime Minister), 184
Building Confidence For Dummies (Burton and Platts), 131, 336
Bulwer, John
Chirologia: or the Natural Language of the Hand, 12
burnout, signs of, 63
Burns, George (comedian), 210
Burton, Kate
Building Confidence For Dummies, 131, 336
Neuro-linguistic Programming For Dummies, 87, 131, 273, 341
Bush, George W. (U.S. president), 58
business situations. *See also* interviews; meetings
authority, projecting, 273–275
eye signals in, 92

facing directly to display serious attitude, 278–279
45-degree angle used to create a relaxed atmosphere, 277–278
movement, using purposeful, 275
negotiating styles, 281–287
positioning your body for, 276–281
positive environment, creating a, 269–276
rapport, establishing, 270–273
respect, demonstrating, 269–270
buttons on jacket, opening/closing, 287
buttress stance, 190–192

• C •

Cable, Daniel M. (professor), 237
Calero, Henry (researcher), 197, 204
Cameron, David (Prime Minister), 147
Cameron, Samantha (Spouse of Prime Minister), 214, 332
Casino Royale (film), 189
catapult gesture, 54
catecholamines, 320
Cattrall, Kim (actor), 101
celebrities. *See also* actors
preening gestures, 192
red carpet walk of, 249
sunglasses, 206–207
chairs
on casters, 280–281
choosing, 279–281
height of, 280, 281
placing, 281
Chaplin, Charlie (actor), 46
character, posture revealing, 126–127
Charles, Prince of Wales, 28, 147
chewing on lips, 105–106
chimpanzees, 38, 39
chin stroking, 65
China. *See also* Asian cultures
affection, displaying, 291
greetings and farewells, 293
Chirologia: or the Natural Language of the Hand (Bulwer), 12
Churchill, Winston (Prime Minister), 40, 210
cigar smokers, 210

claiming your space
environment, acquainting yourself with
the, 282–283
filling your space, 283
overview, 282
seat, choosing your, 283
cleaning eye glasses, 204–205
Cleaver, Eldridge (Black Panthers leader),
188
Clegg, Nick (Deputy Prime Minister), 171
clenched hands
and crossed arms, 142
fig leaf, 167
in front of face, 166, 167
in mid position, 166
overview, 166
Clinton, Bill (U.S. president), 71–72,
87, 261, 320
Clinton, Hillary Rodham (U.S. Secretary of
State), 184, 214, 261
close intimate space, 221
closed palm, finger-pointed gesture,
162–163
closed-lip grin, 115–116
clothing
adjusting, 202
buttons on jacket, opening/closing, 287
and communication, 342–343
courting behaviour, 249
men's, 214–215
overview, 213
women's, 213–214
cocking your head, 60
codpiece, 188, 257
cold shoulder, 146, 228
collar, tugging, 322
combative position, 231–232
'come hither' look, 87–88
comfort
cradling head for, 62
personal space revealing, 227–228
Common Sense At Work, 63
communication
behaviour
demonstrating awareness of, 343
feedback on, asking for, 344
clothing and, 342–343
excellent communication behaviour,
modelling, 340

improving, 339–344
interest in others, showing an, 339–340
mirroring others, 341
perceived, acting how you want to be, 343
posture aiding, 131–135
practicing gestures, 341
synchronising gestures, 342
thoughts, clearly expressing your, 340
timing, developing, 341–342
conclusions drawn when reading body
language, 309–313
confidence
building, 284
in negotiations displaying, 284–285
confrontation, avoiding, 94
constricted pupils, 84, 86, 88
contact lenses, 207
contempt, 78–79
context, 39, 313
conversation
dominance in, 90
eye contact in, 90
eye glasses as prop for controlling, 206
cool, eye glasses as prop for appearing,
206–207
cooperative positioning, 230–231, 278
courting behaviour
attracting attention, 242–250
availability, showing, 250–258
clothing, 249
eye contact, 245
facial expressions, 250
gender differences, 246–250
matching, 259
men's gestures, 256–258
preening, 245
pupils, dilated, 258
smiling, 245
space, filling, 248–249
stages of, 245–246
talking, 245–246
together, displaying signs you belong,
259–261
touching, 246
walking, wiggling, and swaggering,
247–248
women's gestures, 250–256
cradling head for comfort, 62
Craig, Daniel (actor), 89, 189, 331

Cross-Cultural Selling For Dummies (Lee and Roberts), 305

crossed-arm position
  clenched fists and crossed arms, 142
  deception indicated by, 322
  gripped crossed arms, 142
  overview, 140–142
  thumbs up and crossed arms, 142–143

crossing your legs, 45

crouching in defence, 296

Cruise, Tom (actor), 273

Cruz, Penelope (actor), 101

crying, 30

cufflinks, fiddling with, 147

cultural differences
  adapting to, 301–305
  affective displays, 41
  bowing, kneeling, and curtseying, 297–298
  crossing your legs, 45
  difficult situations, handling, 302
  eye contact, 85, 302–304
  greetings and farewells, 291–294
  high status behaviour, 295–298
  humor, 301
  illustrators, 41
  laughing, 300–301
  low status behaviour, 295–298
  okay sign, 300
  overview, 36, 289–290
  personal space, 290–291
  positioning, 290–291
  punctuality, 329
  respecting, 301–305
  standing to attention, 298–299
  thumbs up sign, 299–300
  universal gestures and, 299–301

Curtis, Tony (actor), 247

curtseying, 297–298

cuticles, biting, 202

cylindrical objects, fondling, 253–254

• *D* •

Dalgiesh, Tim (clinical psychologist), 107

Darwin, Charles
  The Expression of the Emotions in Man and Animals, 12, 38
  naturalist, 61, 115

De Boulogne, Guillaume (neurophysiologist), 76

deception
  arms, crossing, 322
  blinking more often than normal, 99
  body, maximising touching, 322
  collar, tugging, 322
  ears, fiddling with, 322
  emotions, masking, 318
  eyes revealing, 319
  facial expressions, suppressing, 318
  feet, fidgeting, 323
  hand gestures, minimising, 321–322
  legs, crossing, 322
  micro facial expressions, catching, 317–318
  mouth-covering gesture, 319–320
  neck, scratching, 322
  nose
    rubbing, 322
    touching, 320
  position, shifting, 323
  smile, faking a, 321
  speech pattern, changing, 323
  spotting, 317–323

deep breathing to combat anger, 80

defensive barriers
  arm gestures, 139–146
  cold shoulder, 146
  crossed-arm position
    clenched fists and crossed arms, 142
    gripped crossed arms, 142
    overview, 140–142
    thumbs up and crossed arms, 142–143
  placing objects in front of yourself, 144–145

defiance, tossing your head in head gestures, 55

diagonal position (seating arrangements), 232

Diana, Princess of Wales, 23, 97, 113, 332

difficult situations, handling, 302

dilated pupils, 84, 86

dipping and ducking head, 61

dipping eyes, 97

disapproval, displaying, 52–53

discomfort, revealing, 227–228

discovering actions for yourself, 44

disgust and contempt, 78–79

displacement activities
  drumming your fingers, 182
  fiddling with objects, 182, 202
  fingernails, biting, 184, 202
  hand gestures
    hand to cheek, 183
    hand to chin, 184
    hand to nose, 182–183
  overview, 27–28, 181
displeasure, 88
dominance
  in conversation, 90
  eye contact, 89–91
  in reprimands, 90
  in touching, 151–152
  unflinching stare, 91
double chop, 171
double-handed handshake,
    149, 150, 178–179
Douglas, Michael (actor), 126
downward facing palm, 161–162
drop-jaw smile, 113–115
drumming fingers, 182
Duchess of Cambridge, 259
ducking head, 61
Duke of Cambridge, 259

• E •

ears, fiddling with, 322
Eastwood, Clint (actor), 89
Edward IV (King of England), 188
Edward VII (King of England), 210
Eibl-Eibesfeldt, Irenaus (scientist), 43
Ekman, Paul (professor), 13, 40, 76, 199
elevating yourself, 236–238
emblems, 40–41
emotions
  deception, revealing, 318
  facial expressions masking, 73–74
  hiding emotions by wearing dark
    glasses, 86
  intensity of emotion shown through
    posture, 124–126, 134
encouragement and agreement
  eyebrow flashing, 100
  head gestures, 56–58
  with nodding, 56–58

offering, 326–327
  understanding, showing, 57
energy, displacing your. *See* displacement
    activities
entrance, making, 266
entwining your legs, 194
environment, acquainting yourself with
    the, 282–283
equality in seating arrangements, creating,
    232–234
ethology, 12
Europeans, 295. *See also specific countries*
evaluating your own posture, 122–123
Evil Eye, 91
excellent communication behaviour,
    modelling, 340
exiting interviews, 267–268
*The Expression of the Emotions in Man and
    Animals* (Darwin), 12, 38
eye contact
  attractive people using, 325–326
  avoiding, 90, 93–97
  breaking, 93–97
  in conversation, 90
  courting behaviour, 245
  cultural differences, 85, 302–304
  displeasure, showing, 88
  dominance, showing, 89–91
  overview, 83–85
  rapport, building, 86–87
  in reprimands, 90
  unflinching stare, 91
eye glasses
  cleaning, 204–205
  conversation, eye glasses as prop for
    controlling, 206
  cool, eye glasses as prop for appearing,
    206–207
  frameless, 207
  at office, 207
  power and authority, eye glasses as prop
    for, 205–206
  resistance, eye glasses as prop for
    showing, 206
  stalling for time, eye glasses as prop for,
    204–205
  women's, 207
eye rubbing, 319

eye signals
  attraction, indicating, 87–88
  blinking, 98–99
  in business situations
    bore, controlling a, 92
    overview, 92
    power lift, 92–93
  'come hither' look, 87–88
  deception, revealing, 319
  dipping, 97
  eye shuttle, 94–95
  flashing eyes, 101
  flicking eyes, 101
  fluttering eyes, 101
  held gaze, 83–93
  inability to look you in the eye, 319
  interest, showing, 85–88
  overview, 83
  sideways glance, 95–96
  widening your eyes, 100–101
  winking, 97–98
eyebrows, flashing, 99–100

• *F* •

Facial Action Coding System (FACS), 13
facial expressions
  anger, 79–80
  courting behaviour, 250
  deception indicated by, 318
  disgust and contempt, 78–79
  emotions, masking, 73–74
  fear, 81–82
  hang-dog, 73
  happiness, 75–77
  interest, demonstrating, 82
  liveliness in face, showing, 326
  micro facial expressions, catching,
    317–318
  mixed messages, 69–72
  observing secretly, 332–333
  posture revealing intensity of emotion
    shown through, 134
  reading, 308
  sadness, 77–78
  surprise, 80–81
  verbal message and, 69–72
  when words are inappropriate, 67–69
facial nerve (cranial nerve VII), 68

facing directly to display serious attitude,
    278–279
fake gestures, 25–26
Far East. *See also specific countries*
  eye contact, 303
  no-touching rule, 294–295
fast head shake, 53
fear
  eyebrow flashing, 100
  facial expressions, 81–82
  reading, 308
fear-crouch reflex, 296
feet. *See also* stance
  deception indicated by, 323
  fidgeting, 196, 323
  jiggling, 203
  knotted ankles, 197–198
  overview, 195
  pointing toward desired place, 195–196
  twitching, flicking, or going in circles,
    198–199
  walking styles, 199–200
fiddling with objects, 182, 202
fig leaf, 144, 145, 167
filling your space, 283
fingernails, biting, 184, 202
fingers
  air punch, 170
  double chop, 171
  drumming, 182
  energy, displacing your, 181–184
  the finger, 40
  gripping hands, wrists, and arms, 173
  hair, running fingers through, 202
  jab, 163
  nervous gestures, 286–287
  opening or closing, 286–287
  overview, 167–168
  power chop, 171
  power grip, 170–171
  precision grip, 168–169
  scissors, 171
  steeple gesture, 172
  thumbs, gesturing with, 173–174
  wag, 163
firm handshake, 181
first impressions, 264–268
first move made by women, 244

first seven seconds of meeting someone, image projected during, 11–12
flashing eyebrows, 99–100
flashing eyes, 101
flicking eyes, 101
flirting. *See* courting behaviour
fluttering eyes, 101
folded hands, 165
Ford, Betty (First Lady of the United States), 332–333
Ford, Harrison (actor), 113
45-degree angle
  in business situations, 277–278
  in interviews, 267
frameless eye glasses, 207
France
  greetings and farewells, 291, 293
  management style, 291
  okay sign, 301
Freud, Sigmund (father of psychoanalysis), 210
friendliness and honesty, conveying, 146
Friesen, W. V.
  Facial Action Coding System, 13
  professor, 40, 76, 199
front of face, clenched hands in, 166, 167
full-blown grin, 116

• G •

gender differences. *See also* men; women
  courting behaviour, 246–250
  touching, 151
Germany
  kissing, 292
  thumbs up sign, 300
gestures
  displacement, 27–28
  fake, 25–26
  to illustrate what you are saying, 15–16
  interviews, using gestures for maximum effect in, 268–269
  learned
    absorbed actions, 44
    described, 44
    discovering actions for yourself, 44
    refined actions, 45–46
    trained actions, 44–45

micro, 26–27
overview, 21
practicing, 341
to reinforce your message, 16–18
signature, 23–25
spoken language evolved from, 38–39
unintentional, 21–23
universal
  blushing, 29–30
  crying, 30
  described, 28
  shrugging, 30–31
  smiling, 28–29
Ghost (film), 253
Gone with the Wind (film), 60
Gosling, Ryan (actor), 331
Grant, Cary (actor), 34
Grant, Hugh (actor), 25, 113
Greece, 291, 295
Greenwood, Ramon (career counsellor), 63
greetings and farewells, 291–294
gripped crossed arms, 142
gripping hands, wrists, and arms, 173
Gross, James (researcher), 107
group's power, seating position affecting dynamics of, 233
guarding your personal space, 226–227
Gulf States, greetings and farewells in, 293

• H •

hair
  flicking, 250
  running fingers through, 202
half-hugs, 144
Hall, Edward T.
  anthropologist, 32, 221
  Hidden Dimension, 221
hand gestures. *See also* fingers; handshakes
  clenched hands
    fig leaf, 167
    in front of face, 166, 167
    in mid position, 166
    overview, 166
  closed palm, finger-pointed, 162–163
  deception indicated by, 321–322
  double-handed handshake, 149, 150
  downward facing palm, 161–162

folded hands, 165
hand to cheek, 183
hand to chin, 184
hand to nose, 182–183
hiding your hands, 164
holding hands, 260
minimising, 321–322
mouth, covering, 319–320
observing secretly, 333
open palm
  connection, making a, 158–161
  honesty, showing, 158, 159
  overview, 158
overview, 157–158
resting your head in your hand, 63, 65
rubbing palms together, 164–165
saluting, 160
Hand Salute, 160
handbag, 147, 254–255
handshakes
  bone cruncher, 176
  double-hander, 178–179
  firm shake, 181
  initiating, 175
  interviews, 266–267
  the leach, 179
  left side advantage, 181
  overview, 174
  personality and, 176–181
  power shake, 177–178
  space invader, 180
  wet fish, 176–177
hang-dog facial expression, 73
Hanks, Tom (actor), 127
happiness, 75–77, 308, 311
head gestures
  aggression, displaying, 51–52
  agreement and encouragement, showing, 56–58
  arrogance, demonstrating, 50–51
  assertiveness, demonstrating, 51
  attention and interest, displaying, 58–61
  beckoning with your head, 55
  boredom, showing, 63–64
  canting, 251
  chin stroking, 65
  cocking your head, 60
  cradling head for comfort, 62

  defiance, tossing your head in, 55
  dipping, 61, 252
  disapproval, displaying, 52–53
  ducking, 61
  encouragement, offering, 326–327
  hand, resting your head in your, 63, 65
  head clasp, 63
  for intimidation, 54
  micro nodding, 57–58
  nodding, 56–58
  observing secretly, 333
  for power and authority, 49–55
  rejection, conveying, 53
  shaking head, 53
  sitting tête à tête, 60–61
  submissiveness or worry, indicating, 61–63
  superiority, signalling, 50
  thought, showing, 64–65
  tilting (canting) your head, 58–60
  touching someone on the head, 55
Hecht, Marvin (professor), 112
held gaze, 83–93
Henry VIII (King of England), 188
Hess, Eckhard (bio-psychologist), 258
Hidden Dimension (Hall), 221
hiding emotions by wearing dark glasses, 86
hiding your hands, 164
high heels, 248
high social status, 295–298
Hilton, Paris (American socialite), 113
history of body language
  overview, 37–38
  primates and body language, 38–39
  spoken language evolved from gesture, 38–39
history of smoking, 210
holding hands, 260
honesty, conveying, 146
horizontal positioning, 234–235
hugging
  arrivals, during, 155
  departures, during, 155
  half-hugs, 144
hugging/stroking yourself, 144
humor and cultural differences, 301
hybrid expression, 115

• I •

illustrators, 41
immediate outer space, 222
importance of personal space, 219–220
impression, using body language to convey a particular, 33–35
improving your reading of body language, 313–314
inborn responses, 43–44
influence, increasing your, 153–154
initiating handshakes, 175
inner space, 222
inner turmoil shown through interaction with accessories, 202–203
intensity of emotion shown through posture, 124–126, 134
interest. *See* attention and interest
internal status, 297
interviews
    approachable, showing that you are, 266
    entrance, making your, 266
    exiting, 267–268
    first impressions, 264–268
    45 degree angle from interviewer, sitting at a, 267
    gestures for maximum effect, using, 268–269
    handshake, 266–267
    nodding to obtain information, 57
    overview, 264
    positioning yourself, 267
    preparing for, 264–265
    reflection before, 282
    space, claiming your, 265–266
intimate space, 221
intimidation, 54
Italy
    greetings and farewells, 291
    laughing, 301
    personal space, 290–291

• J •

Japan
    bowing, 298
    difficult situations, handling, 302
    eye contact, 303
    no-touching rule, 294
    okay sign, 301
    smiling in, 29
    thumbs up sign, 301
jewellery, 213
jiggling feet, 203
John, Elton (singer), 207
Jolie, Angelina (actor), 260
Judge, Timothy A. (professor), 237

• K •

Keating, Paul (Australian Prime Minister), 152
Kennedy, John F. (U.S. president), 31
kinesics
    adaptors, 42–43
    affective displays, 41
    emblems, 40–41
    illustrators, 41
    overview, 33, 40
    regulators, 42
The King and I (play), 131
Klein, Hans-Michael (chairman of Knigge Society), 292
knee pointed in direction of attraction, 255
kneeling, 297–298
Knigge Society, 292
knotted ankles, 197–198
knowledge, signalling lack of, 137
Kuhnke, Elizabeth *(Persuasion & Influence For Dummies)*, 19, 30, 51, 70, 87, 110, 124, 131, 146, 231, 270, 281, 323, 330

• L •

labia, 253
LaFrance, Marianne (professor), 112
Latin countries, 290–291, 292
laughter
    cultural differences, 300–301
    overview, 117
leach handshake, 179
leaning forward to show interest and liking, 134–135
learned gestures
    absorbed actions, 44
    described, 44
    discovering actions for yourself, 44

refined actions, 45–46

trained actions, 44–45

Lee, Michael Soon

Cross-Cultural Selling For Dummies, 305

left side advantage for handshakes, 181

left wing, 233

legs

  crossing, 45, 322

  entwining, 256

Lemmon, Jack (actor), 247

levator labii superior muscles, 103–104

lips. _See also_ smiling

  changing thoughts and behaviours, lips
    closing to indicate, 111–112

  chewing on, 105–106

  enhancing, 253

  lip to lip bite, 106

  loose, 105

  lower lip bite, 106

  muscles controlling, 103–104

  overview, 103–104

  pouting, 107–109, 252

  pursing, 109–110

  stiff upper lip, 106–107

  tensing your lips and biting back words,
    110–111

  tight, 104–105

  upper lip bite, 106

  wetting, 252

lipstick, 253

liveliness in face, showing, 326

loose lips, 105

lop-sided smile, 113, 114

low social status, 295–298

lower lip bite, 106

lowered steeple gesture, 172

lowering yourself, 235–236

lying. _See_ deception

lying down posture, 130

• _M_ •

maintaining your personal space, 228–229

makeup

  advantages of, 211–212

  to enhance appearance, 212

  men wearing, 212

  at office, 212

  women, 211–212

Mandela, Nelson (President of South
  Africa), 40

mannerisms, 184

Manwatching (Morris), 12

Maori haka, 314

Margulies, Juliana (actor), 224

Marx, Groucho (comedian), 210

matching, 259, 271, 272, 273

Max Planck Institute for Behavioural
  Physiology, 43

meetings. _See also_ business situations

  negotiating styles, 281–287

  standing up in, 286

Mehrabian, Albert

  professor, 10, 13, 134

  Silent Messages, 132

men

  accessories, 214–215

  clothing, 214–215

  courting behaviour, 256–258

  fig leaf, 144

  hand gestures, minimising, 321

  knotted ankles, 198

  lowering yourself, 235–236

  makeup, wearing, 212

  reading women's signals, 244

  sexual appeal of, 243

  smoking, 208–209

  straddle stance, 187–189

  thumbs hooked over waistband, into belt
    or into top of trouser pockets, 256–257

  thumbs up and crossed arms, 142–143

  ties, straightening, 147

  tilting head, 58

mental state reflected through accessories,
  201–204

mentalis muscles, 103–104

message reinforcement with touching,
  152–153

method acting, 281

micro gestures

  facial expressions, 317–318

  nodding, 57–58

  overview, 26–27

mid position, clenched hands in, 166

Middle East

  eye contact, 303

  greetings and farewells, 293

  local customs, 301

Middle East *(continued)*
okay sign, 301
public touching, 292
thumbs up sign, 300
mirroring, 271–272, 341
mixed messages
facial expressions, 69–72
reading, 311–313
Monroe, Marilyn (actor), 101, 247, 248
mood, determining a person's, 310–311
Moore, Demi (actor), 253
Moore, Roger (actor), 147
Morris, Desmond
Manwatching, 12
The Naked Ape, 12
zoologist, 80, 136, 202, 220, 253
mouth-covering gesture, 319–320
movement
matching mood and, 276
using purposeful, 275
walking styles
overview, 199–200
walking, wiggling, and swaggering,
247–248
Murdoch, Rupert (CEO of News
Corporation), 99
muscles
levator labii superior, 103–104
mentalis, 103–104
orbicularis oculi, 76
orbicularis oris, 103–104
zygomatic major, 76

• *N* •

Nadal, Rafael (tennis player), 25, 125
The Naked Ape (Morris), 12
neck
scratching, 322
showing, 251
negotiations
claiming your space, 282–283
confidence, displaying, 284–285
nervous gestures, avoiding, 285–287
overview, 281–282
reflection before, 282
styles of, 281–287

nervous gestures
avoiding, 285–287
fingers, opening or closing, 286–287
gripping arm behind back, 173
overview, 285
Neuro-linguistic Programming For Dummies
(Ready and Burton), 87, 131, 273, 341
neuromuscular therapy, 239
New Zealand
greetings and farewells, 291
Maori haka, 314
Nierenberg, Gerard (researcher), 197, 204
Nigeria, 300
Nixon, Richard (U.S. president), 31, 99
Nixon-Kennedy election debate, 31
nodding
to encourage speaker to continue, 56
information, nodding to obtain, 57
micro nodding, 57–58
to show understanding, 57
Nordic countries
eye contact, 303
personal space, 291
toasting, 303
nose
rubbing, 322
touching, 320

• *O* •

Obama, Barak (President of the United
States), 292
Obama, Michelle (First Lady of the United
States), 152, 214, 292, 332
observing someone secretly
appearance, 335–336
arm gestures, 334
eye gestures, 331–332
facial expressions, 332–333
hand gestures, 333
head movements, 333
positioning, 334–335
posture, 334
synchronising gestures, 336–337
time management, 336
touching, 335
voice, 337–338

office. *See also* business situations
  eye glasses in, 207
  makeup in, 212
okay sign, 41, 169, 300
Onassis, Aristotle (shipping magnate), 86
open gestures, 327
open palm
  connection, making a, 158–161
  honesty, showing, 158, 159
  overview, 158
orbicularis oculi muscles, 76
orbicularis oris muscles, 103–104
orientation. *See* positioning
ownership, demonstrating, 225–226

• *P* •

Pacino, Al (actor), 273
pale-faced fury, 80
parallel stance, 189–190
Parrott, Andy (psychologist), 211
pausing for thought, using accessories
    while, 203–204
Paz, Octavio (poet), 239
perceived, acting how you want
    to be, 343
personal space, 32, 221. *See also* seating
    arrangements
  claiming your space
    environment, acquainting yourself with
      the, 282–283
    filling your space, 283
    overview, 282
    seat, choosing your, 283
  comfort, revealing, 227–228
  courtship behaviour, 248–249
  cultural differences, 290–291
  discomfort, revealing, 227–228
  guarding your, 226–227
  importance of, 219–220
  maintaining your, 228–229
  overview, 219–220
  ownership, demonstrating, 225–226
  personality and, 223
  proxemics, 221–222
  respecting, 328
  status and, 224
  submission, showing, 226
  using, 225–229

personality
  handshakes revealing, 176–181
  personal space revealing, 223
  posture revealing, 126–127
Persuasion & Influence For Dummies
    (Kuhnke), 19, 30, 51, 70, 87, 110, 124,
    131, 146, 231, 270, 281, 323, 330
phallic displays, 189
physically supporting the spoken word,
    16–18
Pinocchio Response, 320
pipe smokers, 210–211
Pitt, Brad (actor), 260
Platts, Brinley
    Building Confidence For Dummies,
      131, 336
playing with accessories, 202
pocket, playing with a, 147
pointing feet toward desired place, 195–196
poker face, 318
politicians
  gestures of, 169
  power grip, 170
Pollick, Amy (researcher), 39
positioning
  asymmetrical, 238–239
  of attractive people, 328
  in business situations, 276–281
  cooperative, 278
  cultural differences, 290–291
  facing directly to display serious attitude,
    278–279
  45-degree angle used to create a relaxed
    atmosphere, 277–278
  horizontal, 234–235
  for interviews, 267
  observing someone secretly, 334–335
  overview, 234
  shifting, 323
  subordinates, sitting with, 278
  vertical, 235–238
positive environment, creating a, 269–276
posture
  attitude changed by changing, 130–131
  character revealed through, 126–127
  communication, using posture to aid,
    131–135
  evaluating your own, 122–123
  intensity of emotion shown through,
    124–126, 134

posture *(continued)*
  leaning forward to show interest and
    liking, 134–135
  lying down, 130
  observing someone secretly, 334
  overview, 121–122
  personality revealed through, 126–127
  showing interest through your, 327
  sitting, 129
  standing, 128–129
  status shown through, 132–133
  types of, 127–130
pouting lips, 107–109
power and authority. *See also* dominance;
    status
  aggression, displaying, 51–52
  arrogance, demonstrating, 50–51
  beckoning with your head, 55
  business situations, 273–275
  defiance, tossing your head in, 55
  disapproval, showing, 52–53
  eye glasses as prop for, 205–206
  gripping hands, 173
  head gestures, 49–55
  horizontal positioning, 234–235
  intimidation, catapult gesture used for, 54
  rejection, conveying, 53
  space invader handshake, 180
  steeple gesture, 172
  straddle stance, 187–189
  superiority, signalling, 50
  touching someone on the head, 55
  vertical positioning, 235–238
  vocabulary as indicator of status/power/
    position, 269
power chop, 171
power grip, 170–171
power handshake, 177–178
power lift, 92–93
power seats, picking, 279–281
practicing reading body language, 313–314
precision grip, 168–169
preening, 192, 245
preparing for interviews, 264–265
presentations, visual aids in, 92
props. *See* accessories
proxemics, 32, 221–222
public arena, 222

public personalities, arm gestures used by,
    147
public space, 222
public speaker, 170
punctuality of attractive people, 329
pupilometrics, 258
pupils
  constricted, 84, 86, 88
  dilated, 84, 86, 258
pursing lips, 109–110

• *Q* •

Queen Elizabeth II, 151–152, 331–332

• *R* •

raised steeple gesture, 172
rapport
  defined, 270
  eye contact, 86–87
  matching, 271, 272, 273
  mirroring, 271–272
  overview, 270–271
  reflecting gestures used to establish, 33
  touching to create a bond, 149–150
reading body language
  anger, 308
  boredom, signalling, 310–311
  conclusions, drawing, 309–313
  context, considering, 313
  facial expressions, 308
  fear, 308
  happiness, 308, 311
  improving, 313–314
  mismatch between spoken and non-
    verbal messages, 311–313
  mood, determining a person's, 310–311
  overview, 307–309
  practicing, 313–314
  and responding appropriately, 35
  sadness, 308
  stress, signalling, 310
  sum total of gestures, looking at, 309–311
  surprise, 308
Ready, Romilla
  *Neuro-linguistic Programming For
    Dummies,* 87, 131, 273, 341

Reagan, Nancy (First Lady of the United States), 332
red carpet walk of celebrities, 249
refined actions, 45–46
reflection before negotiations, 282
regulators, 42
rejection, conveying, 53
relaxed, friendly conversation, seating arrangements for, 230
reprimands, 90
resistance, eye glasses as prop for showing, 206
respect
  in business situations, 269–270
  cultural differences, 301–305
revealing thoughts, attitudes and beliefs, 18–21
Rhetorical Gestures (Siddons), 65
Richards, Jane (researcher), 107
right wing, 233
Roberts, Ralph R.
  Cross-Cultural Selling For Dummies, 305
Robinson, Anne (TV presenter), 89
Roddick, Andy (tennis player), 125
Rodin, Auguste _(The Thinker),_ 64
rubbing
  eyes, 319
  nose, 322
  palms together, 164–165

• S •

sadness
  in facial expressions, 77–78
  reading, 308
saluting, 160
Sarkozy, Nicolas (President of France), 273
Saudi Arabia. _See also_ Middle East
  greetings and farewells, 293–294
  time management, 336
Schwarzenegger, Arnold (actor), 91
scissor stance, 22–23, 192–194
Scott, Walter
  St Ronan's Well, 228
seating arrangements. _See also_ personal space
  choosing your seat, 283
  combative position, 231–232
  for cooperation, 230–231

diagonal position, 232
equality, creating, 232–234
group's power, seating position affecting dynamics of, 233
involved, technique for making people feel, 233
overview, 229
for relaxed, friendly conversation, 230
secretly observing someone. _See_ observing someone secretly
self-touching movements, 144, 183
sexual appeal, 243
sexual display, smoking as, 208–209
shoe, dangling, 255
short people, 237
shoulder
  cold shoulder, giving, 146
  glancing sideways over raised, 254, 255
shrugging
  elements of, 136
  lack of knowledge, signalling, 137
  overview, 30–31, 136–137
  submissive apology, implying, 138
  unwillingness to get involved, showing, 137–138
Siddons, Henry
  Rhetorical Gestures, 65
sideways glance, 95–96
sign of the cuckold, 40
signature gestures, 23–25
Silent Messages (Mehrabian), 132
sitting
  chairs for, 279–281
  posture, 129
  power seats, picking, 279–281
  tête à tête, 60–61
slow head shake, 53
smiling
  attractive people, 326
  closed-lip grin, 115–116
  courting behaviour, 245
  drop-jaw smile, 113–115
  faking, 321
  full-blown grin, 116
  laughter, 117
  lop-sided smile, 113, 114
  overview, 28–29, 75–77, 112
  tight-lipped smile, 112–113
  turn-away smile, 115

smoking
  cigar smokers, 210
  history of, 210
  methods of, 209–211
  overview, 208
  pipe smokers, 210–211
  as sexual display, 208–209
  specialty smokers, 209
  stress and, 211
  women, 208–209
social space, 221–222
sombre expression, 73
Some Like It Hot (film), 247
Sommer, Robert (psychologist), 32, 229
South America, 300
space. *See* personal space
space invader handshake, 180
Spain, 290–291
spatial awareness, 32
specialty smokers, 209
speech pattern, changing, 323
spoken language evolved from gestures,
    38–39
St Ronan's Well (Scott), 228
stalling for time, eye glasses as prop for,
    204–205
stance. *See also* feet
  attitude shown through, 185–186
  bent blade, 193
  buttress, 190–192
  cultural differences, 298–299
  entwining your legs, 194
  in meetings, 286
  overview, 185–186
  parallel, 189–190
  posture, 128–129
  scissor, 192–194
  straddle, 187–189
Stanislavski, Constantine (director), 281
status
  high social status, 295–298
  low social status, 295–298
  and personal space, 224
  shown through posture, 132–133
  stance reflecting, 186
  vocabulary as indicator of status/power/
    position, 269

steeple gesture, 172
Stewart, James (actor), 127
stiff upper lip, 106–107
Stiff Upper Lip, Jeeves (Wodehouse), 107
Stone, Sharon (actor), 101, 256
straddle stance, 187–189
stress
  signalling, 310
  and smoking, 211
submissive apology, implying, 138
submissive gestures
  eye contact, breaking, 94
  eye dip, 97
  head gestures, 61–63
  personal space, 226
  scissor stance, 193
subordinates, sitting with, 278
substituting behaviour for spoken word,
    13–14
successful use of body language
  anticipation of movements, 32–33
  impression, using body language to
    convey a particular, 33–35
  overview, 31–32
  rapport established through reflecting
    gestures, 33
  reading signals and responding
    appropriately, 35
  spatial awareness, 32
Sugar, Alan (entrepreneur), 280
sum total of gestures, looking at, 309–311
sunglasses, 206–207
sunny expression, 73
superiority, signalling, 50
superstition, touching and, 149
surprise
  eyebrow flashing, 100
  facial expressions, 80–81
  reading, 308
Swanson, Gloria (actor), 46
Swayze, Patrick (actor), 253
synchronising gestures
  attractive people, 330
  communication, 342
  observing someone secretly, 336–337

• T •

tall people, 237
tensing your lips and biting back words, 110–111
tension
  fingernails, biting, 184, 202
  gestures relieving, 202–203
  tight lips, 104–105
territorial parameters. *See* personal space
testosterone, 244
Thatcher, Margaret (Prime Minister), 74
The Thinker (Rodin), 64
thought
  clearly expressing your, 340
  head gestures showing, 64–65
thumbs
  gesturing towards another person with your, 173–174
  hooked over waistband, into belt or into top of trouser pockets, 256–257
  protruding from a person's pockets, 173
  sucking, 184
  thumbs up gesture
    and crossed arms, 142–143
    cultural differences, 299–300
    overview, 173
tie, straightening a, 147
tight lips, 104–105
tight-lipped smile, 112–113
tilting (canting) your head, 58–60
time management
  of attractive people, 329
  observing someone secretly, 336
tossing head, 250
touching
  arrivals, during, 155
  bond, creating a, 149–150
  to connect, 328
  courting behaviour, 246
  departures, during, 155
  dominance, demonstrating, 151–152
  gender and, 151
  how long to touch, 148
  influence, increasing your, 153–154
  message reinforcement, 152–153
  observing someone secretly, 335
  overview, 148–149

someone on the head, 55
  and superstition, 149
  themselves, women's courtship behaviour, 252–253
  when to touch, 148
  where not to touch, 148
  where to touch, 148
trained actions, 44–45
Trump, Donald (entrepreneur), 89
turn-away smile, 115
twitching, flicking, or going in circles, feet, 198–199

• U •

uncertainty, hand gesture showing, 169
unconscious transmission of messages, 12–13
understanding, nodding to show, 57
unflinching stare, 91
unintentional gestures, 21–23
universal gestures
  blushing, 29–30
  crying, 30
  cultural differences, 299–301
  described, 28
  shrugging, 30–31
  smiling, 28–29
unwillingness to get involved, showing, 137–138
upper lip bite, 106

• V •

verbal message and facial expressions, 69–72
vertical positioning
  elevating yourself, 236–238
  lowering yourself, 235–236
  overview, 235
victory sign, 40
'visor eyes,' 89
visual aids in presentations, 92
visualisation, 131
vocabulary as indicator of status/power/position, 269
voice, 70, 330, 337–338

• W •

Waal, Frans de (researcher), 38, 39
walking styles
  overview, 199–200
  walking, wiggling, and swaggering,
    247–248
well-modulated voice, technique for
    developing, 70
wet fish handshake, 176–177
widening your eyes, 100–101
winking, 97–98
Wodehouse, P. G.
  Stiff Upper Lip, Jeeves, 107
women
  accessories, 213–214
  clothing, 213–214
  courtship behaviour
    cylindrical objects, fondling, 253–254
    hair, flicking, 250
    handbag placed in close proximity,
      254–255
    head, canting, 251
    head, dipping, 252
    knee pointed in direction of attraction,
      255
    legs, entwining, 256
    lips, pouting and wetting, 252
    neck, showing, 251
    shoe, dangling, 255
    shoulder, glancing sideways over raised,
      254, 255
    tossing head, 250
    touching themselves, 252–253
    wrists, exposing, 253
  eye glasses, 207
  eyes, widening, 100–101
  first move made by, 244
  half-hugs, 144
  hand gestures, increasing, 322
  handshakes, 175
  height of, 237
  high heels, wearing, 248
  knotted ankles, 198
  leg twine, 194
  lowering yourself, 236
  makeup, 211–212
  sexual appeal of, 243
  smoking, 208–209
  tilting head, 58–59
work environment. *See* business situations
wrists, exposing, 253

• Y •

Yerkes National Primate Research
  Center, 38
yoga, 239

• Z •

Zeta Jones, Catherine (actor), 225
zygomatic major muscles, 76

FOR DUMMIES®

Making Everything Easier! ™

UK editions

BUSINESS

978-0-470-97626-5

978-0-470-97211-3

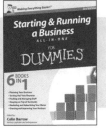

978-1-119-97527-4

REFERENCE

978-0-470-68637-9

978-0-470-97450-6

978-0-470-74535-9

HOBBIES

978-0-470-69960-7

978-0-470-68641-6

978-0-470-68178-7

Asperger's Syndrome For Dummies
978-0-470-66087-4

Basic Maths For Dummies
978-1-119-97452-9

Boosting Self-Esteem For Dummies
978-0-470-74193-1

British Sign Language
For Dummies
978-0-470-69477-0

Cricket For Dummies
978-0-470-03454-5

Diabetes For Dummies, 3rd Edition
978-0-470-97711-8

English Grammar For Dummies
978-0-470-05752-0

Flirting For Dummies
978-0-470-74259-4

IBS For Dummies
978-0-470-51737-6

Improving Your Relationship
For Dummies
978-0-470-68472-6

Keeping Chickens For Dummies
978-1-119-99417-6

Lean Six Sigma For Dummies
978-0-470-75626-3

Management For Dummies,
2nd Edition
978-0-470-97769-9

Neuro-linguistic Programming
For Dummies, 2nd Edition
978-0-470-66543-5

Nutrition For Dummies, 2nd Edition
978-0-470-97276-2

FOR DUMMIES®

A world of resources to help you grow

UK editions

SELF–HELP

978-0-470-66541-1

978-1-119-99264-6

978-0-470-66086-7

Origami Kit For Dummies
978-0-470-75857-1

Overcoming Depression For Dummies
978-0-470-69430-5

Positive Psychology For Dummies
978-0-470-72136-0

PRINCE2 For Dummies, 2009 Edition
978-0-470-71025-8

Project Management For Dummies
978-0-470-71119-4

Psychometric Tests For Dummies
978-0-470-75366-8

Reading the Financial Pages
For Dummies
978-0-470-71432-4

Rugby Union For Dummies, 3rd Edition
978-1-119-99092-5

Sage 50 Accounts For Dummies
978-0-470-71558-1

Self-Hypnosis For Dummies
978-0-470-66073-7

Study Skills For Dummies
978-0-470-74047-7

Teaching English as a Foreign Language
For Dummies
978-0-470-74576-2

Time Management For Dummies
978-0-470-77765-7

Training Your Brain For Dummies
978-0-470-97449-0

Work-Life Balance For Dummies
978-0-470-71380-8

Writing a Dissertation For Dummies
978-0-470-74270-9

STUDENTS

978-0-470-68820-5   978-0-470-74711-7   978-1-119-99134-2

HISTORY

978-0-470-68792-5

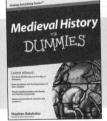

978-0-470-74783-4

978-0-470-97819-1